Popular Science®
WOODWORKING PROJECTS

1991 Yearbook

Edited by Al Gutierrez

Meredith® Press
New York

Cover Photo by: Jonathan Press

For Meredith® Press:
    Director: Elizabeth P. Rice
    Editorial Project Manager: Connie Schrader
    Assistant: Ruth Weadock
    Production Manager: Bill Rose
    Copy Reader: Daniel Early
For Jonathan Press:
    Produced by: Jonathan Press, Cannon Falls, MN
    Producer/Executive Director: Al Gutierrez
    Copy Editor: Berit Strand
    Copy Editor: Cheryl Clark
    Copy Editor: Barb Machowski
    Technical Consultant: Gary Branson
    Illustrator: Geri Klug
    Woodworking Technician: Pat Manion

Book Design: Jonathan Press

Special thanks to:
    American Plywood Association, Tacoma, WA
    California Redwood Association, Novato, CA
    Cherry Tree Toys, Inc., Belmont, OH
    Delta International Machinery Corp., Pittsburgh, PA
    Georgia-Pacific Corporation, Atlanta, GA
    Ryobi America Corp., Bensenville, IL
    Shopsmith, Inc., Dayton, OH

The projects presented in this book have come from a variety of sources. The plans and instructions have been developed by many different writers. We have tried to select those projects that will assure accuracy and safety. Due to differing conditions, tools, and individual woodworking skills, Meredith® Press assumes no responsibility for any injuries suffered, damages or losses incurred during, or as a result of, the construction of these projects.

Before starting on any project, study the plans carefully; read and observe all the safety precautions provided by any tool or equipment manufacturer and follow all accepted safety procedures during construction.

Preface

This year's yearbook includes some of the most functional furniture and toy projects around. Whether you want a step stool to reach tall kitchen cabinets, an outdoor planter, a comfortable chair, a display cabinet or a child's sandbox, there is certainly a project to pique your interest and meet your needs.

Most of the 36 woodworking projects feature simple construction and, consequently, do not require the use of complex and expensive tools, such as thickness planers. However, there are several projects included that will challenge even the most advanced woodworker's skill.

We have carefully provided a comprehensive story, diagram and photos for each project that will take you through every aspect of construction. Our step-by-step construction photos are worthy of special note. They help to clarify critical steps in making a project part and show alternative tools and methods that can be used to accomplish project construction.

One special-purpose tool which you'll see in some of the construction photos is the abrasive sander or band sander. Refer to Fig. 2 on page 37. This often overlooked power bench tool is invaluable for sanding inside and outside edges. It looks like a miniature band saw with a sanding belt. The sanding belt is approximately 1 in. wide and moves around two wheels. Near the table is a removable platen which supports the back of the belt so you can exert sanding pressure. An abrasive sander supplied with a curved platen lets you sand inside curves and is ideal for dressing edges of smaller projects because it does such a thorough, quick sanding job. The sanding belts come in a wide variety of grits for sanding wood or filing metal.

The task of compiling projects for this yearbook was made easier due to special assistance from Shopsmith, Inc. About one dozen of their projects grace our pages. They are very kind to work with, and I would like to personally thank them for their efforts.

Over the years we have come to depend on your comments about our projects and always enjoy looking at the projects you have built from our plans. Send us a black-and-white photo of your project or a question about woodworking that we might include in a special woodworking techniques section in a future yearbook. Please send your project photos and questions to Popular Science® Q&A, Jonathan Press, P.O. Box 19, Cannon Falls, MN 55009.

Again, thank you for your interest and dedication to this year's yearbook.

Al Gutierrez

Contributors

American Plywood Association ♦ The American Plywood Association (APA) is a nonprofit trade association whose member mills produce approximately 80 percent of the structural wood panel products manufactured in the United States. Founded in 1933 as the Douglas Fir Plywood Association and widely recognized today as the voice of the structural wood panel industry, APA performs numerous functions and services on behalf of panel product users, specifiers, dealers, distributors, schools and universities and other key groups. Among the most important of these functions is quality inspection and testing. APA trademarks appear only on products manufactured by APA member mills and signify that panel quality is subject to verification through APA audit — a procedure designed to assure manufacture in conformance with APA performance standards or U.S. Product Standard PS 1-83 for Construction and Industrial Plywood. APA maintains seven quality testing laboratories in key producing regions, including a 37,000-square-foot research center at Association headquarters in Tacoma, Washington.

California Redwood Association ♦ The California Redwood Association, founded in 1916, is one of the oldest trade groups in the country. Its members are the major producers of redwood lumber. The Association's activities include advertising, product promotion and providing technical assistance to anyone with questions about using redwood. The CRA has a staff wood technologist and publishes a wide variety of informational written material about redwood products.

George Campbell ♦ George has been a professional writer for numerous woodworking and how-to magazines for over a decade. George's philosophy of design stresses functionality. He believes that a design that does its job will naturally be attractive. To a large degree he is influenced by Shaker and Scandinavian designs, which are the epitome of simplicity and beauty. His projects are designed for creation with modern power tools. He has also authored *The Backyard Builder's Book of Outdoor Building Projects* for Rodale Press. George resides in California.

Georgia-Pacific Corporation ♦ Georgia-Pacific is one of the world's largest forest products companies, with more than 60,000 employees in more than 400 facilities throughout the United States. Founded in 1927, the company grew rapidly as a distributor, and later a producer, of lumber and other building materials. In the 1950s, the company entered the pulp and paper business, and is now one of the larger producers of pulp and paper. Georgia-Pacific reforests timber sites with nursery-grown seedlings — about 30 million each year.

Gene and Katie Hamilton ♦ The Hamiltons write a weekly syndicated newspaper column, "Do-it-Yourself or Not?" and are regular contributors to many of the home how-to magazines. They've written three books about woodworking and contribute to several of the *Reader's Digest* projects books. As school teachers in suburban Chicago, they worked on houses in the summer months learning new skills as they tackled more difficult projects. Today they're writing about and working on their 14th house on the eastern shore of Maryland.

Shopsmith, Inc. ♦ Shopsmith is a major contributor to our yearbook and has provided us with more than a dozen stories. They are well known for the quality, multipurpose tools which are synonymous with their name. They are based in Dayton, Ohio.

Dennis Watson ♦ With a constant flow of suggestions and ideas from his wife, Missourian Dennis Watson found he enjoyed being a part-time woodworker and began designing pieces that were not only functional but also artistic. Right up to his death from leukemia in October of 1988, one of his greatest joys was working with his son and daughter on woodworking projects such as bug cages, hand-carved dinosaurs, a variety of wood toys and his last project, a gun cabinet for his teenage son. Even though Dennis was a full-time aerospace engineer, he found time to be a member of St. Louis Woodworkers Guild and presented workshops and demonstrations in the St. Louis area. Dennis' work has been featured over the years in *Workbench, The Family Handyman, American Woodworker* and several woodworking books.

Contents

Projects

Techniques

PROJECTS

This project is courtesy of Dennis Watson.

Modern Chair

Relax and think about your next project in this comfortable chair.

With its combination of a natural oil finished oak frame and a dark brown canvas sling, this chair blends well with most styles of furniture and does not appear to crowd a room because of its light, open look.

The chair is lightweight, which allows it to be easily moved as seating requirements demand. Strong, durable oak is used for the frame and, when treated with a natural oil finish, it produces a warm reddish brown color with a bold grain pattern. Though most any hardwood would be fine for the frame, softwoods are not strong enough.

Tips

Construction of the chair requires three basic woodworking joints: open, blind and wedged mortise and tenon joints. The open and wedged mortise and tenon joints are very strong and also visually attractive, with the end grain and wedge providing contrast with the flat grain. If you prefer not to use the mortise and tenon joint, substitute a dowel joint. The dowel joint can also be wedged to obtain a similar visual effect.

When making an open mortise and tenon joint, it is easier to cut the open mortise first, then cut the tenon to fit. We cut the open mortise on a table saw using a homemade tenoning jig. The piece is clamped to the jig and slid along the rip fence past a hollow-ground or carbide-tipped combination saw blade.

Using this setup, cut the sides of the open mortise into the legs. The remaining wood can be chiseled out or you can make repeated passes past the saw blade. Using the tenoning

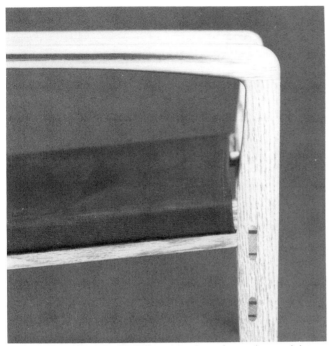

Figure 1. Here is a detail of the wedged mortise and tenon joints. They consist of walnut wedges driven into slots cut into the stretchers (C, D, E).

Figure 2. Lay out and then cut the mortises into the legs (A). Use a sharp wood chisel and stay short of the cutting lines when making your rough cuts. After the hole is rough cut, finish to the cutting line with your wood chisel.

jig, cut the cheek (or side of the tenon) to fit the mortise. (Cut the tenon slightly fat and trim it with a chisel to get a good fit.) To finish up the tenon, make the shoulder cut by setting the depth of the saw blade to cut through the scrap wood, but not into the tenon. Later, square up the corner using a chisel.

Here's a tip to consider when cutting both the open mortise and the tenon cheeks. Use one side of the board as a reference and place it against the tenoning jig. This prevents any thickness variation in the board from being transferred to the tenon or mortise and causing a poor fit.

The blind mortise can be cut in several ways. A mortising chisel in a drill press will cut clean, square mortises. A router with straight cutter and a straightedge clamped to the base will produce a good mortise with round ends. (Use a radial arm saw with a drill chuck attached to the power take-off side of the arbor.) A straight router bit or a bottoming end mill, as used in metalworking, will produce very clean, round corner mortises.

Construction

Cut all of the project parts to size and lay out any required designs, such as the curve on the armrest (G).

Using the methods described in the Tips section, mortise the front and back legs (A, B).

Cut the joints for the armrest (G) and seat rail (F) and dry-fit the legs (A, B) together to make sure the joints pull up tight. Lay out the through-mortise for the four stretchers (C, D, E). When cutting the through-mortise, use a back-up block to prevent the wood from splintering as the router bit or bottoming end mill comes through the wood. Cut the taper on the legs. Round the corner on the upper part of the leg slightly fat and finish to the line when the sides are glued up. Use a

¾ in. rotary rasp and a ¼ in. drill to round the corners. The slot in the seat rail is cut on a table saw and then squared up with a wood chisel.

Round the corners of the seat rail (F) on a shaper or router to prevent the canvas from being torn or ripped. Dry-fit the side together one more time before gluing and clamping. Remember, when gluing an open mortise and tenon joint, it is necessary to clamp the cheek of the joint. This is easily done with a C-clamp.

Cut the tenon for the stretchers (C, D, E). Round the tenon carefully using a chisel or knife. Start at the base and work out toward the end, then finish with a file. The tenon should be rounded as near to a perfect circle as possible, but the force from the wedge and the moisture from the glue will deform the wood fibers slightly to produce a good fit.

Using a fine-tooth backsaw or dovetail saw, make the saw cuts in the tenon for the wedges. We usually place the wedges just past the half-round of the tenon, and slant them inward

	BILL OF MATERIALS — Modern Chair		
	Finished Dimensions in Inches		
A	Front Leg	1 x 2 x 22 oak	2
B	Back Leg	1 x 2 x 22 oak	2
C	Front Stretcher	¾ x 1¼ x 23¾ oak	1
D	Front Top Stretcher	¾ x 1¾ x 23¾ oak	1
E	Back Stretcher	¾ x 1¼ x 23¾ oak	2
F	Seat Rail	¾ x 2¼ x 25 oak	2
G	Armrest	1 x 1½ x 25¾ oak	2
H	Back Brace	1 x 1 x 21 oak	2
I	Seat and Back	29¾ x 33½ canvas	1

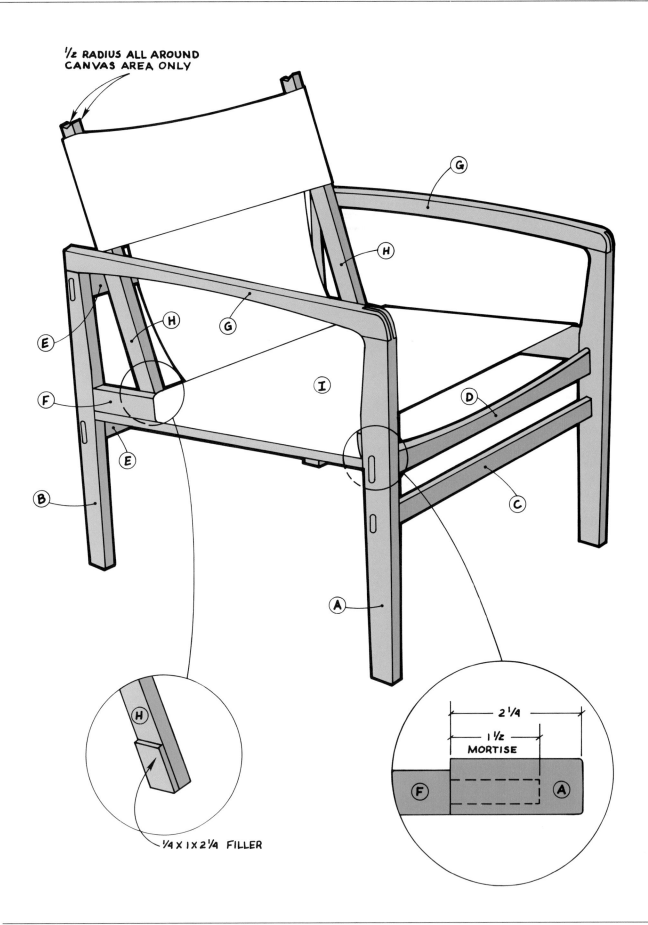

½ RADIUS ALL AROUND
CANVAS AREA ONLY

G

H

E

H

G

F

I

D

E

B

C

A

¼ X 1 X 2¼ FILLER

H

2¼

1½
MORTISE

F

A

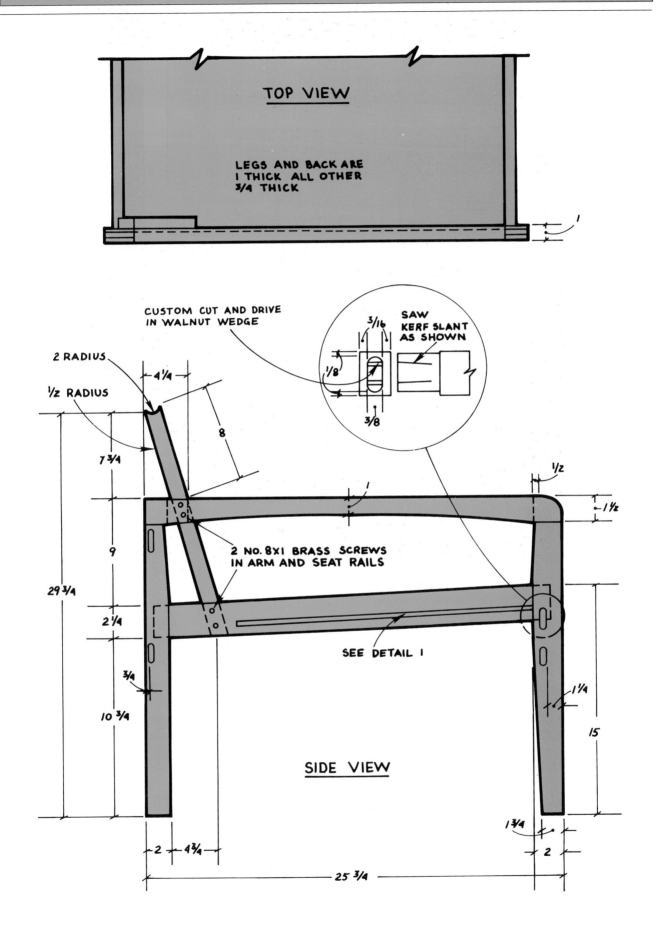

TOP VIEW

LEGS AND BACK ARE
1 THICK ALL OTHER
3/4 THICK

CUSTOM CUT AND DRIVE
IN WALNUT WEDGE

SAW
KERF SLANT
AS SHOWN

3/16

1/8

3/8

2 RADIUS

1/2 RADIUS

4 1/4

8

7 3/4

1/2

1 1/2

9

2 NO. 8X1 BRASS SCREWS
IN ARM AND SEAT RAILS

29 3/4

2 1/4

SEE DETAIL 1

3/4

1 1/4

10 3/4

15

SIDE VIEW

2   4 3/4

1 3/4

2

25 3/4

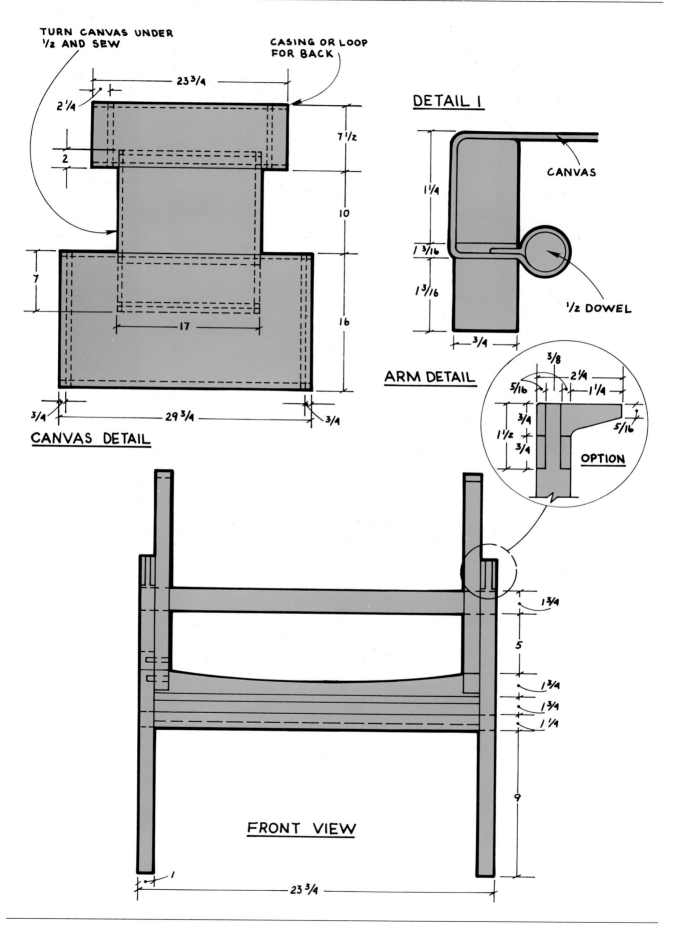

TURN CANVAS UNDER
½ AND SEW

CASING OR LOOP
FOR BACK

23¾

2¼

2

7½

10

7

17

16

¾

29¾

¾

CANVAS DETAIL

DETAIL 1

CANVAS

1¼

1³/₁₆

1³/₁₆

½ DOWEL

¾

ARM DETAIL

3/8

2¼

5/16

1¼

¾

1½

¾

5/16

OPTION

1¾

5

1¾

1¾

1¼

1

FRONT VIEW

23¾

9

Figure 3. Drill holes through the legs (A) for the mortises that will accommodate the stretchers (C, D, E). Use a Forstner bit and drill a series of holes as shown. Use a clamped straightedge to insure that the holes are aligned. Use a back-up board to prevent wood tearout.

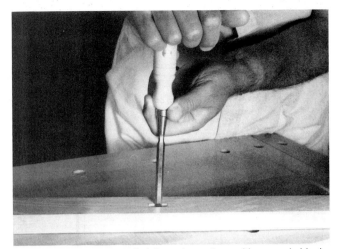

Figure 4. Finish the rounded through-mortises with a wood chisel. Work from the showing side and make sure your chisel is sharp.

Figure 5. Assemble the chair with carpenter's glue and plenty of clamps. After the assembly is tightened, drive in wedges into the slotted tenons.

very slightly so the tenon isn't weakened. Wedges are easily made by planing a darker colored wood (walnut, in this case) to the same thickness as the tenon and then ripping into ⅛ in. wide strips. Use a chisel to cut a taper on both sides of the wood strips. The taper should be long enough for the wedge to go in almost the full length of the tenon.

When gluing up the chair, place clamps on each side of the stretchers to allow room to drive the wedges home.

Use a saber saw to shape the armrests, then finish with a file and sandpaper. Round all corners slightly to remove any possible splinters.

Cut the back brace (H) and round the edges where the canvas goes. Clamp the back brace in place, then insert the canvas sling. The sling simply slides on the back and is wrapped around the seat rail through the slot. A ½ in. dowel is slid into a casing sewn into the sides of the canvas to hold the canvas seat in place. The canvas should be stretched tightly initially because it will stretch slightly with use.

We found in making the chair that the placement of the back brace and the backward tilt of the brace will determine the chair's comfortability. We made two chairs and ended up with the backs in two different positions; one for *her* and one for *him*.

So sit in the chair and try different positions for the back support. When the chair feels right, use No. 8 by 1 in. brass flathead screws to attach the back brace to the seat rail and the armrest.

The canvas sling is made from canvas chair duck available from any awning supply store. It consists of three rectangular pieces that are sewn together. The canvas for the back support has a casing sewn in each side that slides down over the back support. The seat piece has casings sewn in the sides for a ½ in. dowel. The canvas can be sewn on most home sewing machines using polyester thread.

We finished the chair with two coats of Watco oil, followed by paste wax. The only disadvantage you'll encounter with the chair is your tendency to spend too much time sitting in it, thinking about your next project, and not enough time working in the shop. □

This project is courtesy of Dennis Watson and Workbench magazine.

Contemporary Wine Rack

Build this compact wine rack for elegant entertaining.

This unique wine rack features clean lines, exposed joints and space for four wine bottles and six large stemmed glasses. Its small size makes it easy to move from one place to another, and it will add a decorative touch to any gathering spot.

This is a challenging project and a rewarding one. Carefully read our instructions and review the illustrations and construction photos before beginning.

Tips

Select straight, knot-free walnut and oak lumber for this project. Choose interesting patterns for extra appeal.

Construction

Start construction by making the frame assembly that will hold the bottles (D, E). Cut pieces of ½ in. oak stock to the dimensions shown. Miter the corners and make dadoes to accommodate the cross frames (E). Finish the dado with a ¼ in. wood chisel.

Temporarily assemble the frame and measure the cross frames (E) to suit. Then custom cut each on your table saw and cut half-lap joints where the cross frames overlap. Cut these half-laps with a band saw, carefully staying next to the cutting line. Use a ½ in. blade to prevent the blade from wandering.

Assemble the sides and the cross frames of the frame, fastening them in place with carpenter's glue. Use band clamps, but do not overtighten. Make sure the assembly is square.

Cut the walnut splines from leftover ¼ in. walnut scrap, using a band saw. Cut the material from longer lengths to prevent working with short workpieces that may position your fingers too close to the band saw blade. Shape the connectors (G) on a stationary belt sander. These connectors must be nearly perfect, so practice on scrap before you begin working on the final connectors.

After the glue has set on the frame assembly, cut dadoes across the corners to accept the walnut splines and the connectors (G). Note that on diagonally opposite corners these connectors are allowed to project so they can fit into leg tenons. The dadoes can be cut by hand, but a tenon jig, either shop-made or a commercial unit, can be used on a table saw. We used a ¼ in. dado blade, making sure that the groove was a good fit for the splines. File down the splines for a snug but not tight fit. If the fit is tight, the moisture in the white glue will cause the tenons to swell, making it extremely difficult to slip the tenons into the mortises.

Next, make the table, which consists of the legs (B), brace (C) and top (A). Glue up ¾ in. walnut stock for the legs and rip them to size on a table saw or band saw. Mortise each leg to accommodate the brace (C) and connector (G). Also drill a ⅜ in. diameter dowel hole to hold the top.

Figure 1. Use a shop-made or commercial jig to hold the assembled frame (D, E) while cutting a ¼ in. by ¼ in. deep groove to accept a spline.

Figure 2. Cut the glass hangers (F) by making a groove from longer material as shown. Keep the wood firmly against the fence. Make the deeper cut first.

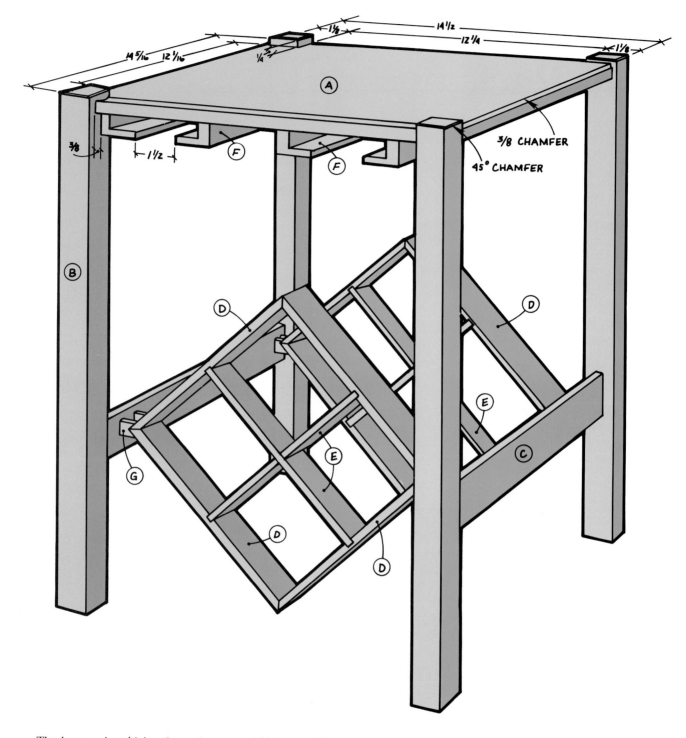

The legs project ¼ in. above the top and ¼ in. outside each edge of the top. The tops and edges of the legs are also chamfered slightly, about ⅛ inch.

Select the hardwood for the top and cut it 1/16 in. oversize. Joint the edges until you get to final size. Then edge-glue the top and allow the glue to cure.

Form ⅜ in. chamfers along the edge of the top and cut 1⅛ in. by 1⅛ in. notches in each corner. Use a ⅜ in. chamfering bit, with pilot, in your router to form the chamfer.

Cut the brace (C) to length and form the tenons, using a

table saw equipped with a dado blade. Round the ends of the tenons with a wood chisel. Also cut the leg tenons that secure the assembled wine rack frames (D, E). Note that the rear rack is ¾ in. lower than the front rack. This allows a standard size bottle to fit with the cork end pointing slightly downward so the cork stays wet. *Note that the photo shows the bottles inserted improperly.*

Dry-assemble the legs, brace, frame assembly and top, along with the splines and connectors. Check for any misaligned joints. Make necessary corrections, then glue and

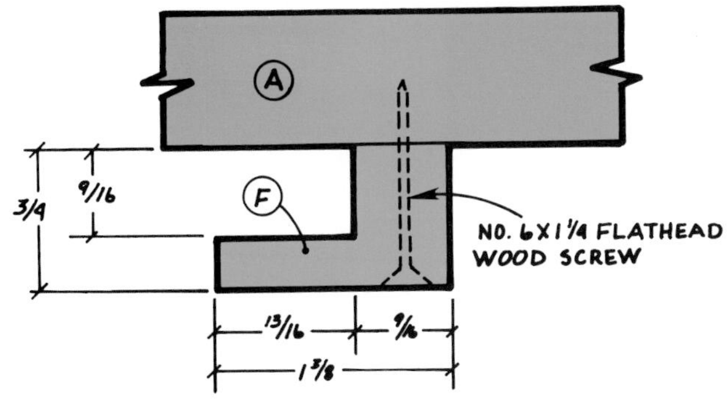
A
F
3/4
9/16
NO. 6 X 1 1/4 FLATHEAD WOOD SCREW
13/16
9/16
1 3/8

GLASS HANGER DETAIL

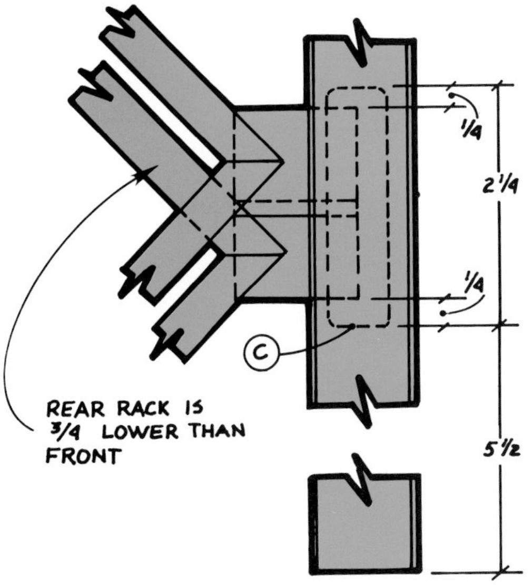
1/4
2 1/4
1/4
C
REAR RACK IS 3/4 LOWER THAN FRONT
5 1/2

FRONT VIEW DETAIL

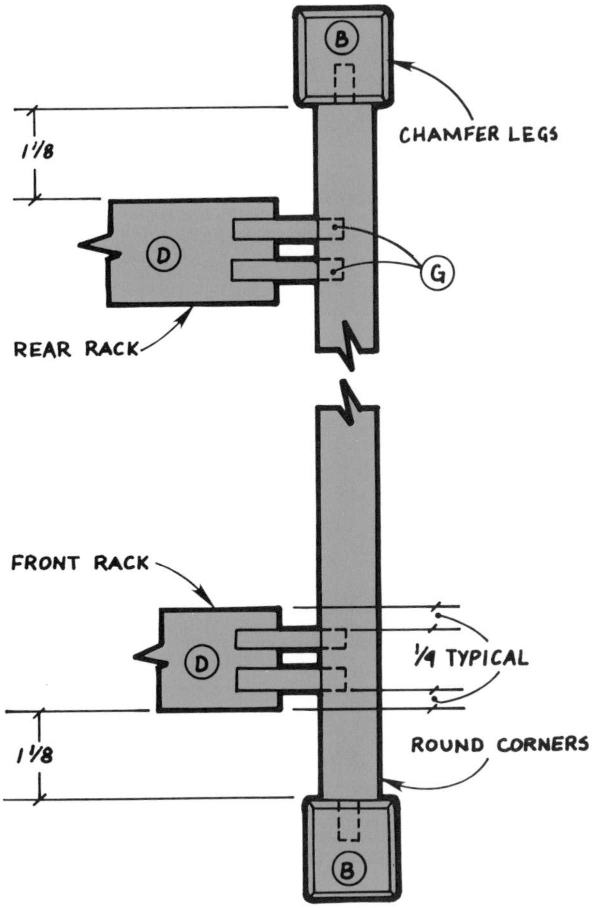
B
CHAMFER LEGS
1 1/8
D
G
REAR RACK
FRONT RACK
D
1/4 TYPICAL
1 1/8
ROUND CORNERS
B

TOP SECTION

clamp the complete project. Make sure that all four legs rest solidly on a flat surface and that the assembly is square. Let the project stand overnight to make sure the glue sets completely, then remove the clamps and do your final sanding and finishing.

Cut the hangers for the glasses (F) from long walnut stock. Cut the rabbet on your table saw. First make the deeper, 13/16 in. cut, then the 9/16 in. cut, to finish the rabbet. Finish sand the glass hangers and secure to the top with glue and countersunk No. 6 by 1 1/4 in. flathead wood screws.

BILL OF MATERIALS — Contemporary Wine Rack

Finished Dimensions in Inches

A	Top	3/4 x 14 5/16 x 14 1/2 walnut	1
B	Leg	1 1/4 x 1 1/4 x 19 3/8 walnut	4
C	Brace	3/4 x 2 1/4 x 13 1/16 walnut	2
D	Frame	1/4 x 1 1/4 x 8 1/4 oak	8
E	Cross Frame	1/4 x 1 1/4 x 8 oak	4
F	Glass Hanger	3/4 x 1 3/8 x 14 5/16 walnut	4
G	Connector	1/4 x 1 x 1 3/8 walnut	8

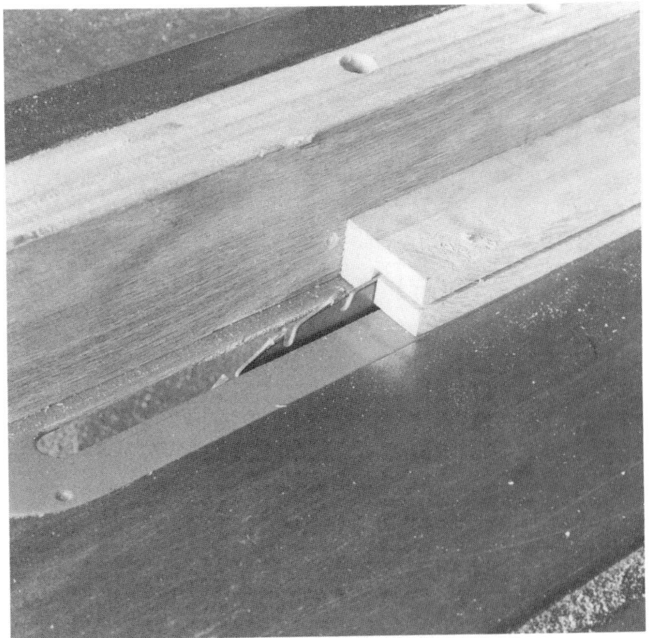

Figure 3. Finish the glass hangers by making the shallower cut as shown. The waste will fall away from the workpiece.

Figure 4. Form the tenons for the braces (C) using your table saw. Make the first cut using a miter gauge, with a dado blade installed. Flip the workpiece over and make the second cut.

Finishing

If you prefer, you can prefinish the various parts after the dry-assembly. If you do, be sure to keep stain and finish off the tenons and out of mortises or any other pieces that are to be glued together.

We finished the project with two coats of Danish oil, the last coat being burnished with 600 grit waterproof sandpaper. This was followed by buffing all surfaces with paste wax. ☐

Figure 5. After forming the brace (C) shoulders, reset the dado blade and position the brace on edge as shown. Make another pass on the table saw, flip the workpiece 180 degrees and complete the shoulder.

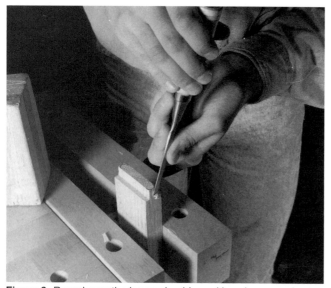

Figure 6. Round over the brace shoulders with a sharp wood chisel. Use a wood file to smooth the radius.

Figure 7. Glue the entire assembly, making sure the legs sit solidly and the unit is square. Allow the glue to cure for at least 24 hours.

This project is courtesy of Carl Coombs and Shopsmith, Inc.

Children's Chalkboard

Give your children a gift that lasts with this wall-mounted chalkboard.

All children love to draw and doodle. Crayons or markers on paper are fine, but with a chalkboard and a selection of colored chalks, your children can look forward to hours of self-entertainment. This space-saving, wall-mounted chalkboard also features drawers for storing chalk, erasers and all the other "essentials." Our complete plans make it easy for you to give your favorite "little one" an exciting and educational gift.

Tips

Use maple stock for the majority of the project. It is durable and great to work with.

Build the Framework

Thickness plane the stock for the stiles and rails (A, B, C) to ¾ in. and cut to size per the Bill of Materials. Joint one edge

BILL OF MATERIALS — Children's Chalkboard

Finished Dimensions in Inches

A	Stile	3/4 x 2 x 28 maple	2
B	Rail	3/4 x 2 x 36 maple	2
C	Inner Rail	3/4 x 2½ x 33 maple	1
D	Top	½ x 5 x 36 maple	1
E	Bottom	½ x 5 x 36 maple plywood	1
F	Partition	½ x 5 x 3 1/16 maple	2
G	Side	½ x 5 x 3 9/16 maple	2
H	Side	½ x 2½ x 5 maple	6
I	Front	½ x 2½ x 11 5/16 maple	3
J	Back	½ x 2½ x 11 5/16 maple	3
K	Bottom	¼ x 4 7/16 x 10 11/16 maple plywood	3
L	Runner	1/32 x ½ x 4½ maple	6
M	Chalkboard	¼ x 24¾ x 32¾	1

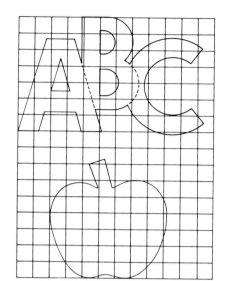

and plane the stiles (A) and rails (B) all at the same time for the straightest and most consistent stock. Be sure to take note that the inner rail (C) is ½ in. wider than the other rails.

Using a dado accessory, cut the lap joints in the stiles (A) and rails (B) with your table saw. The most accurate method of doing this is to set the dado blade depth at one-half the thickness of the stock (3/8 inch). Then make a pass over the blade with a 3/4 in. thick piece of scrap stock. Turn the scrap stock over and make a second pass directly under the first cut. Adjust the depth of cut until after making two passes there is only a sliver of stock remaining in the center.

When all the table saw adjustments are complete, cut the lap joints slightly wider than 2 in. to allow for sanding flush later.

Lay out and cut the mortises and tenons in the stiles (A) to attach the inner rail (C). The tenons are ¼ in. wide by 2 in. long by ½ in. deep. To prevent the tenons from "bottoming out," make the mortises slightly over ½ in. deep. We found the best way to cut the mortises is with an overhead routing system. Of

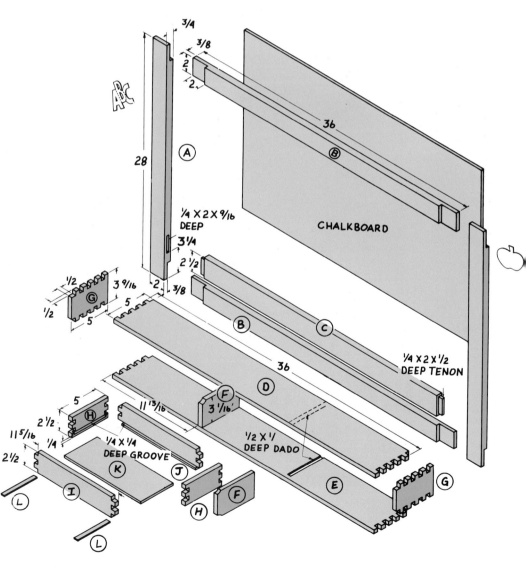

Figure 1. Use a thickness planer to thickness the material. Make light passes to reduce excessive wood tear.

course, a mortising accessory will also do the job.

Cut the tenons on the ends of the inner rails (C), then sand the inside edges of all framework pieces. Glue and assemble the stiles (A), rails (B) and inner rail (C). Use C-clamps during gluing, and square the assembly.

Build the Drawer Box and Drawers

Again, start by thickness planing the stock. This is a good time to plane all the remaining pieces of ½ in. stock that are needed for the chalkboard drawer box and drawers. Cut and joint all the common widths for the drawer box and drawers, and then cut the pieces to length following the Bill of Materials.

Create the finger joints on your table saw by using a dado blade set to cut ½ in. fingers. You will need to make a cutting jig as illustrated in the construction photos.

Set up the table saw's dado and cut the stopped dadoes for the drawer box top (D) and bottom (E). Follow the diagram for positioning. Use a band saw or scroll saw to cut off the front corners of the partitions (F) to fit in the stopped dadoes.

Sand the inside surfaces of all drawer box pieces and dry-fit. When you're sure you have a good, snug fit, disassemble the drawer box pieces and glue and clamp them together. Check the drawer box for squareness and wipe away any excess glue immediately with a damp cloth.

Figure 2. Cut half-laps into the edges of the stiles (A) and rails (B) with your table saw set to one-half the wood's thickness. Use a dado blade to make these cuts.

Figure 3. Make repetitive cuts in the half-lap areas. Use a pencil mark, placed on tape, to help you position the stock for dadoing.

Figure 4. Clean up the marks left by dadoing with a wide, sharp wood chisel. Clamp the workpiece to prevent fingers from getting in front of the wood chisel.

Figure 5. Make a finger joint jig from scrap plywood screwed to a table saw's miter jig. Cut two slots ½ in. wide, spaced ½ in. apart. Cut a guide pin to fit snugly inside one of the pins. This pin fits snugly but is removable.

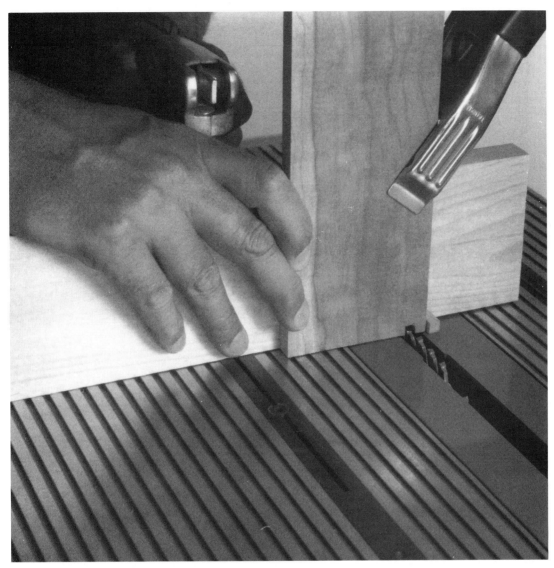

Figure 6. Make the first cut by sliding the workpiece against the guide pin. For additional cuts, place the workpiece's slot over the guide pin for spacing. Follow this same technique for cutting all box joints.

Rout the ¼ in. grooves in the inside of the drawer sides (H), fronts (I) and backs (J) ½ in. up from the bottom edges to hold the drawer bottoms (K). The grooves in the drawer fronts and backs run the full length of the stock, while the grooves in the drawer sides stop ¼ in. in from each end so that they won't show when assembled. Cut the drawer bottoms to size (¼ in. by 4⁷⁄₁₆ in. by 10¹¹⁄₁₆ in.) from maple plywood. Dry-assemble all drawer pieces, then disassemble, glue and clamp, and check for squareness. After making any necessary adjustments, put the drawers aside to dry. Once the drawers have properly dried, sand all assemblies smooth and flush with a belt sander.

Chalkboard Attachment

Chalkboards are available through office supply centers and many specialty stores. If you prefer, you can make your own by spraying tempered Masonite with a special chalkboard paint available at craft stores. Rout a ⅜ in. wide by ¼ in. deep rabbet in the back of the frame assembly to hold the chalkboard.

Finish sand the frame, drawer box and drawers. Be sure to use sandpaper to dull any sharp corners or edges that children could injure themselves on.

Final Assembly

Attach the completed drawer box to the frame with No. 8 by 1¼ in. wood screws. Drill pilot holes in the chalkboard and frame to accommodate No. 6 by ⅝ in. wood screws, but do not attach the assemblies at this time. Cut the runners (L) and glue them to the bottom of the drawers. These ¹⁄₃₂ in. by ½ in. by 4½ in. strips make the drawers slide easier and give you an equally spaced gap around the drawers.

If you desire, you can add the decorative appliqués that are made from ¼ in. plywood and cut out on a scroll saw.

Finishing

Paint the appliqués with a high-gloss enamel. You can also paint the drawer pulls with the same enamel. Finish the chalkboard project with a coat of semi-gloss polyurethane. Mount the chalkboard in the frame, attach the appliqués (if desired) and install the drawer pulls. □

This project is courtesy of the American Plywood Association.

Modular Wall System

Divide a room or accent a wall with this modular wall system.

Standing over 5 ft. tall and 5 ft. across, this modular wall system is ideal for your stereo equipment. There is even a handy compartment for storing records and tapes. A second compartment features a fold-down lid that doubles as a desk. Four adjustable shelves add even more versatile space.

Tips

The modular wall system is constructed from ¾ in. APA plywood sanded on both sides. Make sure that you select warp-free material for this project.

Construction

Cut out all of the project parts to their overall width and length using your table saw or handheld circular saw equipped with a plywood cutting blade. Then dress all of the edges. Joint the larger workpieces on a jointer, but use a disk sander for smaller places like the rails (B) and the frame supports (C).

Draw the patterns for the doors (H), desk lid (G) and frame supports (C). Then cut them out with a saber saw.

Now miter the edges of the top/bottom (E) and sides (F) on your table saw. You can also use a circular saw set to 45 degrees and guided by a straightedge. Make some test cuts on scrap material first to insure a perfect 45 degree miter. Then rabbet the back edges of these workpieces to accommodate the back (I).

Begin assembly by drilling mating dowel holes where the rails (B) adjoin the stiles (A). Drill these dowel holes to accommodate two ⅜ in. diameter by 2 in. dowels.

Now glue the rail to the stiles with carpenter's glue, and use a bar clamp to hold each of the three rail and stile assemblies. Make sure that the joints are snug and the units are square.

BILL OF MATERIALS — Modular Wall System

Finished Dimensions in Inches

A	Stile	¾ x 5 x 66 plywood	6
B	Rail	¾ x 5 x 8 plywood	3
C	Frame Support	¾ x 2 x 2 plywood	6
D	Shelf	¾ x 16 x 30 plywood	4
E	Top/Bottom	¾ x 15¼ x 30¼ plywood	4
F	Side	¾ x 15¼ x 16 plywood	4
G	Lid	¾ x 16 x 30¼ plywood	1
H	Door	¾ x 15⅛ x 16 plywood	2
I	Back	¾ x 15¼ x 30¼ plywood	2
J	Divider	¾ x 2 x 14½ plywood	4

Figure 1. Miter the cabinet sides (F) by running a circular saw set to 45 degrees along a straightedge. Use this T-square design and clamp it securely to the workpiece.

Figure 2. If your blade causes too much wood tearout, run a utility knife along a clamped carpenter's square. Then cut up to this line, not on it, with your saw. This scored line must be on the tearout side of the blade.

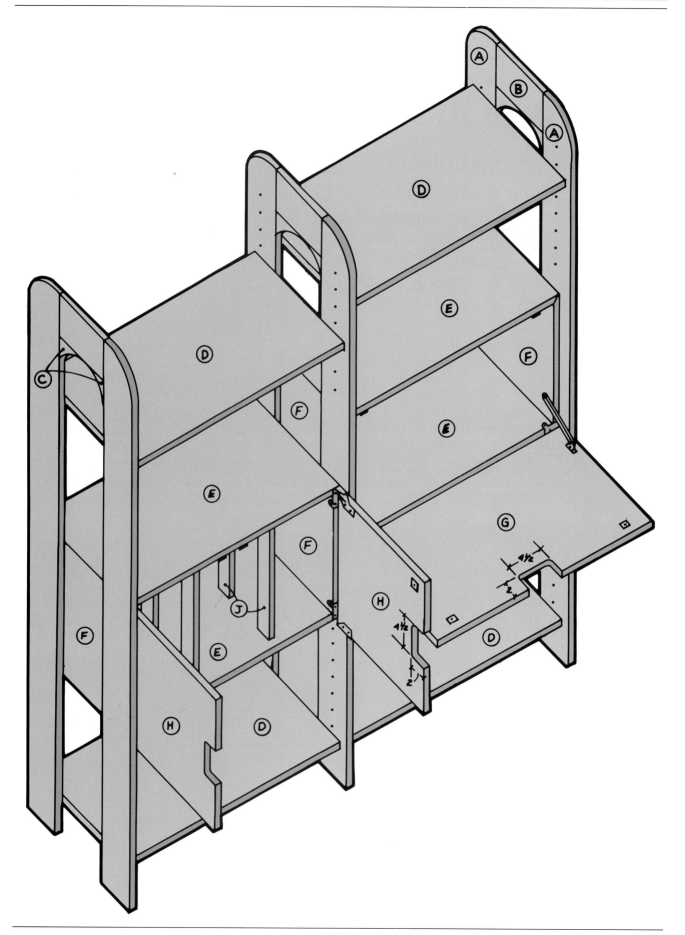

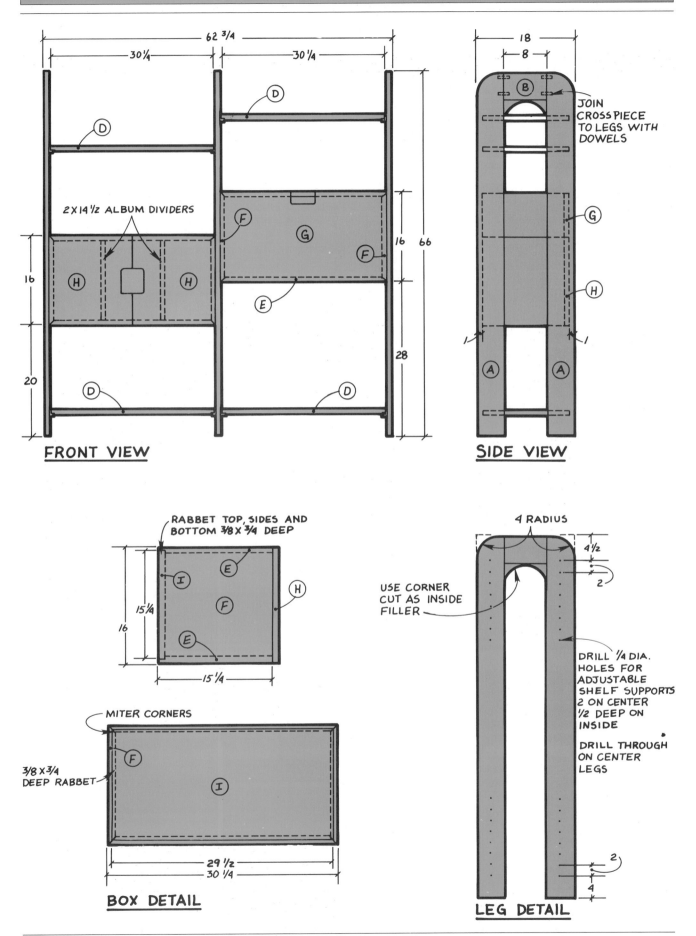

FRONT VIEW

62 ¾

30 ¼   30 ¼

D   D

2 X 14 ½ ALBUM DIVIDERS

F

G

16   66

F

H   H

E

16

28

20

D   D

SIDE VIEW

18

8

B

JOIN CROSSPIECE TO LEGS WITH DOWELS

G

H

1   1

A   A

BOX DETAIL

RABBET TOP, SIDES AND BOTTOM ⅜ X ¾ DEEP

I   E

F   H

15 ¼

16

E

15 ¼

MITER CORNERS

3/8 X ¾ DEEP RABBET

F

I

29 ½

30 ¼

LEG DETAIL

4 RADIUS

4 ½

2

USE CORNER CUT AS INSIDE FILLER

DRILL ¼ DIA. HOLES FOR ADJUSTABLE SHELF SUPPORTS 2 ON CENTER ½ DEEP ON INSIDE

DRILL THROUGH ON CENTER LEGS

2

4

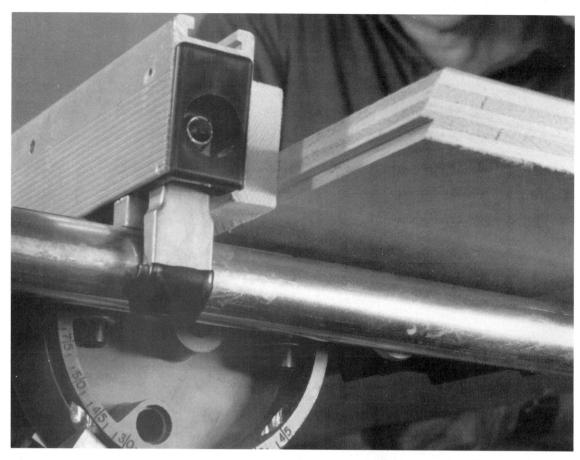

Figure 3. If you do not have a dado blade to make the rabbet in the cabinet top/bottom (E) and sides (F), make repetitive grooves on your table saw.

After the rail and stile assemblies are dry, glue the frame supports (C) in place. Make sure that you remove any excess glue that may interfere with the insertion of these frame supports.

Now draw the corner radius onto the stiles and cut out the shape with a saber saw. Sand these three rail-stile assemblies, and drill holes to accommodate shelf pins for the adjustable shelves (D).

Assemble the enclosed cabinets by securing the top/bottom workpieces (E) to the sides (F) along with the back (I). Secure with carpenter's glue and 4d finishing nails. Sink in all nail heads and fill in any recesses with a nontoxic wood filler. Then insert four album dividers (J) into the cabinet that will have the two hinged doors.

Assemble the modular wall system on a flat surface, and secure the two cabinets to the stiles with No. 10 by 1¼ in. flathead wood screws (counterbored). Make sure you pre-drill these fastener holes.

Attach the two doors to the cabinet with two sets of hinges. You must use pin hinges because conventional hinges such as straight pin hinges will interfere with the stiles. Then install two magnetic catches (one for each door).

Likewise, install the lid (G) with a set of pin hinges and a left and right lid support. Again, install two sets of magnetic catches in each corner of the lid.

Now insert the shelf pins and position the adjustable shelves (D) to insure that everything fits properly.

Install edging on the front of the shelves (D) and other showing surfaces where necessary.

Finishing

Remove all of the hardware, and finish sand the project. Slightly round the edges and corners with sandpaper. Then remove all of the dust with a lint-free, damp cloth.

Apply a base coat or primer to the project and sand lightly after dry. Then give it a final finish coat in the color or colors of your choice.

Reinstall the hardware, lid and shelves to complete your project. □

Figure 4. Clean out the rabbeted area (see previous photo) using a sharp wood chisel. Always clamp the workpiece to prevent one hand getting in harm's way in case of a slip.

This project is courtesy of Shopsmith, Inc.

Cheval Mirror

Enhance your home with this elegant cheval mirror.

The traditional design combined with the natural beauty of oak will make this cheval mirror a family treasure for generations. Its quality construction calls for a 4 ft. mirror that swivels on two turned pins for a full view. Ornately crafted legs, spindles and rails raise the unit to a full 5 ft. height.

Tips

Buy only straight, knot-free oak for this special project. You may also wish to buy a beveled mirror, which must be custom ordered. If you do, give the retailer the precise dimensions of the frame opening and rabbet details. You may have to make

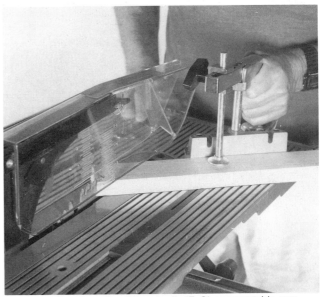

Figure 1. Miter the stiles (E) and rails (F, G) on your table saw. Use a combination saw blade to produce a smoothly cut surface.

Figure 2. Cut grooves in the stiles and rails to accept splines. Clamp a straightedge to the workpiece. The straightedge rides along the fence top. Move the workpiece into the wood and keep fingers well away from the blade.

Figure 3. Custom cut the splines (J) to fit the grooves you made in the stiles and rails. The spline's grain runs perpendicular to the longest length shown here. This makes the joint strong.

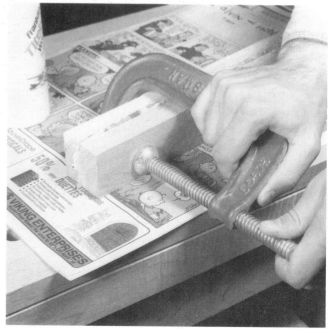

Figure 4. Surface-glue long pieces of material to form the spindle stock (A). Use carpenter's glue and secure the stock with C-clamps.

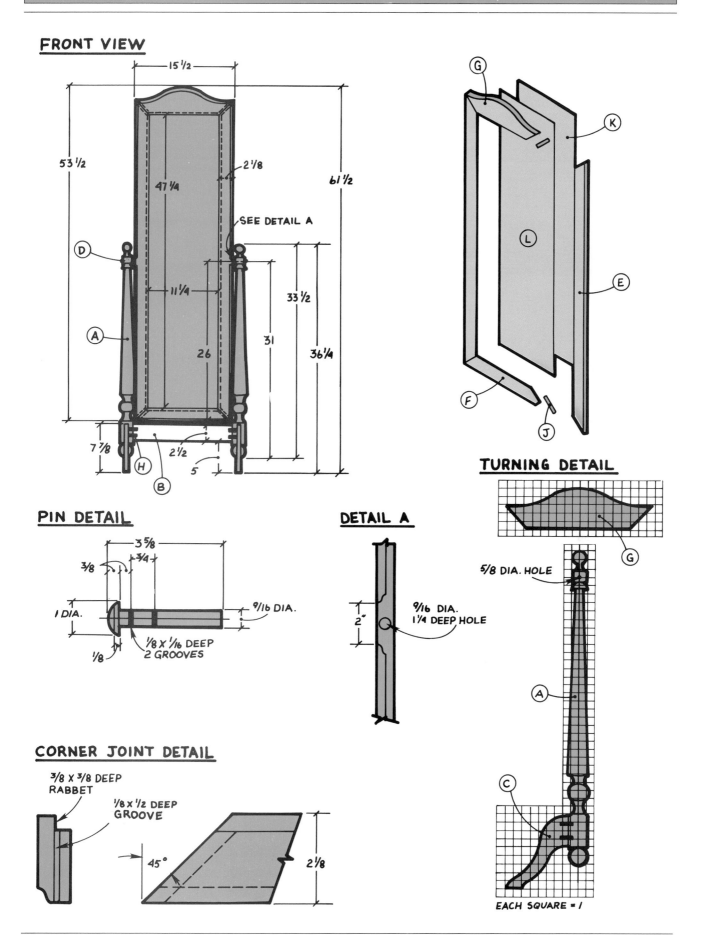

FRONT VIEW

15 1/2
53 1/2
47 1/4
2 1/8
61 1/2
SEE DETAIL A
D
11 1/4
33 1/2
31
A
26
36 1/4
7 7/8
2 1/2
H
5
B

G
K
L
E
F
J

PIN DETAIL

3 5/8
3/4
3/8
1 DIA.
9/16 DIA.
1/8 × 1/16 DEEP
2 GROOVES
1/8

DETAIL A

2"
9/16 DIA.
1 1/4 DEEP HOLE

TURNING DETAIL

5/8 DIA. HOLE
G
A
C
EACH SQUARE = 1

CORNER JOINT DETAIL

3/8 × 3/8 DEEP
RABBET
1/8 × 1/2 DEEP
GROOVE
45°
2 1/8

Figure 5. Taper the spindle stock (A) with a bench plane. This saves time and wear on your lathe tools.

modifications to the frame to accommodate the mirror, so do not cut the rabbets until you have the glass.

Construction

Start this project by gluing up stock for the spindles (A). Make sure that these pieces can be cut to a full 2 in. by 2 in. by 34 inches. Using a drill press, drill dowel holes in the spindle stock for the legs (C) and stretcher (B), along with the pivot pinholes. Use a bench plane to taper this spindle stock on all four sides ¼ in. over a length of 26 in. from the top end, and then turn the stock on a lathe.

Figure 6. Lay out the leg (C) pattern, and carefully cut it out on a band saw equipped with a ⅜ in. blade. Stay to the outside of the cutting line.

BILL OF MATERIALS — Cheval Mirror

Finished Dimensions in Inches

A	Spindle	2 x 2 x 33½ oak	2
B	Stretcher	¾ x 2½ x 16 oak	1
C	Leg	¾ x 3½ x 10½ oak	4
D	Pivot Pin	1 dia. x 3⅝ oak	2
E	Stile	¾ x 2⅛ x 51⅜ oak	2
F	Bottom Rail	¾ x 2⅛ x 15½ oak	1
G	Top Rail	¾ x 4¼ x 15½ oak	1
H	Dowel Pin	5/16 dia. x 2 oak	8
J	Spline	⅛ x 1 x 3½ oak	4
K	Mirror Back	⅛ x 12 x 48 plywood	1
L	Mirror	⅛ x 12 x 48	1

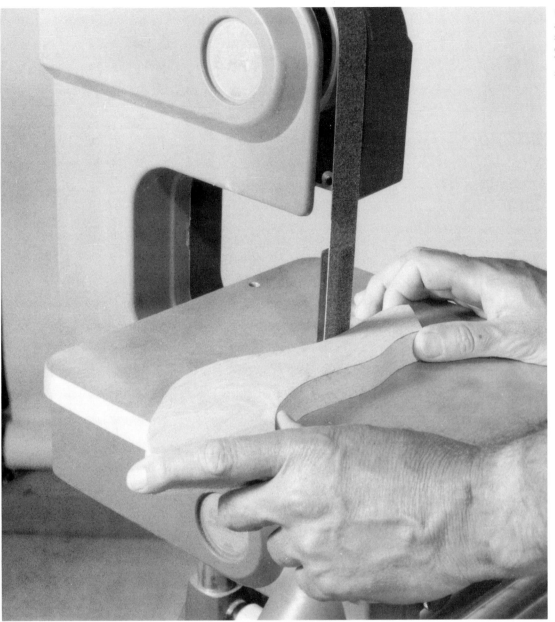

Figure 7. Use an abrasive sander to smooth the edges of the legs (C). Work in long, smooth strokes.

Turn the pivot pins (D) in the same manner. Be careful to turn them exactly to the dimensions given in the drawings.

Cut the stock for the mirror frame (E, F, G), stretcher (B) and legs (C) to size on the table saw. Use a dado blade to cut the ⅜ in. deep by ⅜ in. wide rabbet in the back of the frame stock. Then use a band saw and a drum sander to shape the legs, and a drill press to drill the dowel holes in the legs and the stretcher.

Miter the ends of the mirror stiles (E) and rails (F, G) with a carbide-tipped or a hollow-ground blade. Then cut the ½ in. deep spline kerfs on the ends of each piece. Cut and sand the contour on the top rail with a band saw. Make the splines (J) and dry-assemble the frame and base assembly. Mark the location of the ⅝ in. pivot pinholes on the stiles and drill them.

Round the top edges of the legs and stretcher with a ¼ in. quarter-round shaper cutter or router bit. For a decorative edge on the mirror frame, use an ogee shaper cutter, but be careful to stop and then start the cut around the pivot pinhole so as not to cut into it.

Glue and clamp the base assembly and the frame assembly and apply a final finish. Install the mirror in the frame and back it with ¼ in. hardboard or plywood (K). Use mirror retainer clips to secure the mirror and plywood back in place.

Mount the mirror frame to the base with the pivot pins and ⅜ in. inner diameter O-rings. The latter are available wherever faucet repair parts are sold. Used here, the O-rings supply the friction needed to keep the mirror positioned as you desire.

Fasten the pins to the frame with No. 8 by ¾ in. flathead wood screws (2 screws for 2 pins), secured from the back through the pivot pins. □

This project is courtesy of Shopsmith, Inc.

Traditional Drop-Leaf Table

Quality craftsmanship and authentic detailing make this versatile table a prize-winning project.

Our traditional drop-leaf table is a versatile, compact piece of furniture that offers a multitude of uses in your home decorating plans. For example, you can open both leaves and place it beside your couch to showcase a special lamp. Or, you can open one leaf and use the table as a bedside accent to support your reading lamp and telephone. Thanks to its versatility, the drop-leaf table has as many possibilities as your imagination can conjure.

This small drop-leaf table is patterned after a traditional Pembroke table. Mortise and tenon joinery is used in this project to make a table that is long-lasting and quite durable. Drop-leaf or rule joints are used to enhance the table's lines and eliminate the otherwise visible gap between leaves and table top.

Tips

A lathe duplicator is the perfect accessory for producing identical legs. Of course, you don't have to use a lathe duplicator to complete the drop-leaf table project, but it is safer, easier and far more precise than freehand turning — and all your table legs will match perfectly.

If you don't have a lathe, we have also supplied the design for a tapered leg.

BILL OF MATERIALS — Traditional Drop-Leaf Table

Finished Dimensions in Inches

A	Leg	1¾ x 1¾ x 25 hardwood	4
B	Side	¾ x 6 x 14½ hardwood	2
C	Front Top Rail	¾ x 1¾ x 16½ hardwood	1
D	Front Bottom Rail	¾ x 1¾ x 16½ hardwood	1
E	Back	¾ x 6 x 16½ hardwood	1
F	Drop-Leaf Support	¾ x ¾ x 10 hardwood	2
G	Drawer Guide	¾ x 1¹/₁₆ x 13 hardwood	2
H	Drawer Front	¾ x 4½ x 15 hardwood	1
J	Drawer Side	¾ x 4½ x 15¼ hardwood	2
K	Drawer Back	½ x 3⅜ x 14 hardwood	1
L	Drawer Bottom	¼ x 14 x 15¼ hardwood	1
M	Table Top (before joinery)	¾ x 36 x 19 hardwood	1
N	Dowel	⅜ dia. x 1½ hardwood	2

Construction

Cut all the wood stock to size according to the Bill of Materials.

Since you will likely use several pieces of stock glued together for the table top (M), we suggest cutting the edges of that stock with a very sharp glue joint shaper bit (Fig. 1). This gives you a self-aligning, unitized spine/groove combination, increases the gluing surface and provides a stronger bond. The rough top to be squared later should measure 19 in. by 36 in., thus providing ample stock to cut the drop-leaf joint. Hint: keeping the worktable at waist level makes controlling the workpiece easier.

To cut in the drop-leaf joints (Fig. 2) before the edges of the table are shaped, use a drop-leaf joint shaper and slowly ease it into the stock — about ¼ in. each pass. This two-knife set requires that one be raised from underneath and one be lowered onto the workpiece.

The mortise and tenon joints give real strength to your table and minimize the wobble found in less structurally sound joints. Use this as one of the locking joints, since it helps form the rugged and sturdy framework. To prevent mixing the faces as you cut the joinery, carefully mark and identify the table legs' (A) stock relative to their final positions. Mark locations for eight mortises and two dovetails (see illustration).

Turn the legs (A) on the lathe or taper them on a band saw (both options are included in the illustration). Next, use a sharp ⅜ in. mortising bit/chisel to cut mortises (Fig. 3). (Always cut mortises before tenons, as it is easier to adjust a miscut mortise than a tenon.) An option is to use a ⅜ in. brad point drill bit to cut the mortises, cleaning up the edges with a hand chisel, or you can even rout them.

Cut the dovetail slots in the top of the front legs. The locking dovetails anchor the entire front of the table assembly, and lock the legs and the front top rail (C) firmly together. Mark the top of the legs with a sharp knife. For initial roughing out, use a ½ in. brad point bit installed in a drill. Finish with a ½ in. wood chisel. Use a band saw to cut the male dovetail on the front top rail (C). Finish fit with a chisel and wood rasp.

Next, use a dado and an extension fence (Fig. 4) to cut the eight tenons and custom-fit your mortises. Use a sharp knife to mark tenons (this prevents splinters as you make dado cuts). To leave room for glue to expand, cut tenons ⅛ in. less in length than the depth of the corresponding mortises.

To make dowel joints on the drop-leaf supports (F), use a dado blade with the miter gauge set at 45 degrees to cut the opening in the sides (Fig. 5). A 45 degree miter on each end makes these supports self-aligning and flush to the side when closed. Next, cut the supports and drill for the dowel pins. Rub a little soap on the dowels and insert them in the supports and sides.

To add decoration around the base of the apron (B, E), use a quarter-round and bead moulding cutter positioned halfway onto the surface of the bottom edge of the stock. For safety, use a push stick or push block.

Next, drill ⅜ in. screw pockets (Fig. 6) in the sides (B) and back (E) to hold the top in place. (The table base and top form a simple butt joint and need this reinforcement.)

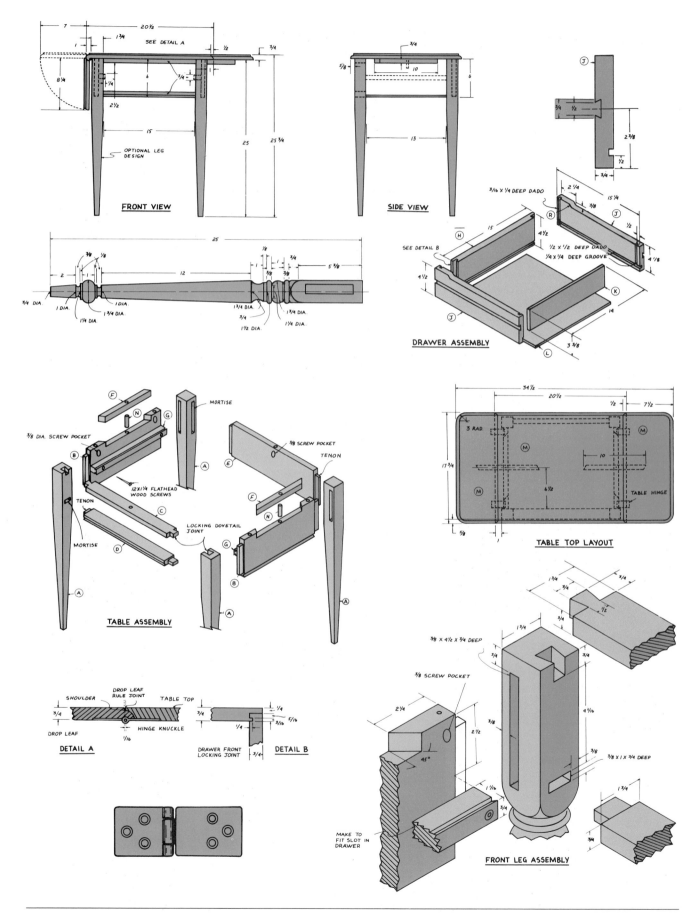

FRONT VIEW

SIDE VIEW

DRAWER ASSEMBLY

TABLE ASSEMBLY

TABLE TOP LAYOUT

DETAIL A

DETAIL B

FRONT LEG ASSEMBLY

Dry-assemble the legs (A) to the apron pieces (B, C, D, E). Check the fit and apply masking tape at each joint. Disassemble and carefully apply glue to each mortise and tenon and dovetail. Reassemble, check squareness and clamp

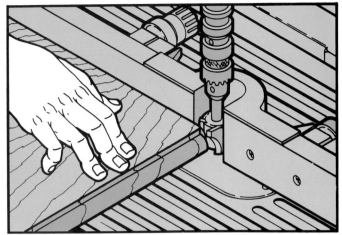

Figure 2. Cut in the drop-leaf joints before the edges of the top are shaped. For clarity, guards not shown.

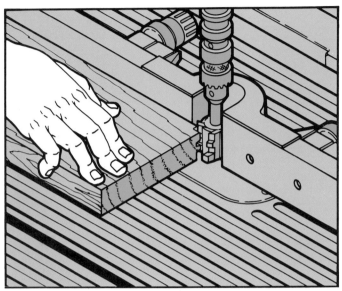

Figure 1. Cut a glue joint into the table top (M) with a very sharp glue-joint shaper bit. For clarity, guards not shown.

together for 24 hours. The tape keeps excess glue from seeping onto the face of the wood.

To withstand the pressure exerted on the drawer case, we used a combination dado/spline joint to connect the drawer

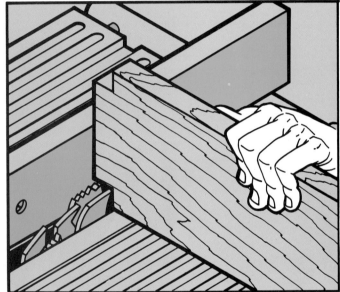

Figure 4. Use a dado installed in your table saw to cut the tenons (note the use of extension fence).

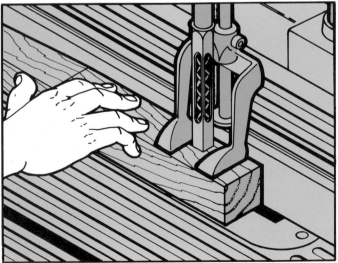

Figure 3. Cut the mortises in the legs (A) with a sharp ⅜ in. mortising bit/chisel.

front (H) to the drawer sides (J). Turn the drawer front on edge and use a dado blade to cut the 5/16 in. by ¾ in. deep dado. Then use a regular blade to cut the 3/16 in. by ¼ in. deep spline. Next, cut the ½ in. stopped dado for the drawer end with

Figure 5. Cut the opening for the drop-leaf supports in the sides (B) with a dado blade. Cut one-half the depth at one time.

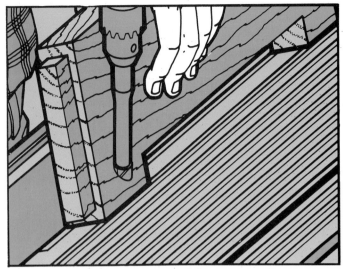

Figure 6. Drill screw pockets in the sides (B). Drill at a 10 degree angle, with a ½ in. Forstner bit, to within ⅜ in. of the bottom. Use a ¼ in. brad point bit to make pilot holes for the No. 12 round head screws. For clarity, guards not shown.

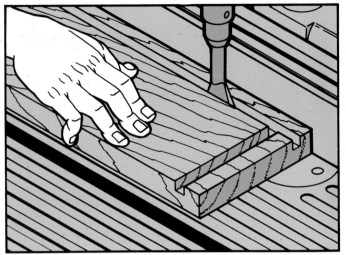

Figure 7. Rout a ¼ in. groove into the drawer front (H), sides (J) and back (K) to accommodate the drawer bottom. For clarity, guards not shown.

either a dado blade or a router. The strength of these joints eliminates the need for glue-blocks.

To cut the self-aligning sliding dovetails in the drawer sides (J), use a Mark V set in the drill press mode (or router table) with a ⁹⁄₁₆ in. dovetail router bit (Fig. 8). Next, rout the drawer guides (G) (Fig. 9).

relief cut for the hinge's cylinder or pivot.

Next, fit the top into place. (No glue is needed; screws will hold it and permit expansion/contraction.) Once the top

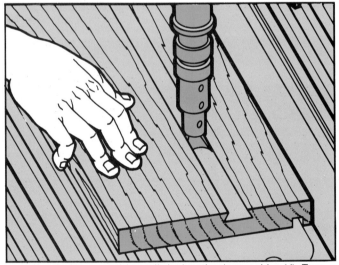

Figure 8. Also rout a dovetail slot into the drawer sides (J). Two passes are needed, both at a full ¼ in. depth. For clarity, guards not shown.

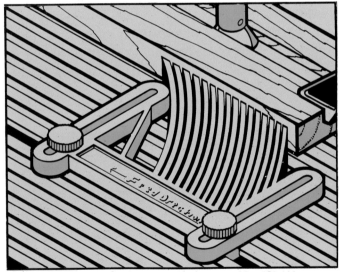

Figure 9. Now, rout the dovetail in the drawer guides (G) with a feather board firmly holding the wood stock against the fence. Push against the router rotation. For clarity, guards not shown.

is secured, mount the drawer guides, again without using glue. Rub with soap for smoothness.

Drill and countersink holes for attaching the guides to the inside of the aprons on the sides (B). Assemble and glue the drawer, but not the bottom (L), as final fitting may be necessary. Mark for the drawer guides (G) and drill pilot holes, but don't attach them yet.

The position of the drop-leaf hinges is critical (see Detail A). From the shoulder of the joint, move the hinges ¹⁄₁₆ in. toward the leaf. This prevents binding as the leaf moves. As you make the shallow mortise to accept the hinge, form a

Finishing

Finally, remove the drop-leaf hinges. Finish sand and apply stain and finish. Now that you are finished, give yourself a hearty pat on the back and show your new custom-crafted, drop-leaf table to someone you care about. Congratulations. Now is when the satisfaction and reward really begin. ☐

This project is courtesy of Cherry Tree Toys, Inc.

Log Truck

This is a toy that children will turn to time and time again.

It is the simple toys, like this truck, that capture a child's imagination. You can almost hear the motor running as this log truck rolls out of the woods with a full load. You may want to make several of these trucks, as they are easy to construct and make great gifts.

Tips

This log truck is constructed from cherry lumber and will take many years of rugged punishment. Buy knot-free lumber.

Some of the parts, like the wheels, can be made or purchased. Cherry Tree Toys, Inc. offers full-size patterns, project parts, cherry workpieces and even a finished truck. For information and a catalog, write to the address listed in the Bill of Materials.

Construction

Transfer our pattern onto graph paper. Then, using carbon paper, trace out all of the pieces on nonsplintering wood of the proper thickness.

Cut out the body (G), bed (K), cab (H), cab top (J) and hood (I) on your band saw. Use a fine-tooth blade to reduce the amount of sanding required.

The headlamps (A), radiator cap (B) and wheels (C) can be purchased as indicated in the Bill of Materials, but they also can be made. Substitute ½ in. diameter doweling for the headlamps and radiator cap. Allow these parts to protrude ½ in. above the hood. Cut the 2¼ in. diameter wheels using a hole saw or turn them on your lathe.

BILL OF MATERIALS — Log Truck

Finished Dimensions in Inches

A*	Headlamp	#3 cherry	2
B*	Radiator Cap	#4 cherry	1
C*	Wheel	#15 cherry	4
D	Stake	⅜ dia. x 2¾ cherry dowels	4
E	Axle	⅜ dia. x 4¹³⁄₁₆ cherry dowels	2
F	Log	¾ dia. x 6¼ cherry dowels	12
G	Body	1¾ x 3¼ x 10 cherry	1
H	Cab	1¾ x 3 x 3⅜ cherry	1
I	Hood	1¾ x 1½ x 2¼ cherry	1
J	Cab Top	¾ x 2¾ x 4¼ cherry	1
K	Bed	¾ x 4½ x 6½ cherry	1

* These parts are available from Cherry Tree Toys, Inc., Dept. PSW, 408 S. Jefferson St., Belmont, OH 43718 (614) 484-4363.

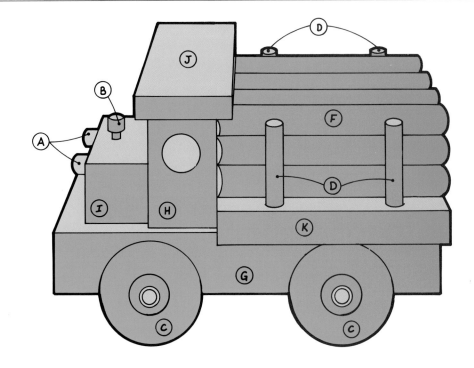

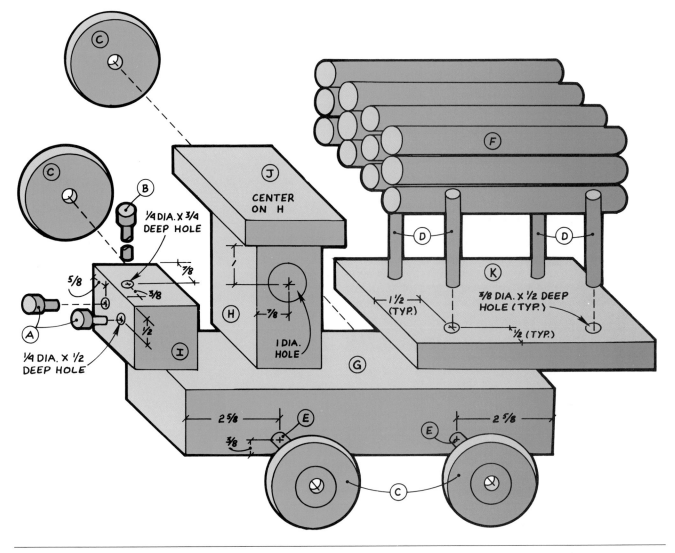

Now cut the axles (E), stakes (D) and logs (F) to their proper lengths on a band saw. Finish sand all of the project parts on a stationary belt sander.

Next, drill all holes as indicated in the illustrations with your drill press or drill guide. Use a backer board to prevent wood tear-out.

The next phase requires assembling the log truck. Dry-assemble the parts first, then use carpenter's glue or another nontoxic glue. To ease assembly, clamp one or two parts at a time, but no more. Otherwise, the parts may move around on you.

You might want to secure the cab top and bed with brass brads to avoid clamping. If you use brads, pre-drill all nail holes.

Glue the hood, cab and cab top to the body. Do not use too much glue.

After this assembly has dried, glue the bed in place. Afterwards, glue and install the headlamps, radiator cap and stakes.

The axle turns freely inside the truck body but must be glued to the wheels. Make sure the axle turns freely before gluing the axle ends to the wheels. Also, make sure the wheels are parallel to the truck body.

Finishing

Finish sand the entire project, making sure all edges and corners are blunt. Then apply a child-safe finish to the project, including the logs.

Now, load up the logs and this log truck is ready to roll to the saw mill. □

Figure 1. Cut the dowels for the logs (F) to length on your band saw. Hold the dowel firmly while cutting to prevent it from turning and binding.

Figure 2. The axle holes must be perpendicular to the truck body. Use a brad point bit and frequently check your work.

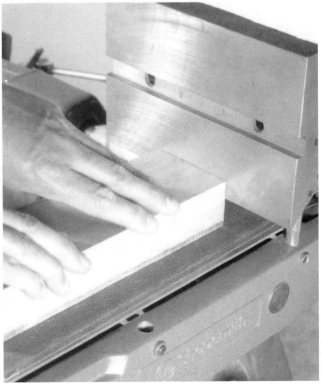

Figure 3. Sand the project parts on a stationary belt sander. Dull the edges and corners too.

This project is courtesy of Shopsmith, Inc.

Colonial Spice Cabinet

Spice up your kitchen with this charming cabinet.

This charming, functional cabinet is made from ½ in., ⅜ in. and ¼ in. pine or hardwood stock that you can prepare on a band saw or a thickness planer.

Construction

Resaw a 5 ft. piece of 1 x 4 stock on your band saw to form the ¼ in. and ⅜ in. pieces. Use the miter gauge with a wooden fence extension and set up the cut so you will end up with ⁹⁄₃₂ in. and ¹³⁄₃₂ in. thick boards. Cut the stock a little oversize to give you room to sand or plane it to proper thickness.

Similarly, prepare a 4 ft. length of 1 x 10 and a 7 ft. piece of 1 x 4 each to a ½ in. thickness.

Cut the back (B) from the wide stock. Then rip the ¼ in. stock to 3⅛ in. for the drawer backs (K, L) and the drawer bottoms (M, N). Rip the sides (A) to 4 inches. Do not rip the back to its finished width yet.

Saw to length all remaining parts according to the Bill of Materials. Tip: Cut the long stock into manageable pieces, then use a stop block on the fence.

Form the rabbets in the backs of the sides (A) with the dado accessory installed in your table saw. Next, cut the rabbets in the drawer fronts (G, H) using the same fence attachment and a miter gauge extension for support. Cut dadoes in the sides (A) and partitions (C, F).

Groove the drawer bottoms in the drawer sides (J) and the drawer fronts (G, H) with the dado accessory. Cut out the contours on the sides (A) using a band saw or jigsaw.

Now dry-assemble the sides (A) and parts C, D, E, F with

clamps and check for fit. Disassemble and then use glue and 4d finishing nails on the outside joints. Use glue only on the interior joints.

Rip the back (B) to width, then cut and sand the top and bottom contours. Drill the ¼ in. mounting hole and then attach the back with 1 in. brads.

Drill the knob mounting holes in the drawer fronts (G, H).

Assemble the drawers with glue and ¾ in. brads. After the glue has dried, sand each drawer to fit. Use a disk or belt sander. Number the drawers on the back for location.

Finishing

Finish sand the entire cabinet and round all edges slightly for a well-worn, Colonial effect. Apply stain, if desired, and finish with a satin polyurethane. Attach the drawer knobs. □

BILL OF MATERIALS — Colonial Spice Cabinet

Finished Dimensions in Inches

A	Side	½ x 4 x 20 pine	2
B	Back	½ x 8½ x 24¾ pine	1
C	Horizontal Partition	½ x 3½ x 8¼ pine	2
D	Bottom	½ x 3½ x 8¼ pine	1
E	Drawer Partition	½ x 3½ x 4 pine	4
F	Vertical Partition	½ x 3½ x 11¾ pine	1
G	Smaller Drawer Front	½ x 3½ x 3¾ pine	6
H	Large Drawer Front	½ x 3½ x 8 pine	1
J	Drawer Side	⅜ x 3½ x 3¼ pine	14
K	Small Drawer Back	¼ x 3⅛ x 3 pine	6
L	Larger Drawer Back	¼ x 3⅛ x 7¼ pine	1
M	Small Drawer Bottom	¼ x 3⅛ x 3¼ pine	6
N	Large Drawer Bottom	¼ x 3⅛ x 7½ pine	1

Figure 1. Cut out the back's (B) contours with a scroll saw. Stay short of the cutting line.

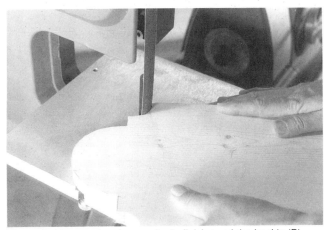

Figure 2. Use an abrasive sander to finish sand the back's (B) contour, finishing up to the cutting line. Sand in long strokes.

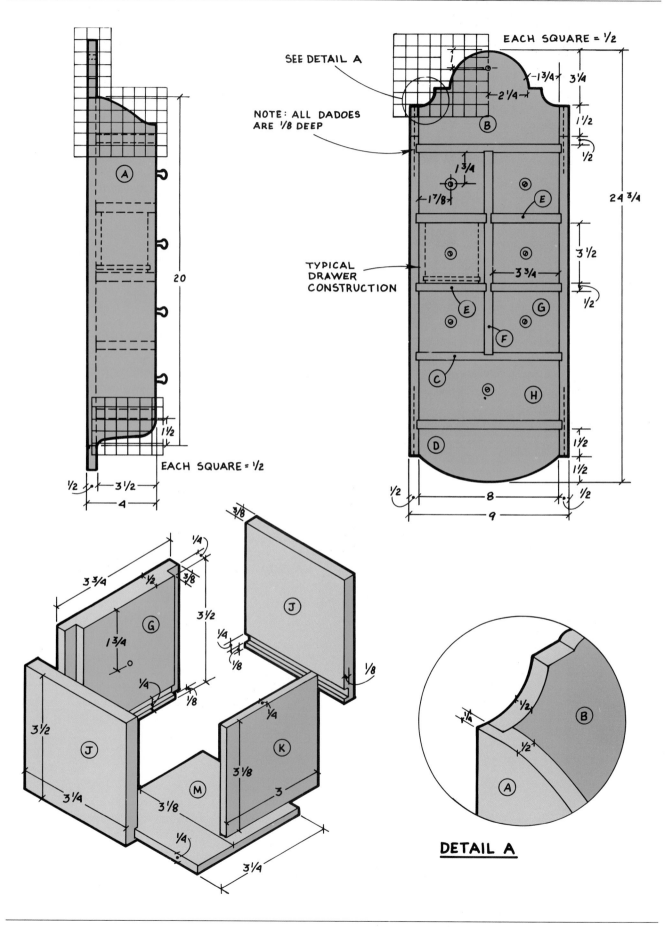

EACH SQUARE = ½

SEE DETAIL A

NOTE: ALL DADOES ARE ⅛ DEEP

TYPICAL DRAWER CONSTRUCTION

EACH SQUARE = ½

DETAIL A

This project is courtesy of Shopsmith, Inc.

Sofa Table

Display your woodworking skills with this finely crafted sofa table.

Wouldn't a beautiful, professional-quality table like this look great in your living room or hall? Maybe against that empty wall you've never quite figured out what to do with. How about behind your couch, a great place for displaying flowers or family photographs. Whatever use you find for it, with these easy-to-follow plans you can create a fine piece of furniture that you'll be proud to display in your home for many years. And you'll be even prouder when you say to your friends and guests, "Thanks! I built it myself!"

Tips

If you prefer, you can substitute doweled joints for the mortise and tenon joints required for this project. Use two dowels at each joint. Also, use carpenter's glue for the project's assembly.

Construction

Glue up stock for the top (A) and let dry for 24 hours. Then cut to size, joint the edges and sand smooth.

Cut parts B, C, D, E, F, G to size according to the Bill of Materials. Allow enough extra material so you can joint the material to final size.

Cut two pieces of stock 2 in. by 2 in. by 25½ inches. Tilt the table of your saw to 45 degrees, and cut each piece of stock lengthwise to make four legs (H) into the shape of right triangles (see Detail 1). Using a shaper or router, lightly round off all three edges of the triangular shape the full length of all four legs.

Using a lathe, turn two pine spindles 2 in. in diameter and 25½ in. in length. Locate the center of the spindles and cut them in half lengthwise to make four leg caps (I). (See Detail 2.)

Assemble the frame rails (B) and frame stiles (C) using ⅜ in. dowel pins and glue. (See Detail 3.)

Cut the 1¾ in. by ⅜ in. by ⅜ in. mortise and tenons in the bottom ends (D) as shown in Detail 4.

Figure 1. Surface glue two pieces of stock together with newspaper sandwiched in between to turn the half-round leg caps (I).

Now, cut the 4½ in. by ⅜ in. by ⅜ in. tenons in the top ends (E) as shown in Detail 5.

Next, make the 1¾ in. by ⅜ in. by ⅜ in. tenons in the bottom rail (F) as shown in Detail 6.

Similarly, make the 4½ in. by ⅜ in. by ⅜ in. tenons in the facings (G) as shown in Detail 7.

Make the 4½ in. by ⅜ in. by ⅜ in. and 1¾ in. by ⅜ in. by ⅜ in. mortises in the legs (H). Follow the diagrams in Detail 1 carefully for placement of the mortises, especially at the bottoms. Use a sharp wood chisel to form the mortises.

Lay out the facings (G), and use a band saw or jig saw to cut out the profiles.

Use a shaper or router to form the decorative ogee design around the perimeter of the assembled top frame. Then cut the bead and bevel designs on the bottom ends (D), top ends (E), facings (G) and both surfaces of the bottom rail (F).

Also rout or shape the round over edge around the perimeter of the top (A), or use a design of your choice.

Before assembling the parts, sand all exposed surfaces smooth with a pad sander.

Assembly

Using Detail 8 as a guide, begin assembly of your sofa table as described below. Be sure to allow ample time for the glue

BILL OF MATERIALS — Sofa Table

Finished Dimensions in Inches

A	Top	¾ x 16 x 56 pine	1
B	Frame Rail	¾ x 3½ x 55½ pine	2
C	Frame Stile	¾ x 3½ x 8½ pine	2
D	Bottom End	¾ x 2½ x 11¼ pine	2
E	Top End	¾ x 5¼ x 11¼ pine	2
F	Bottom Rail	¾ x 2½ x 52½ pine	1
G	Facing	¾ x 5¼ x 51¼ pine	2
H	Leg	2 x 2 x 25½ pine	4
I	Leg Cap	2 dia. x 25½ half-round pine	4

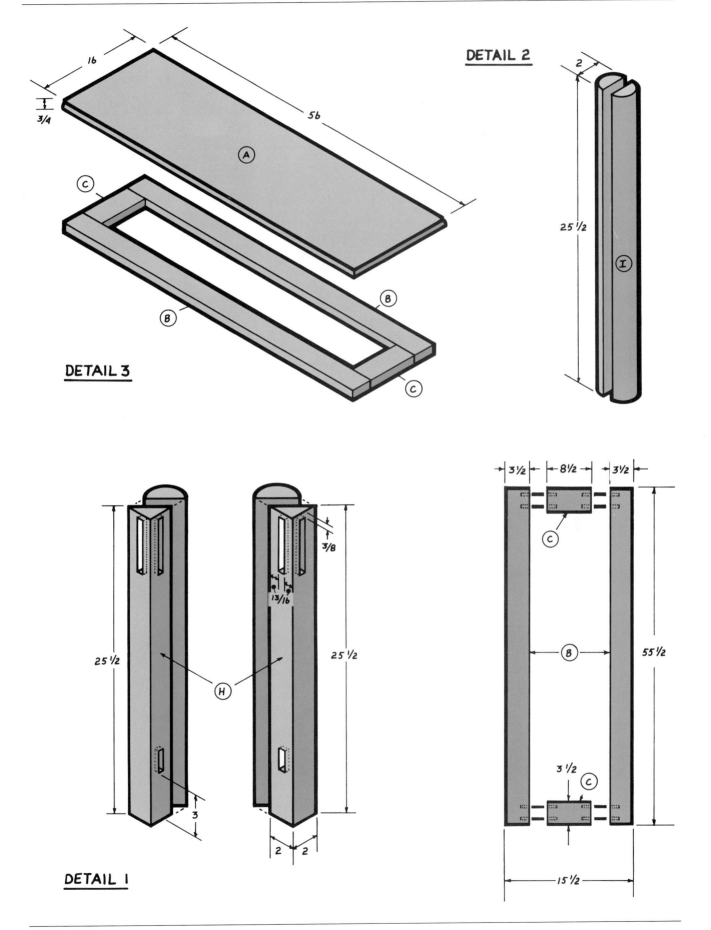

DETAIL 2

DETAIL 3

DETAIL 1

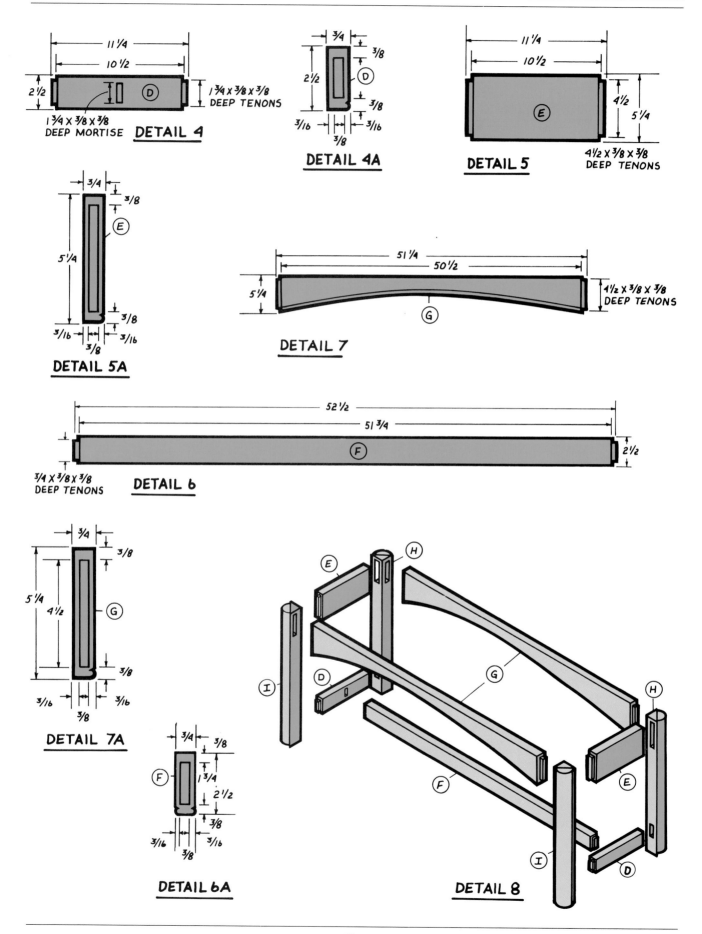

11 1/4
10 1/2
2 1/2
1 3/4 x 3/8 x 3/8
DEEP TENONS
1 3/4 x 3/8 x 3/8
DEEP MORTISE   **DETAIL 4**

3/4
3/8
2 1/2
D
3/8
3/16   3/16
3/8
DETAIL 4A

11 1/4
10 1/2
4 1/2
E
5 1/4
4 1/2 x 3/8 x 3/8
DEEP TENONS
DETAIL 5

3/4
3/8
E
5 1/4
3/8
3/16   3/16
3/8
DETAIL 5A

51 1/4
50 1/2
5 1/4
G
4 1/2 x 3/8 x 3/8
DEEP TENONS
DETAIL 7

52 1/2
51 3/4
F
2 1/2
3/4 x 3/8 x 3/8
DEEP TENONS   **DETAIL 6**

3/4
3/8
5 1/4
4 1/2
G
3/8
3/16   3/16
3/8
DETAIL 7A

3/4
3/8
F
1 3/4
2 1/2
3/8
3/16   3/16
3/8
DETAIL 6A

E   H
I   D   G   H
F   E
I   D
DETAIL 8

to dry on all subassemblies, and wipe away any excess glue with a damp cloth before it dries.

Glue and clamp top (A) to the frames (B, C). (See Detail 3.) Then glue and clamp the legs (H) to the leg caps (I), as shown in Detail 8.

Next, attach the leg assemblies (H, I) to the bottom ends (D) and top ends (E).

Now, glue and clamp the facings (G) to the leg assemblies (H, I), and the bottom rail (F) to the bottom ends (D).

Secure the top assembly (A, B, C) to the leg and frame assembly (D, E, F, G, H, I).

Finishing

After the project has dried, finish sand and stain with the color of your choice. Apply a sanding sealer, then sand lightly after the sealer has thoroughly dried. Spread on a final finish to suit. □

Figure 2. Lay out the areas to be mortised on the triangular legs (H). Then remove the areas with a sharp wood chisel.

This project is courtesy of the American Plywood Association.

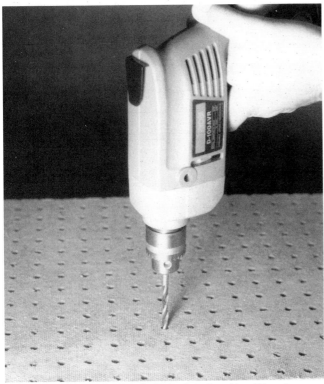

Figure 1. Drill holes for the shelf pins into the sides (A) and cabinet dividers (D) using a scrap of Pegboard to help you locate the holes. Drill holes to suit the diameter of your shelf pins.

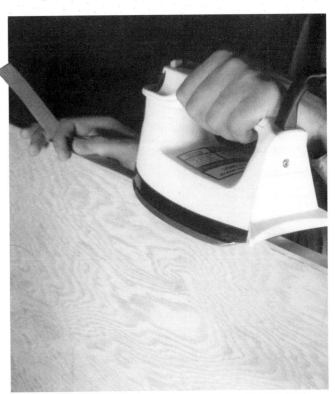

Figure 2. Apply an edging to the plywood edges. This edging is affixed by ironing it on.

Modular Secretary

This secretary features storage cupboards below, adjustable shelves above and a roomy desk in between.

This contemporary styled secretary organizes books, stationery and writing materials and even has enough space for a typewriter or small personal computer. The secretary also features a built-in light and storage space below for files, games and important papers.

Tips

This project uses ¾ in. APA plywood, sanded on both sides. Buying plywood that has been sanded on both sides saves time, since only minimal surface sanding is necessary.

Use 4d finishing nails and carpenter's glue for assem-

bling the modular secretary. For added strength, use doweling. Make sure that you sink all nail heads and fill the recesses with a nontoxic wood filler.

Construction

Cut out all of the project parts to their appropriate widths and lengths from ¾ in. plywood. Rip them to width where

BILL OF MATERIALS — Modular Secretary			
		Finished Dimensions in Inches	
A	Side	¾ x 12 x 79 plywood	2
B	Top	¾ x 12 x 46½ plywood	1
C	Cabinet Bottom	¾ x 12 x 46½ plywood	1
D	Cabinet Divider	¾ x 12 x 26½ plywood	2
E	Cabinet Shelf	¾ x 12 x 15 plywood	3
F	Table Top and Bottom	¾ x 18 x 46½ plywood	2
G	Table Divider	¾ x 4 x 18 plywood	3
H	Desk Bottom	¾ x 12 x 12 plywood	2
I	Desk Side	¾ x 11¼ x 23¾ plywood	2
J	Back	⅜ x 48 x 79 plywood	1
K	Desk Shelf	¾ x 11¼ x 11¼ plywood	3
L	Light Shroud	¾ x 3 x 46½ plywood	1
M	Door	¾ x 11⅞ x 23½ plywood	2
N	Cleat	¾ x ¾ x 11 plywood	2

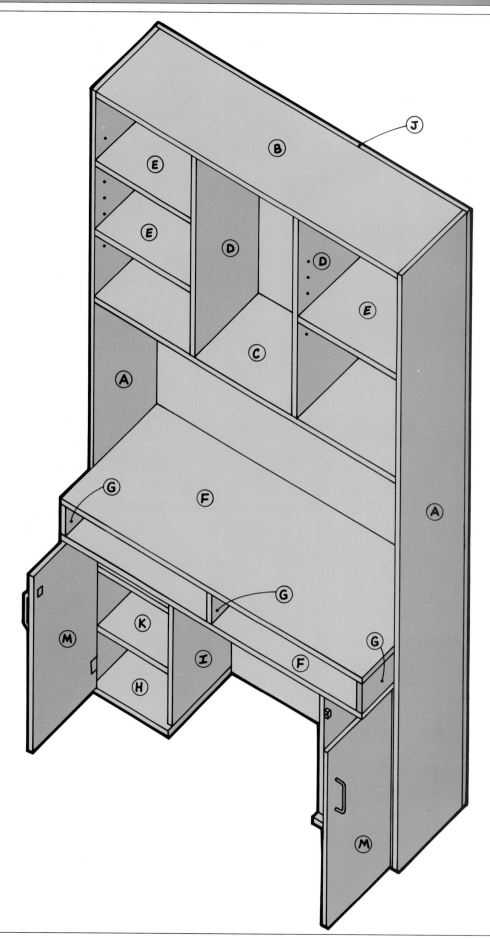

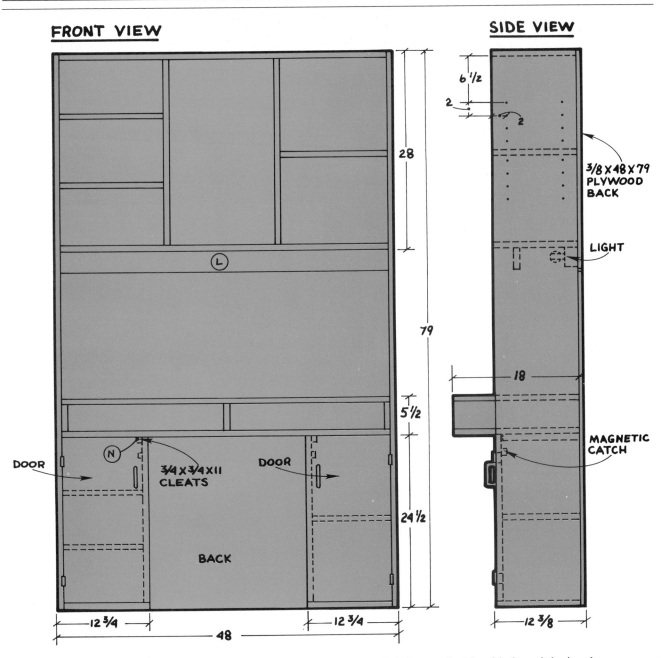

FRONT VIEW

28

79

5½

24½

DOOR

DOOR

BACK

¾ X ¾ X 11 CLEATS

12¾

12¾

48

SIDE VIEW

6½

2

2

⅜ X 48 X 79 PLYWOOD BACK

LIGHT

18

MAGNETIC CATCH

12⅜

possible on a table saw using a combination blade or a plywood cutting blade. A radial arm saw is ideal for crosscutting the workpieces to length. If you use a radial arm saw, cut the workpieces with the good side down. If not, use a circular saw equipped with a plywood cutting blade to crosscut the long pieces, such as the sides (A), guided by a clamped straightedge.

Check to make sure that all of the workpieces for assembly are absolutely square. If they are not, you will have difficulty assembling the project.

The adjustable cabinet shelves (E) rest on shelf pins that are available at hardware stores or lumberyards. Drill holes to accommodate them into the side pieces (A) and the cabinet dividers (D) as indicated in the illustration.

Assemble the sides (A), the top (B), the cabinet bottom (C) and the cabinet dividers (D) with 4d finishing nails and carpenter's glue. Now square the assembly with a framing

square. It is best to do this with the unit laying down on your shop or garage floor.

After the glue has dried, custom cut the back (J) to fit. Now secure the back to the assembly, making sure that the back fits flush with the edges of the sides and top.

Next, assemble the lower desk components. Affix the desk side (I), the desk shelf (K) and the desk bottom (H) to the side and back of the secretary assembly. Note that the lower left desk compartment has two shelves (K).

Custom cut the doors (M). Use two 1½ in. straight pin hinges for each door, and mortise the edge of each door the thickness of a folded hinge. Then mount the doors to the secretary assembly, making sure there is enough clearance so that the doors won't bind against the table when it is installed. Also install a magnetic catch for each door so that it closes properly. Now add contemporary door handles to suit your room style.

Figure 3. Remove excess edging by filing into the edge as you move the file forward. Work slowly. Then sand the edge to suit.

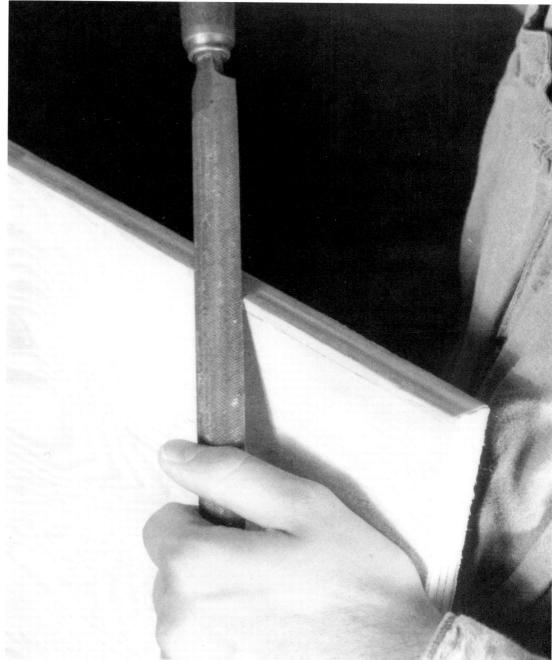

The next phase consists of constructing the table assembly. Make sure that the table top and bottom workpieces (F) fit into the secretary cavity. They should fit squarely, with no unsightly gaps. Then secure the table top and bottom to the table dividers (G). Square the unit and allow it to dry thoroughly. Once the glue has cured, install two cleats (N) to the table bottom. Next, attach the desk to the secretary and secure. Note that the desk sides (I) are secured to the cleats. During this installation, make sure that the door has cleared the desk.

Install a single-tube fluorescent light fixture underneath the cabinet bottom and position a light shroud (L) in place. Drill a hole in the back of the secretary to accommodate the cord for the fluorescent light.

Fill in all blemishes with a nontoxic wood filler. For a more finished appearance, apply an appropriate edging to the exposed surfaces of the secretary. These edgings are available from a number of mail order sources and home centers.

Remove the drawer hardware and fluorescent light fixtures and sand the project thoroughly. Round over all sharp edges and corners. Before you paint, wipe the dust away with a damp cloth.

Spray on an appropriate wood sealer and allow it to dry, then sand the sealer thoroughly. Next, give it a final coat of paint and allow it to dry thoroughly.

Move the modular secretary to where it will be used before installing the fluorescent light, hardware and shelf pins, along with the adjustable shelves (E). □

This project is courtesy of Karl Baker, Cal Brandow and Shopsmith, Inc.

Sewing Thread Holder

This thread holder is great for the sewing room and a unique way to display and organize thread.

If you or your spouse has ever sewn or know someone who sews quite often, keeping the ever-growing collection of threads handy, organized and within reach can be a real chore. Some of the more infrequently used colors usually end up at the bottom of the sewing basket, possibly never to be seen again! Wouldn't it be helpful to have all the thread colors available for easy access? This holder organizes and shows at a glance what colors and amounts of threads are available and is a great-looking addition to any sewing room. It features pivot shelves that allow you to easily insert or remove thread.

Cut the Stock

We made our thread holder from pine, but you can substitute the wood of your choice. Use used ¾ in. and ½ in. pine. You will either have to buy the ½ in. stock from a lumberyard or thickness it yourself. The easiest way to obtain ½ in. stock is

to pass it through a thickness planer or stationary jointer.

Using a table saw, begin by cutting the top (A), bottom (B), shelves (C), sides (D) and upper back (E) to the sizes shown in the Bill of Materials. Also cut the ¼ in. diameter by 1⅜ in. dowel pins (G) to length. Although the plans described here are designed for two shelves, more shelves can be added. For each additional shelf, simply extend the length measurements of the sides (D) and lower back (F) by 3½ in. per shelf.

Transfer the pattern for the upper back (E) shown in the grid detail to the stock, and use a band saw to cut out the profile. (Use a ⅜ in. band saw blade.)

Drill the Peg and Assembly Holes

Mount a ¼ in. diameter brad-point drill bit in the drill press and set the depth gauge for ⅜ inch. Drill all the holes for the dowel pins (G) for proper positioning in shelves (C).

Change to a ⅜ in. diameter brad-point bit and drill the eight ½ in. deep assembly holes on the outside of the top (A) and bottom (B). Complete these assembly holes by drilling them through with a ⁵⁄₃₂ in. diameter bit. Follow Detail 4 closely for proper positioning of assembly holes. The sides (D) are ⅜ in. in from the ends of the top (A) and bottom (B), and the sides also must be flush with the back edge of the top and bottom.

Make the Final Cuts

Assemble the top (A), bottom (B) and sides (D) using No. 8 by 1¼ in. flathead wood screws. Do not glue. Then use a router with a ¼ in. straight bit to rout a ¼ in. wide by ¼ in. deep rabbet around the back of the framework to hold the

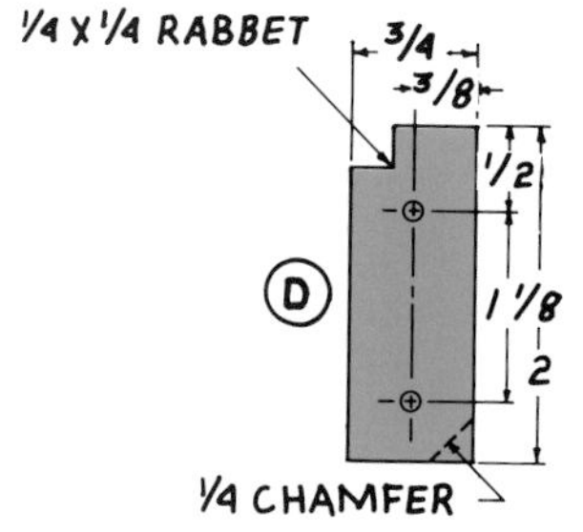
1/4 X 1/4 RABBET
3/4
3/8
1/2
D
1 1/8
2
1/4 CHAMFER

DETAIL 2

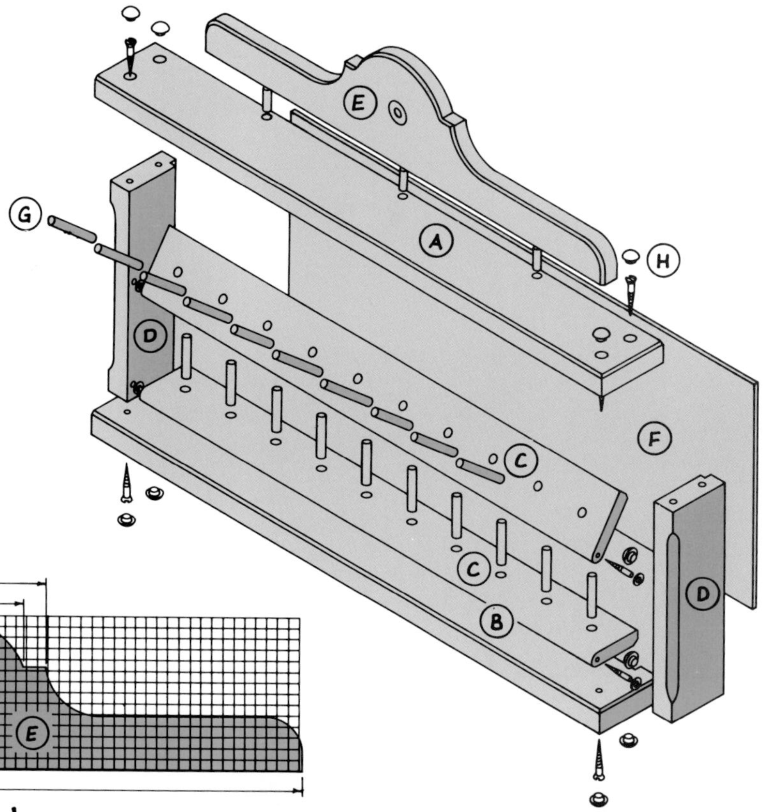
E
G
D
A
H
C
F
C
B
D

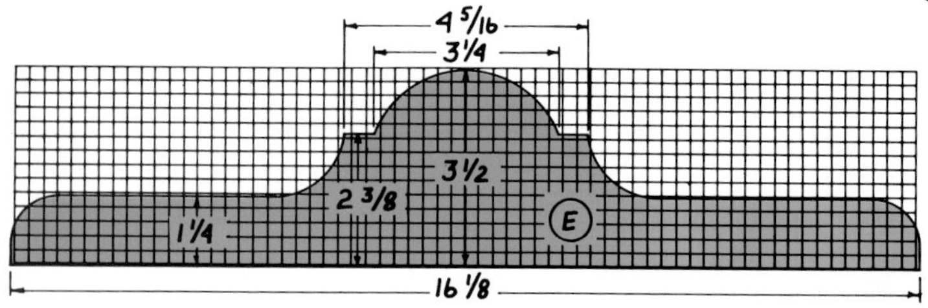
4 5/16
3 1/4
3 1/2
2 3/8
1 1/4
E
16 1/8

EACH SQUARE = 1/4

DETAIL 1

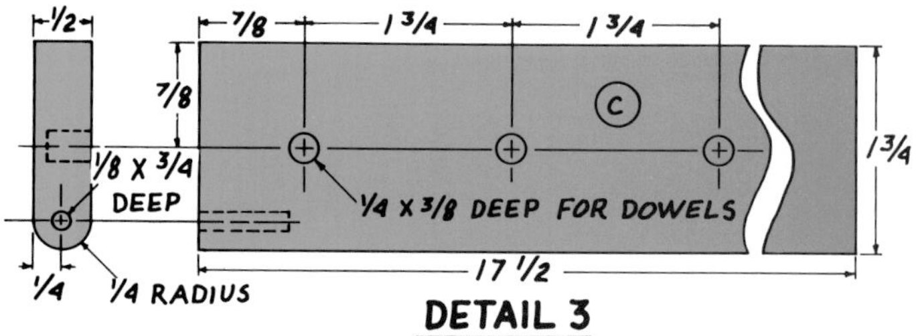
1/2
7/8
1 3/4
1 3/4
7/8
C
1/8 X 3/4
DEEP
1/4 X 3/8 DEEP FOR DOWELS
1 3/4
17 1/2
1/4
1/4 RADIUS

DETAIL 3

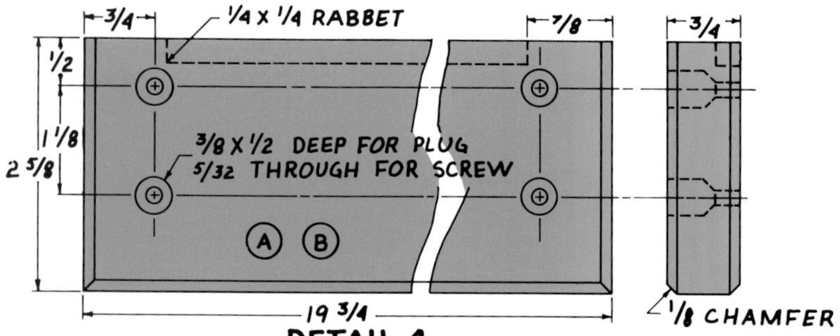
3/4
1/4 X 1/4 RABBET
7/8
3/4
1/2
1 1/8
2 5/8
3/8 X 1/2 DEEP FOR PLUG
5/32 THROUGH FOR SCREW
A B
19 3/4
1/8 CHAMFER

DETAIL 4

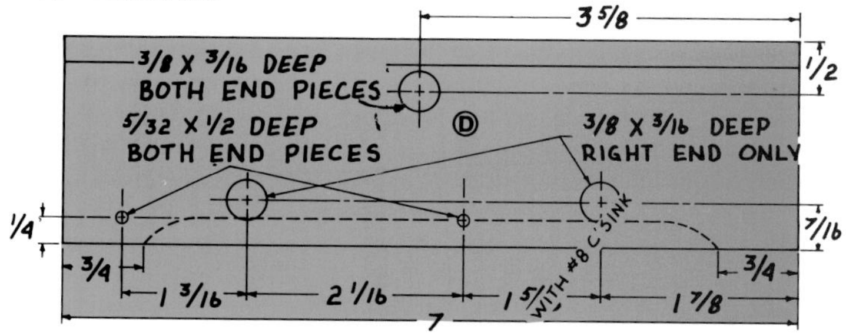
3 5/8
3/8 X 3/16 DEEP
BOTH END PIECES
1/2
5/32 X 1/2 DEEP
BOTH END PIECES
D
3/8 X 3/16 DEEP
RIGHT END ONLY
WITH #8 C'SINK
1/4
7/16
3/4
3/4
1 3/16
2 1/16
1 5/8
1 7/8
7

DETAIL 5

Figure 1. Rabbet the sides (D) on your table saw using a dado blade. Work from a long length of material, since short lengths can be difficult to mill on a table saw.

Figure 2. Lay out the design for the upper back (E) and cut out with a scroll saw. Keep the blade guard ⅛ in. or less above the wood.

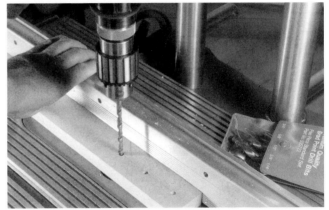

Figure 3. Carefully locate the positions for the dowel pins (G) on the shelves (C). Then drill ¼ in. diameter by ⅜ in. deep holes into the shelves with a drill press. Use the drill's depth stop.

lower back (F). While still assembled, take the measurements for the lower back and cut it from ¼ in. pine.

Disassemble the top, bottom and sides assembly. Using a router with a chamfer bit, bevel the sides (D) on the front edge only. Bevel the underside rear of the shelves (C) so they will not bind when tipped. We suggest that you also bevel the edges of the top (A), bottom (B) and the upper back (E) for a pleasing appearance. Change to a ¼ in. rounding over bit and rout the front edge of shelves (C).

Drill and countersink ⅛ in. diameter holes in the ends of shelves (C) and insert No. 10 by 1¼ in. flathead wood screws. (See Detail 3.) Drive the screws until the thread is not visible and cut off the screw heads ¼ in. from the end of the shelves (C). File the shank to dull the metal edges. Drill a ⁵⁄₃₂ in. diameter hole in the sides (D) to accept the metal peg created by the wood screws in the shelves. Then drill the ⅜ in. diameter holes for the dowel plugs (H) that the shelves will rest on. (See Detail 2.)

BILL OF MATERIALS — Sewing Thread Holder

Finished Dimensions in Inches

A	Top	¾ x 2⅝ x 19¾ pine	1
B	Bottom	¾ x 2⅝ x 19¾ pine	1
C	Shelf	½ x 1¾ x 17½ pine	2
D	Side	¾ x 2 x 7 pine	2
E	Upper Back	½ x 3½ x 16⅛ pine	1
F	Lower Back	¼ x 7½ x 18 pine	1
G	Dowel Pin	¼ dia. x 1⅜ pine	20
H	Dowel Plug	⅜ dia. pine	12

Finish and Assembly

Sand all the pieces smooth. Before applying the finish, we recommend that a metal washer be glued to the upper back (E) to hold a magnet. It will come in handy for holding sewing needles and pins.

Give the project several coats of a polyurethane clear finish to give it a rich, natural looking appearance.

The only glue needed for assembly is to secure the dowel pins (G) in the shelves (C), the dowel plugs (H) to the screw heads, and the lower back (F) to the top (A), bottom (B) and sides (D). Follow the exploded diagram to assemble your sewing thread holder correctly. □

This project is courtesy of Georgia-Pacific Corporation.

Modular Entertainment Center

Stack a dozen or more of these cubes to form a unique entertainment system. When you get tired of one arrangement, simply restack them to form another interesting pattern.

This unique entertainment system is made up of individual modules that can be built with or without doors. With about a dozen cubes, you can obtain more than 100 different arrangements that will keep your living room, study or family room looking fresh and interesting. This modular system features mitered corners and simple construction.

Tips

Buy good quality ¾ in. plywood, sanded on both sides, and use a sharp circular saw blade on your table saw or portable circular saw. Secure the joints with carpenter's glue and 4d finishing nails (countersunk).

Construction

Decide on the number of cubes that you want to build, with and without doors.

Rip the sides (A) from longer lengths of material on your table saw. Keep the best side up when ripping. Miter the side pieces with your table saw set to a 45 degree angle. Cut a miter on a scrap piece of material first and check the edge with a carpenter's square to insure squareness. Check the edge to see if there is severe wood splintering. If so, score the cutting line with a utility knife guided by your carpenter's square. Then when you make the cut on your table saw, the blade should

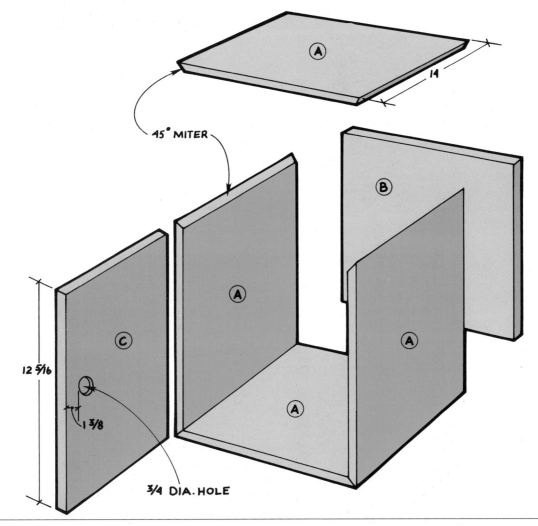

53

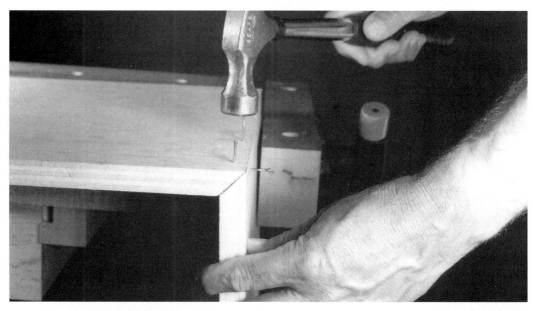

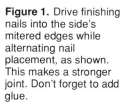

Figure 1. Drive finishing nails into the side's mitered edges while alternating nail placement, as shown. This makes a stronger joint. Don't forget to add glue.

Figure 2. Use a backer board when drilling the hole into the door to prevent excessive wood splintering.

Figure 3. Mark the hinge locations on the door and, using a saber saw, cut mortises the thickness of a folded hinge.

cut next to the line and not on it. This technique will help prevent wood splintering.

Now cut the backs (B) to their appropriate length and width. Then assemble four sides and a back with glue and 4d finishing nails. Drive nails into alternate mitered surfaces. This technique will help make the structure stronger.

Custom cut the doors, if desired, to fit the cube opening and drill a ¾ in. diameter hole to be used as a pull. Make sure you use a backer board to prevent wood splintering, and drill into the good side of the door first.

Finishing

Mark the hinge position on the doors and mortise an area that is the thickness of a folded hinge. Do this for two hinges. Then install the door along with a magnetic latch to the cube. When everything is perfect, remove the hardware and finish sand the pieces, making sure to dull all edges. Fill in all blemishes

BILL OF MATERIALS — Modular Entertainment Center			
Finished Dimensions in Inches			
A	Side	¾ x 14 x 14 plywood	4
B	Back	¾ x 12½ x 12½ plywood	1
C	Door	¾ x 12⁵⁄₁₆ x 12⁵⁄₁₆ plywood	1

in the wood with a good quality, nontoxic wood filler.

Each unit can be painted its own color, or the modules can be painted all the same color. After painting or spraying on a base coat, allow the modules to dry. Then give them a light sanding and apply a second finish coat.

Finally, reattach the hardware and arrange your cubes to form an interesting modular entertainment system. ☐

This project is courtesy of Cherry Tree Toys, Inc.

Wood Chopper

Simple hand tools are all you need to build this wood chopper whirligig. Building and painting it are almost as much fun as watching it spin in the wind.

Whirligigs are delightful wind toys and part of our American folk art heritage. With waving arms, spinning propellers and sweeping wings, whirligigs take many forms — from birds and airplanes to caricatures of witches and Uncle Sam. The more animated mechanical whirligigs often perform such tasks as cranking cars, milking cows or, like this one, chopping wood.

Tips

This whirligig is constructed from pine and plywood and will take many years of rugged punishment. Buy knot-free lumber.

Cherry Tree Toys, Inc. offers full-size patterns, project parts, workpieces and even a finished whirligig. For information and a catalog, write to them at the address given at the end of the Bill of Materials.

Construction

Cut out all of the wooden parts to their overall width and length.

Transfer all of the designs and painting patterns to graph paper. Using carbon paper, trace the designs and patterns to non-splintering wood or plywood of the proper thickness. Note that the painting patterns are for one side only. To make a mirror image of the painting patterns for the opposite side, place a piece of plain paper underneath the painting patterns. Then put a piece of carbon paper with the ink side up underneath the plain piece of paper. Trace over the painting patterns

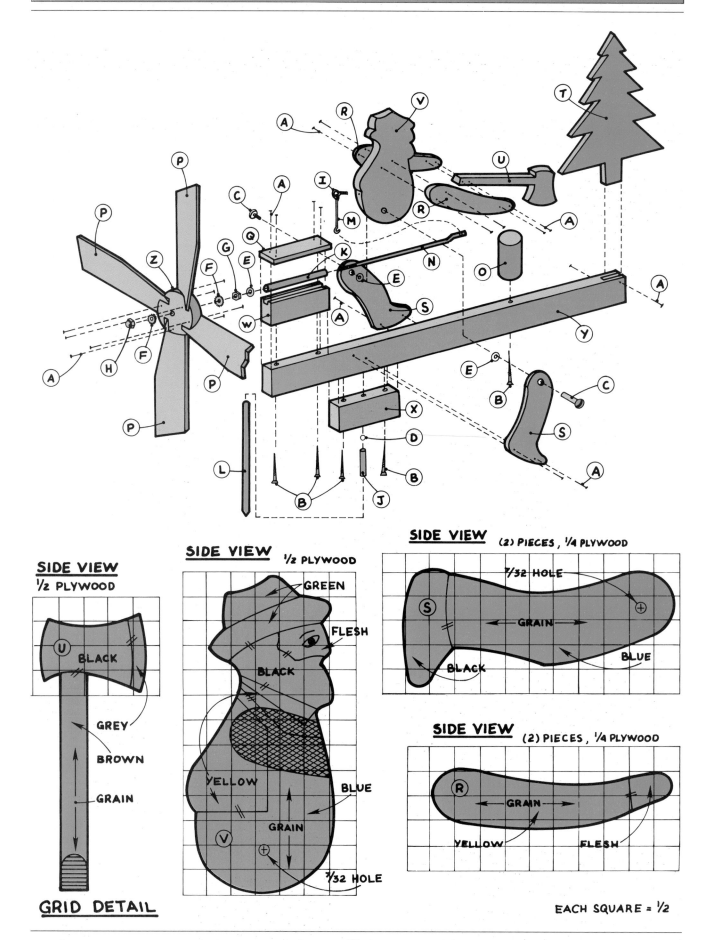

SIDE VIEW
1/2 PLYWOOD

U
BLACK
GREY
BROWN
GRAIN

GRID DETAIL

SIDE VIEW
1/2 PLYWOOD

GREEN
FLESH
BLACK
YELLOW
BLUE
GRAIN
V
7/32 HOLE

SIDE VIEW
(2) PIECES, 1/4 PLYWOOD

7/32 HOLE
S
GRAIN
BLACK
BLUE

SIDE VIEW
(2) PIECES, 1/4 PLYWOOD

R
GRAIN
YELLOW
FLESH

EACH SQUARE = 1/2

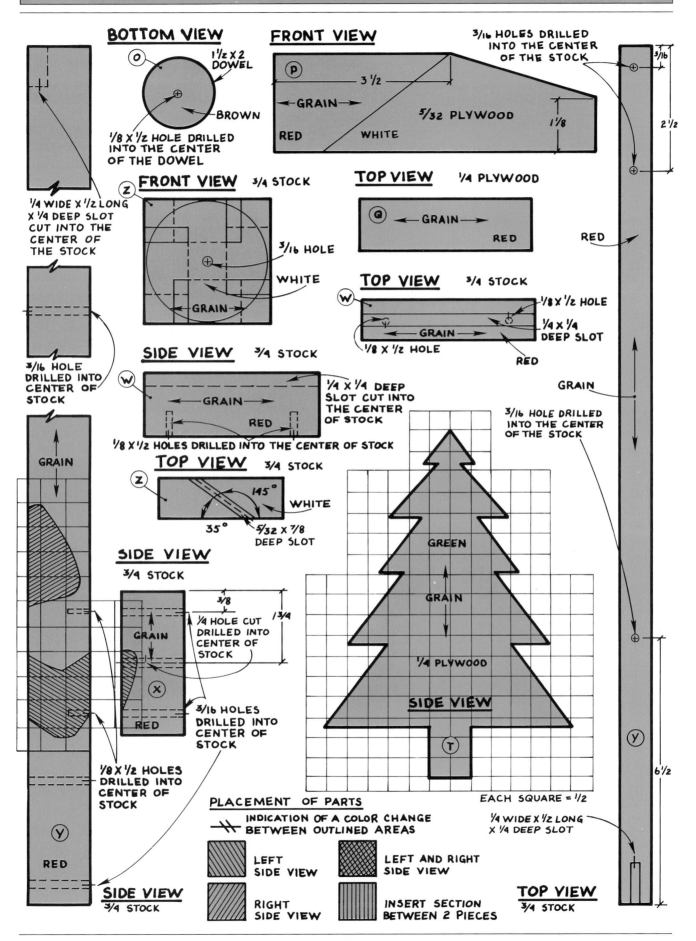

BOTTOM VIEW

O

1½ x 2 DOWEL

BROWN

⅛ X ½ HOLE DRILLED INTO THE CENTER OF THE DOWEL

FRONT VIEW

3/16 HOLES DRILLED INTO THE CENTER OF THE STOCK

P

3½

←GRAIN→

5/32 PLYWOOD

RED   WHITE

1⅛

3/16

2½

FRONT VIEW   ¾ STOCK

Z

3/16 HOLE

WHITE

←GRAIN→

TOP VIEW   ¼ PLYWOOD

Q   ←GRAIN→

RED

RED

TOP VIEW   ¾ STOCK

W

⅛ X ½ HOLE

¼ X ¼ DEEP SLOT

←GRAIN→

⅛ X ½ HOLE

RED

¼ WIDE X ½ LONG X ¼ DEEP SLOT CUT INTO THE CENTER OF THE STOCK

SIDE VIEW   ¾ STOCK

W

←GRAIN→

RED

¼ X ¼ DEEP SLOT CUT INTO THE CENTER OF STOCK

⅛ X ½ HOLES DRILLED INTO THE CENTER OF STOCK

3/16 HOLE DRILLED INTO CENTER OF STOCK

RED

GRAIN

3/16 HOLE DRILLED INTO THE CENTER OF THE STOCK

TOP VIEW   ¾ STOCK

Z   145°

WHITE

35°   5/32 X ⅞ DEEP SLOT

SIDE VIEW   ¾ STOCK

GRAIN

3/8

1¾

¼ HOLE CUT DRILLED INTO CENTER OF STOCK

GRAIN

X

RED

3/16 HOLES DRILLED INTO CENTER OF STOCK

⅛ X ½ HOLES DRILLED INTO CENTER OF STOCK

GREEN

GRAIN

¼ PLYWOOD

SIDE VIEW

T

EACH SQUARE = ½

¼ WIDE X ½ LONG X ¼ DEEP SLOT

Y   RED

SIDE VIEW   ¾ STOCK

PLACEMENT OF PARTS

INDICATION OF A COLOR CHANGE BETWEEN OUTLINED AREAS

LEFT SIDE VIEW

LEFT AND RIGHT SIDE VIEW

RIGHT SIDE VIEW

INSERT SECTION BETWEEN 2 PIECES

RED

Y

TOP VIEW   ¾ STOCK

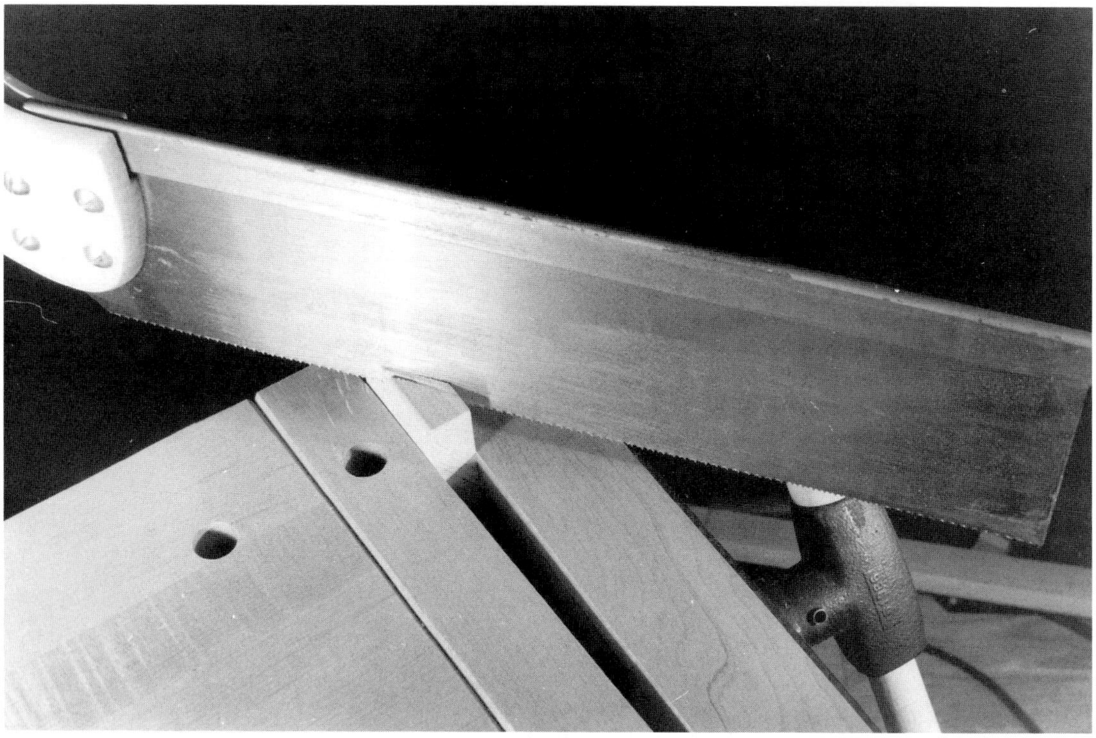

Figure 1. Cut four slots in the hub (Z) with a backsaw after laying out the proper slot angle. Use a wood chisel to finish to the proper width.

BILL OF MATERIALS — Wood Chopper

Finished Dimensions in Inches

A*	#904		26
B*	#907		5
C*	#908		1
D*	#909		1
E*	#910		3
F*	#911		2
G*	#912		1
H*	#913		1
I*	#914		1
J*	#916		1
K*	#917		1
L*	#918		1
M*	#919		1
N*	#921		1
O	Log	1½ dia. x 2 dowel	1
P	Blade	5⁄32 x 2 x 6½ plywood	4
Q	Cover	¼ x 1 x 3½ plywood	1
R	Arm	¼ x 1³⁄₁₆ x 5 plywood	2
S	Leg	¼ x 2⅜ x 5½ plywood	2
T	Tree	¼ x 6 x 8½ plywood	1
U	Ax	½ x 2¼ x 5¾ plywood	1
V	Man	½ x 3⅛ x 6½ plywood	1
W	Block	¾ x 1¼ x 3½ pine	1
X	Bracket	¾ x 1½ x 3½ pine	1
Y	Beam	¾ x 1½ x 21 pine	1
Z	Hub	¾ x 2½ x 2½ pine	1

* These parts are available from Cherry Tree Toys, Inc., Dept. PSW, 408 S. Jefferson St., Belmont, OH 43718 (614-484-4363).

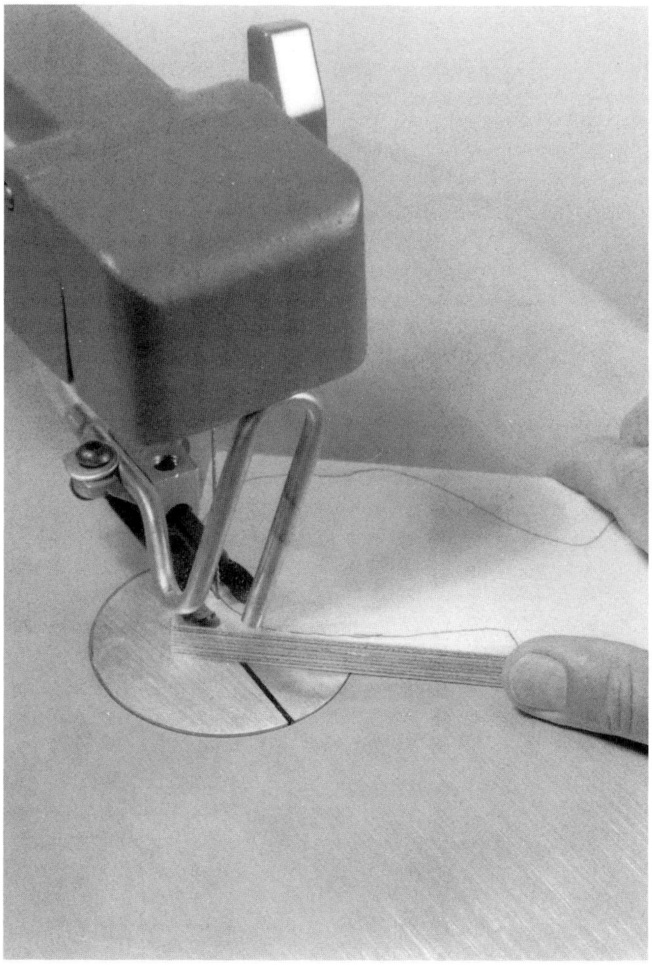

Figure 2. Cut out the man (V) with a scroll saw. Stay outside of the cutting line.

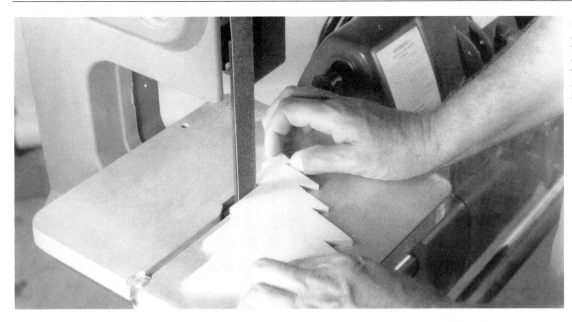

Figure 3. Use an abrasive sander to finish sand the edges of most workpieces. Install a curved platen to sand inside curves.

with a pencil to transfer the painting patterns to the bottom side of the plain piece of paper.

Next, with the hub (Z) still in the shape of a square, cut out both sides of the four slots to the angle specified on the plan. Cut the hub with a handsaw, then clean out the remainder of the wood left in the slots with a chisel. Note that the four slots in the hub are all identical and are cut to the same angle.

Cut all of the remaining project parts to shape with a scroll saw.

Use a backsaw to cut two kerfs into the block (W), along the length of the workpiece. Then clean out the waste area with a chisel.

Mortise the area at the end of the beam (Y) by drilling ¼ in. by ½ in. deep holes adjacent to each other. Clean out the remainder of the wood left in the slot with a wood chisel.

Next, drill all holes as indicated in the drawings and finish sand the project parts. Then paint the parts with an outdoor primer and an exterior grade finish paint. Be creative, adding decorative details that you feel are appropriate.

Figure 4. Cut the groove in the block (W) by making two parallel cuts with a backsaw. Then remove the section in between with a sharp wood chisel. The workpiece must be clamped for this operation.

Assembly

Insert piece K into the slot in the block (W), leaving each end extending an equal distance (see the exploded diagram). Then secure the cover (Q) to the block with glue and nails.

Now glue and screw the block to the end of the beam (Y). Similarly, attach the front of the bracket (X) ⅝ in. from the rear of the block.

Next, glue and drive pieces D and J into the bracket. Screw piece I into the middle of the man (V) ½ in. below the man's belt line.

Attach the legs (S) to the man, making sure the workpieces swing freely. Glue and nail the legs and all of the parts connected to them to the beam.

Glue and nail the two arms (R) to the ax (U) as shown in the plan and the exploded diagram. Also attach the log (O) to the beam.

Glue and nail the subassembly, which consists of the two arms (R) and ax (U), to the man. Make certain the ax strikes

the log directly in the center. Attach pieces E, G and N as shown in the exploded diagram.

Close the half loop of piece M around the groove in piece N with a pliers. Make certain that piece M does not bind when piece N turns.

With the offset in piece N in the highest position and with the ax resting on the log, insert piece M through piece I. Bend piece M with a pliers into the shape of a loop (see the exploded diagram) and cut off any excess wire.

Now, glue and nail the tree (T) to the beam. Also, glue and nail the four blades (P) to the hub (Z), making sure the rear edges of the blades are flush with the rear of the hub. Then install the assembled hub.

Assemble the remainder of the whirligig parts as shown in the exploded diagram.

Touch up the painted surfaces to complete your wood chopper. □

Shaded Sandbox

Bring the beach to your backyard with this covered sandbox.

Sit back, close your eyes and recall those simple days of childhood. Remember the feeling of warm, soft sand beneath your feet...the coolness you'd feel on your fingertips as you'd dig deeper and deeper...the lazy hours whiled away under a cloudless summer sky. Whether your experiences in the sand were on the beach or in a little box in your own backyard, you were a child, innately driven to dig and explore, immersed in the earthy, imaginative fun it provided.

Then and now, kids are kids, and yours can enjoy many happy hours in this freestanding covered sandbox.

Getting it Together

First off, you'll need four 8 ft. 1 x 8s for the sides (A), and shelf (D), shelf back (E) and the canopy frame (G and H). Buy one 8 ft. 1 x 12 for the seats (C) and the cleat strips (L), and one 8 ft. 4 x 4 for the posts (B). You'll also need a half sheet of ¼ in. and ½ in. exterior plywood for the top (K) and bottom (J), along with a quarter sheet of ½ in. exterior plywood for the pivot supports (F).

Cutting the Parts

Cut stock to size as shown in the Bill of Materials. (Note: Cut the seats (C) diagonally from a single, square piece of cut stock.)

With the band saw miter gauge set to 60 degrees, cut the decorative post (B) top angles. *Do not use a table saw for these cuts.*

Use a band saw again to cut notches for the posts and cleat strips in the bottom (J), top (K) and shelf ends (D). Then cut the two front corners from the top (K).

Use your band saw to make the pivot supports (F) from ½ in. plywood. Next, drill a ⅜ in. diameter pivot hole and a ⁷⁄₁₆ in. diameter hole at the end of the pivot slot, drilling through both pieces before you separate them. To cut the pivot grooves in the pivot supports (F), use either a scroll saw or jigsaw.

Then drill ⅜ in. diameter holes in the posts (B) and 1 in. diameter drain holes in the bottom (J).

Assembling the Parts

All sandbox parts should be glued with resorcinol resin waterproof glue, then screwed together with drywall screws.

First, assemble the box by gluing and screwing the sides (A) with No. 6 by 1¼ in. drywall screws. Use a cleat strip (L) in the two front corners to help strengthen this area. Then add the seats (C) to these corners.

Use four lag screws with flat washers (two in each side) and glue to attach the posts (B) to the inside of the box. The bottom of the post must be flush with the bottom of the box sides (A).

Attach the cleat strips (L) to the undersides of the bottom (J) and top (K) with glue and No. 6 by 1¼ in. drywall screws. Slide the bottom (J) in the box and attach it to the side cleat strips (L) with screws only.

Assemble the pivot supports (F) to the canopy sides (G). Then attach the canopy ends (H) to the canopy sides (G). Use two ⅜ in. by 6 in. carriage bolts, washers, hex nuts and wing nuts to fasten the canopy assemblies to the posts (B).

Assemble the shelf (D) and the shelf back (E) with glue and screws, then attach the shelf assembly to the posts.

Finishing

Fill in all blemishes with a nontoxic waterproof wood filler You must also dull all sharp edges and file all protruding bolts

Figure 1. Assemble the sides (A) by driving drywall screws through a corner cleat, into the sides. Pre-drill these holes to prevent the cleat from splitting.

Figure 2. Cut the tapers on the posts (B) on your band saw. Work carefully and support the outboard end to prevent binding.

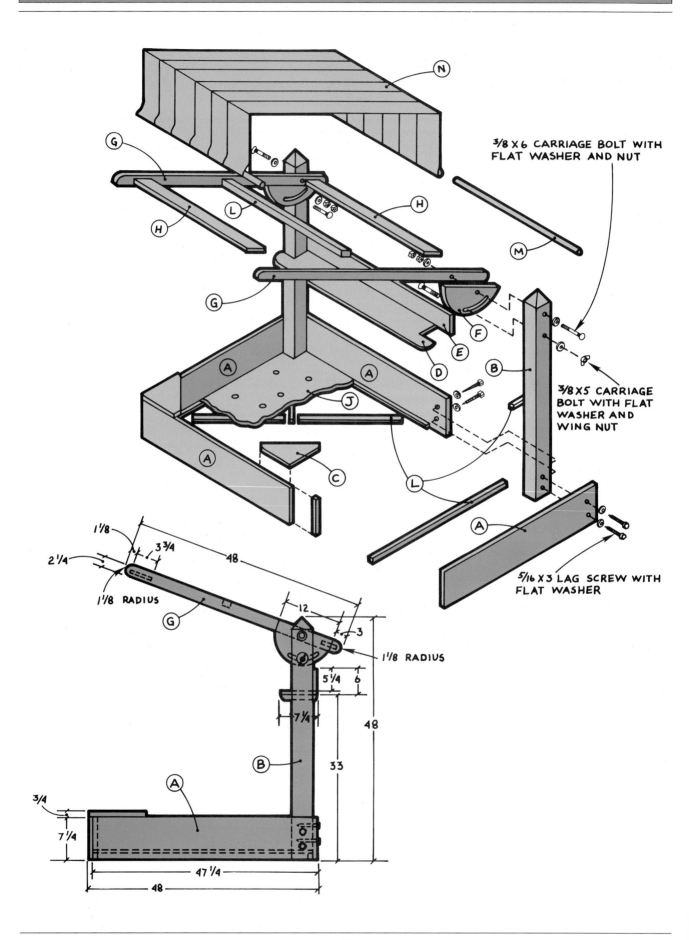

3/8 X 6 CARRIAGE BOLT WITH
FLAT WASHER AND NUT

3/8 X 5 CARRIAGE
BOLT WITH FLAT
WASHER AND
WING NUT

5/16 X 3 LAG SCREW WITH
FLAT WASHER

1 1/8

3 3/4

2 1/4

1 1/8 RADIUS

48

12

3

1 1/8 RADIUS

5 1/4

6

7 1/4

48

33

3/4

7 1/4

47 1/4

48

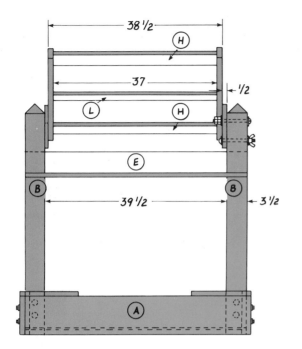

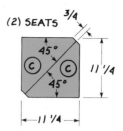

(2) SEATS

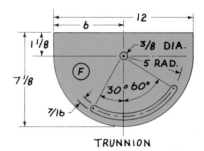

TRUNNION

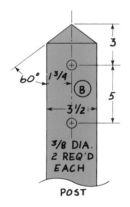

POST

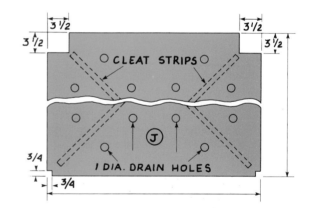

CLEAT STRIPS

1 DIA. DRAIN HOLES

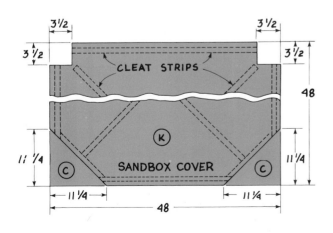

CLEAT STRIPS

SANDBOX COVER

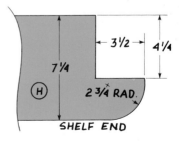

SHELF END

Figure 3. If you do not have a drill press, drill the holes into the posts (B) by drilling a hole at the proper location, but only three quarters of the way in depth. Then drill into the other side until you meet the hole you just drilled.

Figure 4. An overhead router is ideal for making the slot into the pivot support. Drive nail at the pivot point and lower the overhead router into the wood at the proper starting point. Then rotate the workpiece. Make only ⅛ in. deep passes until you achieve final depth. Then drill out the pivot point with a drill press.

(and bolt ends) to prevent injury to children. Finish the sandbox with an exterior natural finish or paint of your choice. *You must use a nontoxic paint.*

Sewing the Canopy

Fold and pin a 3 in. hem on each end of the canvas sun shade (N). Use heavy thread and a heavy-duty needle to sew an open-ended hem in each end of the material. Each hem will hold a dowel rod. Slide the dowel rods (M) into the hems and fasten with a tack or staple in each end. The canopy can be rolled up for storage during bad weather. □

BILL OF MATERIALS — Shaded Sandbox

Finished Dimensions in Inches

A	Side	¾ x 7¼ x 47¼ pine	4
B	Post	3½ x 3½ x 48 pine	2
C	Seat	¾ x 11¼ x 11¼ pine	2
D	Shelf	¾ x 7¼ x 46½ pine	1
E	Shelf Back	¾ x 5¼ x 46½ pine	1
F	Pivot Support	½ x 7⅛ x 12 ext. plywood	2
G	Canopy Side	¾ x 2¼ x 48 pine	2
H	Canopy End	¾ x 3¾ x 37 pine	2
J	Bottom	½ x 46½ x 46½ ext. plywood	1
K	Top	¼ x 48 x 48 ext. plywood	1
L	Cleat Strip	¾ x ¾ x 12 pine	48
M	Dowel Rod	¾ dia. x 36 pine	2
N	Sun Shade	36 x 60 canvas	1

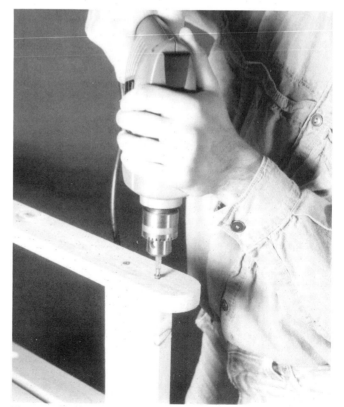

Figure 5. Secure the canopy sides (G) to the canopy ends (H) with No. 6 by 1⅝ in. drywall screws and glue. Pre-drill these holes to prevent the wood from splitting.

This project is courtesy of Georgia-Pacific Corporation.

Two-Step Stool

Simple in design and easy to construct, this is a great project for the novice woodworker.

This Shaker-style two-step stool is perfect for reaching those tall shelves in the kitchen or hall closet. Paint or stain it to match your decor, and add self-adhesive strips to the treads for safety.

Tips

Select quality pine lumber for your project. You also will need glue and finishing nails. Remember to sink all nail heads and fill in the hole recesses with quality wood filler. Be sure to pre-drill all nail holes placed at the edge of the material.

Construction

Begin by forming the two sides (A). These are made up from smaller sections of ¾ in. pine. Make sure you joint the edges on a jointer with a power hand plane, and then edge-glue them together with carpenter's glue. Secure this subassembly with bar clamps, clamped with moderate pressure, until the glue cures.

While the sides are drying, cut the steps (B) and stretchers (C) from select pine. You may want to replace the ⅞ in. thick pine stretchers with ¾ in., since ⅞ in. pine is not readily available in many areas.

Remove the bar clamps from the side panels and sand the wider surfaces flat with a belt sander. If there is any glue squeezed between the joints, remove it with an old wood

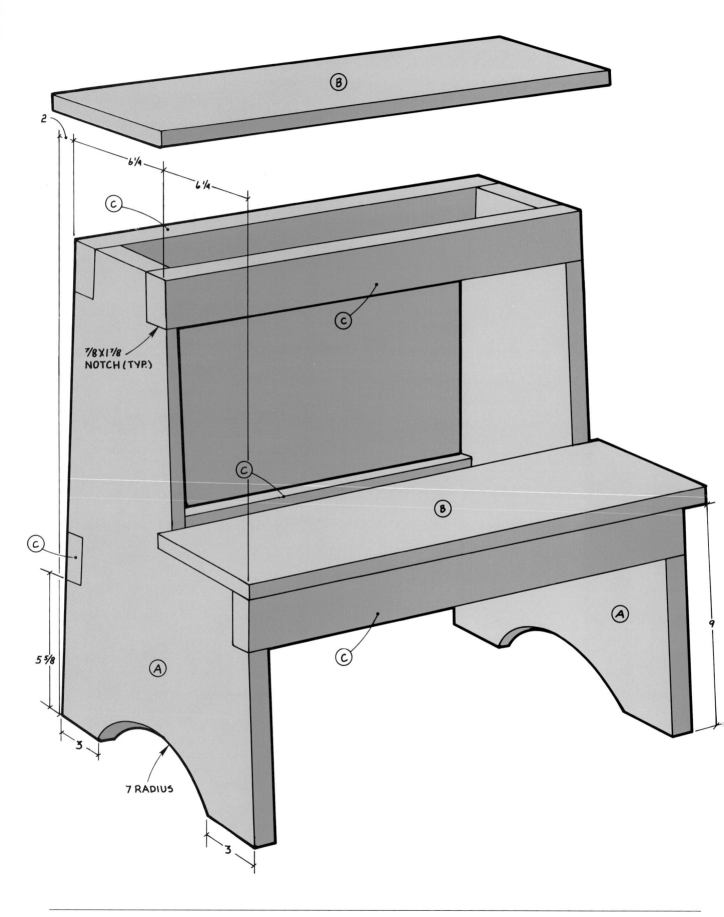

B

2

6 1/4

6 1/4

C

C

C

7/8 X 1 7/8
NOTCH (TYP.)

C

B

C

A

9

C

A

5 5/8

3

7 RADIUS

3

Figure 1. Joint the lumber to be edge-glued to form the sides (A). Use a stationary jointer and make a smooth continuous pass. Keep fingers well away from the cutters.

Figure 2. Cut the sides (A) on a band saw, staying next to the cutting line. Use a ⅜ in. blade and keep the guard ⅛ in. above the wood's surface for safety.

chisel or a paint scraper. Now, lay out the panels for cutting.

Cut out one side silhouette with a saber saw or band saw. Use a band saw to gang-cut both side pieces at one time, making sure that you use a ½ in. wide blade to prevent the blade from wandering. If you have an abrasive sander available, dress the notches where the stretchers will be inserted. If not, use a sanding block, being careful not to tear out the wood.

Rout over the edges of the steps with a ¼ in. rounding over bit equipped with a pilot guide. Then finish sand all of the pieces before you assemble the stool.

Assemble the stool with carpenter's glue and 4d finishing nails. Make sure the assembly is square as you add each workpiece, and try not to overglue.

Finishing

Fill in the holes with a nontoxic wood filler. Then finish sand the assembly with a sanding block or pad sander.

Remove all dust particles with a damp cloth. Apply an appropriate stain and then a sanding sealer. Allow the sanding sealer to dry before giving it a light sanding. Give the stool a final coat of satin polyurethane to complete your project. □

Figure 3. Sand the notches cut into the sides (A) with an abrasive sander, working up to the cutting line.

BILL OF MATERIALS — Two-Step Stool

Finished Dimensions in Inches

A	Side	¾ x 14½ x 19¼ pine	2
B	Step	¾ x 6¾ x 21 pine	2
C	Stretcher	⅞ x 2 x 20 pine	4

This project is courtesy of Dennis Watson.

Bath Cabinet

This country-inspired cabinet is attractive, easy to make and a class above the ordinary metal medicine cabinet.

Tired of that old metal medicine cabinet — the one with a large rust spot on the lower shelf? This pine bathroom cabinet won't rust, provides ample storage space and is an attractive addition to your bathroom.

Tips

Buy the louvered doors (E) and trim them 2 in. in length. Otherwise you may have to trim too much material from the project or the shutters may be entirely too small.

Construction

Start by ripping the sides (A) slightly wider than 5½ in., then hand-plane or use a jointer to finish to 5½ inches. Crosscut to 28 in. long on your table saw.

Rip and crosscut the top and bottom pieces (B) so they finish out to their proper width and length.

Enlarge the grid detail (shown in the illustration) for the sides, and transfer the pattern onto the boards. Cut the sides to shape using a saber saw or band saw, staying just to the outside of the line. Finish up to the line with a spokeshave or rasp. Do the final edge-sanding with a drum sander chucked into a portable drill.

The top and bottom workpieces are housed in a stopped dado. Cut the stopped dado using a dado blade mounted in a table saw or router equipped with a ¾ in. straight bit and guided with a straightedge. Cut the dado just shy of 4½ in. long, then square up the corner and remove the waste with a sharp wood chisel.

Cut a rabbet for the back panel (F) in the top and bottom (B) and the side (A) edges with a rabbeting bit installed in a router table. Next, round over the top, bottom and side edges with a ⅜ in. rounding over bit with pilot. On the top and bottom panels, rout short of the ends by about ¾ inch. After the cabinet is assembled, finish rounding over these edges with a wood chisel and file. (This is easier than trying to cut the stopped dado with a round end.)

Drill the 1 in. diameter hole in the project sides for the towel bar (D) using a Forstner bit or spur bit. Use the drill stop on your drill press. Now, drill ¼ in. holes in the side pieces for the adjustable shelves (G). Buy the adjustable shelf hardware first to insure you drill the proper diameter holes.

Cut the back (F) to size from ¼ in. plywood and the towel rod (D) to length. Now, dry-fit the sides to the top and bottom shelves, along with the back panel and towel rod. Make sure all the joints pull up tight.

Give all the pieces a thorough sanding, then glue and clamp the cabinet together using the back to assure it is square.

Enlarge the squared drawing for the decorative back (C) and transfer the design to ¾ in. pine. Cut out the design,

Figure 1. Cut the contours in the sides (A) with a band saw. Use a ⅜ in. saw blade and keep the blade guard about ⅛ in. above the wood.

Figure 2. Sand the contours using a drum sander inserted in your drill press. Move the material into the drum.

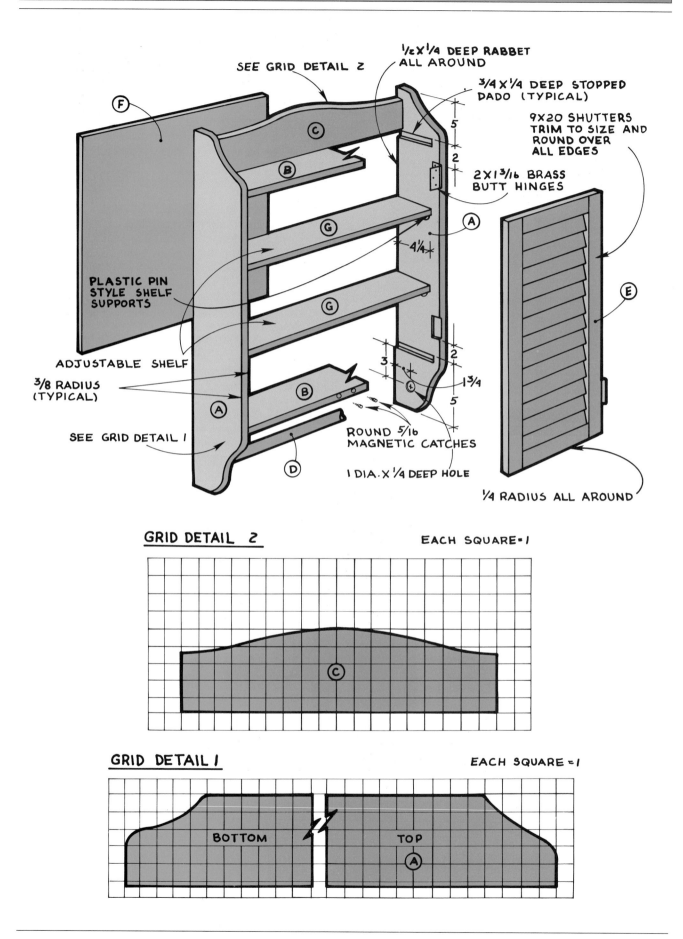

SEE GRID DETAIL 2

½ X ¼ DEEP RABBET ALL AROUND

¾ X ¼ DEEP STOPPED DADO (TYPICAL)

9X20 SHUTTERS TRIM TO SIZE AND ROUND OVER ALL EDGES

2 X 1³/₁₆ BRASS BUTT HINGES

PLASTIC PIN STYLE SHELF SUPPORTS

ADJUSTABLE SHELF

³/₈ RADIUS (TYPICAL)

SEE GRID DETAIL 1

ROUND 5/16 MAGNETIC CATCHES

1 DIA. X ¼ DEEP HOLE

¼ RADIUS ALL AROUND

GRID DETAIL 2   EACH SQUARE = 1

GRID DETAIL 1   EACH SQUARE = 1

BOTTOM   TOP

Figure 3. Cut a stopped dado for the top and bottom workpieces. Carefully mark the stopping points on your saw.

staying just to the outside of the line, then file and sand smooth. Round over the edge similar to the side pieces. Glue and clamp the decorative back in place, next to the sides and top.

The purchased louvered doors (E) each measure 9 in. by

BILL OF MATERIALS — Bath Cabinet

Finished Dimensions in Inches

A	Side	¾ x 5½ x 28 pine	2
B	Top and Bottom	¾ x 4½ x 18½ pine	2
C	Decorative Back	¾ x 5 x 18 pine	1
D	Dowel	1 dia. x 18½ birch	1
E	Louvered Door	⅝ x 9 x 18 pine	2
F	Back	¼ x 19 x 19 fir plywood	1
G	Adjustable Shelf	½ x 4¼ x 18 pine	2

Figure 4. Trim the stopped dado with a sharp wood chisel. Strike the chisel lightly with a wood mallet.

Figure 5. Use Pegboard to help you locate holes for the adjustable shelf pins. Use a drill press or hand drill to drill the holes.

Figure 6. Round over the edges of the partially assembled project. Then round over the area where the top and bottom workpieces join the stopped dado.

Figure 7. Round over the louvered door with a ¼ in. rounding over bit, with pilot, in your router. Work counterclockwise.

20 inches. Cut the doors to 18 in. long. Round over the edges with a ¼ in. rounding over bit, with pilot, in your router. Cut the hinge mortises with a wood chisel and screw the hinges in place. Fit the louvered doors in position, and mark the location of the hinges on the cabinet's sides. Next, cut the mortises in the sides and hang the doors.

Cut the adjustable shelves (G) from ½ in. thick pine. Also round over the front edge with a ¼ in. rounding over bit.

To open the louvered doors, grasp the bottom edge of the door rail. Use a ⅜ in. core box bit and a router to cut a small finger grip in the bottom of the rail.

Install the round magnetic catches by drilling two ⁵⁄₁₆ in. holes in the bottom pieces (B) and driving in the catches. Screw the supplied metal washers to the back of the doors.

Finishing

The wood in the louvered doors varies a lot in texture and color. Therefore, each piece will take the stain slightly differently. Seal the cabinet with a light coat of shellac, cut half and half with denatured alcohol, or use a specially prepared sealer. After the sealer dries, lightly sand the cabinet, then apply the stain. We used Minwax Early American.

Since a bathroom has high humidity, give the project two coats of semi-gloss polyurethane varnish, lightly sanded between coats. Be sure to finish the inside, too.

Mount the cabinet to the wall with four 1¼ in. brass wood screws and decorative washers. ☐

This project is courtesy of Shopsmith, Inc.

Figure 1. Cut the rabbets on your router table. Do not make the cut in one pass; make progressively deeper cuts on each pass. Use a miter gauge to hold the material for cutting.

The Garden Planter

Dress up your home with this custom garden planter.

Want to dress up your deck, patio or front porch with some greenery, but don't want to hire a landscape designer or pay store retail prices to do it? This redwood planter (or even a few of them) can do the trick, and it's easily adapted to suit any pot.

Since these plans offer some flexibility in the size of pot you wish to use, purchase the pot *before* you start cutting. Once you have the pot, measure the height and the outside diameter of the lip. Memorize these measurements, because you'll be using them frequently throughout the project.

At the Lumberyard

Your first purchase is the pot, preferably terra cotta. Our plans call for a 10 in. diameter or 12 in. diameter pot. For the wooden planter, you'll need two 8 ft. 2 x 4s, one 4 ft. 1 x 10, and four 8 ft. 1 x 4s (for the 10 in. pot). We recommend using redwood lumber for the most weather resistance. You also will need to purchase flathead wood screws and galvanized nails.

Sawing the Top and Bottom Frames

Once you have your pot, stock and fasteners, you're ready to start. Begin by cutting the 2 x 4s into eight pieces for the top and bottom frame sides (A, B). *The length(s) of these cuts depends on the outside diameter of your pot.* Add 3½ in. to the diameter of the pot's mouth, then cut four frame sides (B). Cut the four remaining frame sides (A), adding 1½ in. to the mouth diameter.

Next, use a router or saw to cut rabbets into the ends of each of the frame sides. The depth of the cuts is equal to the board's actual width, minus 1 in. (see Detail 2).

Cutting the Sides, Pot Support and Cover

For the 10 in. pot, rip the 1 x 4 side pieces (C) and pot supports (D) to 3⁵⁄₁₆ inches. For the 12 in. pot, rip the 1 x 6s to 3¾ inches. To make the sides (C), cut the ripped boards into 16

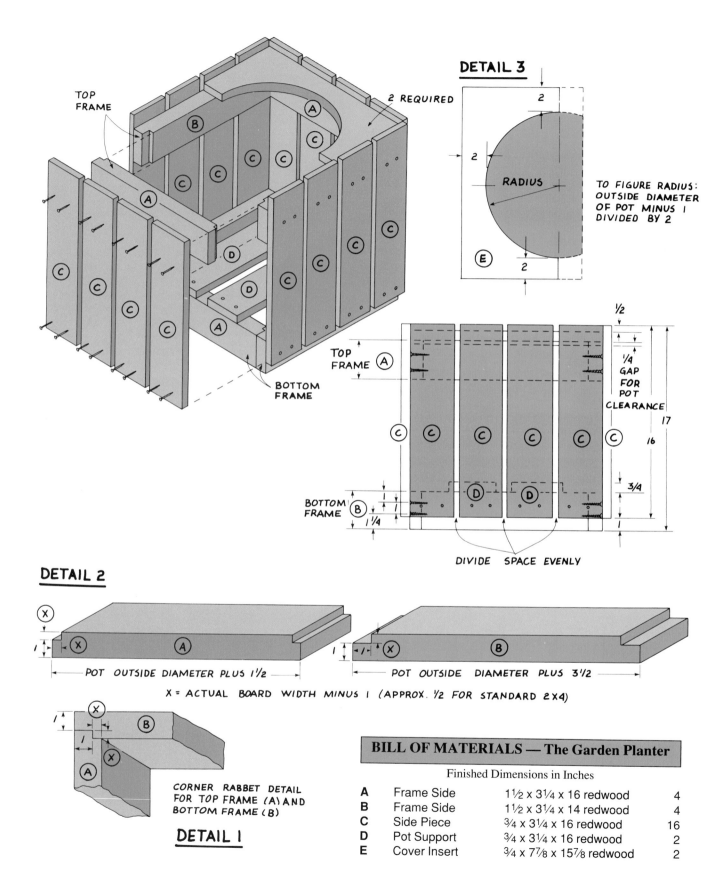

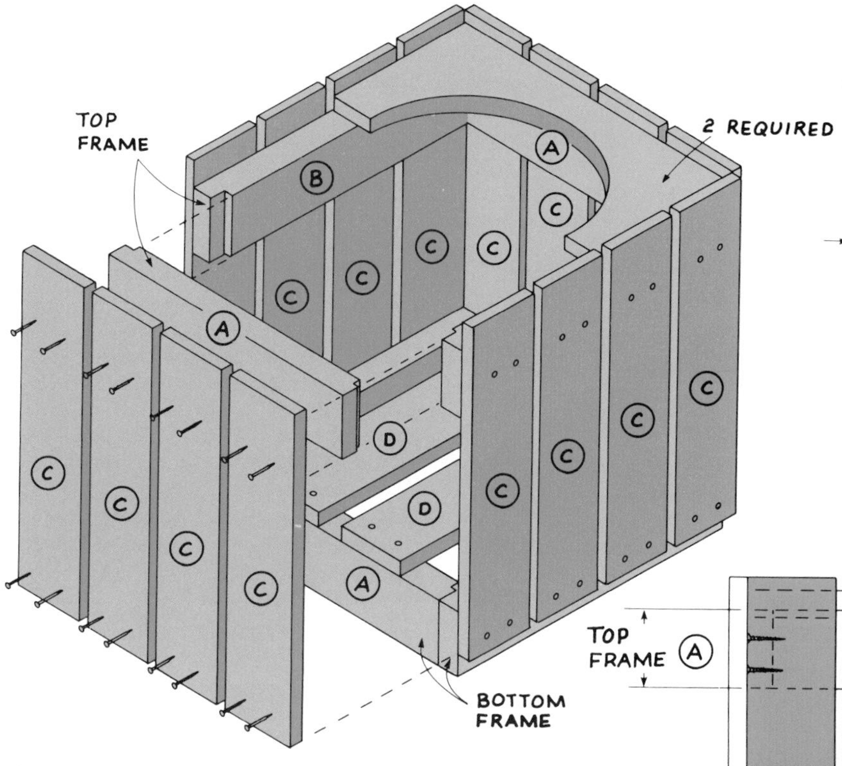
TOP FRAME
2 REQUIRED
A
B
C
D
BOTTOM FRAME

DETAIL 3

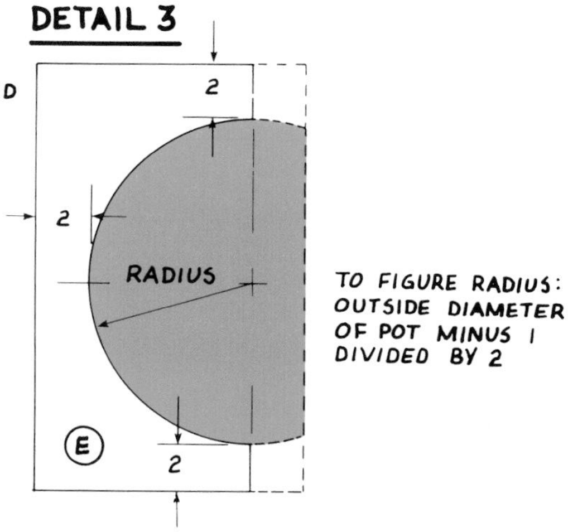
2
2
RADIUS
E
2
TO FIGURE RADIUS: OUTSIDE DIAMETER OF POT MINUS 1 DIVIDED BY 2

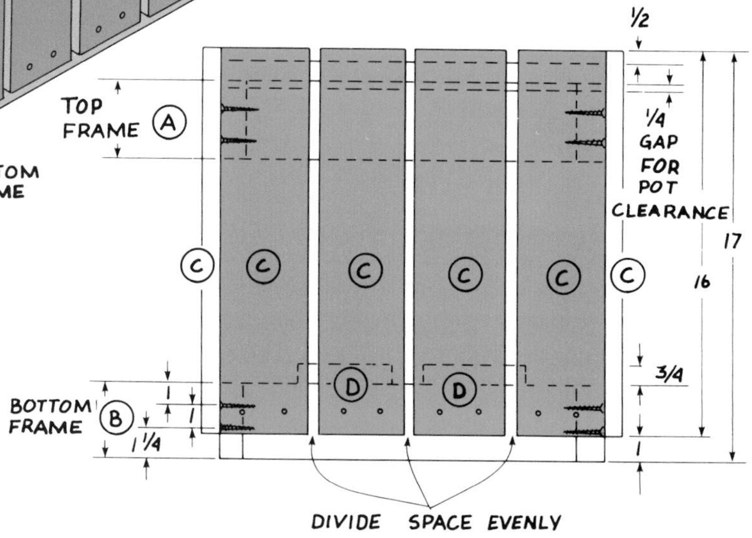
1/2
TOP FRAME A
1/4 GAP FOR POT CLEARANCE
17
16
C
D
3/4
BOTTOM FRAME B
1
1
1 1/4
1
DIVIDE SPACE EVENLY

DETAIL 2

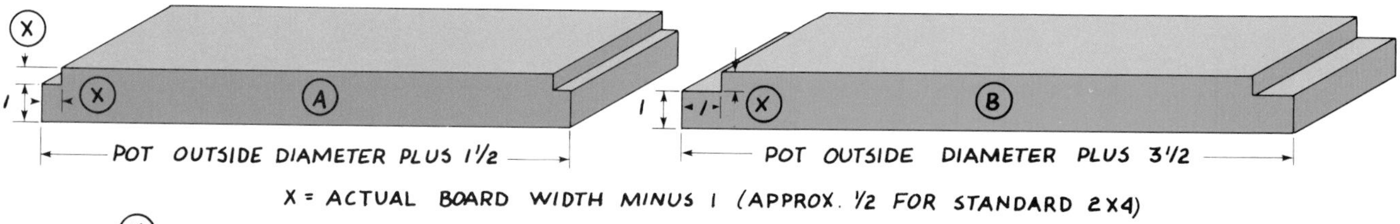
X
1
A
B
POT OUTSIDE DIAMETER PLUS 1 1/2
POT OUTSIDE DIAMETER PLUS 3 1/2
X = ACTUAL BOARD WIDTH MINUS 1 (APPROX. 1/2 FOR STANDARD 2X4)

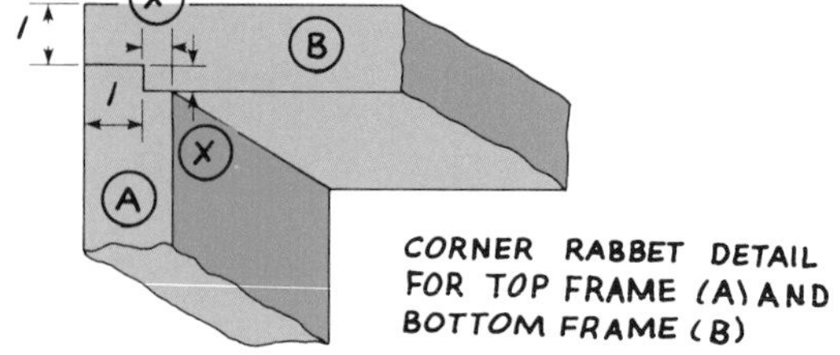
X
1
B
1
X
A

CORNER RABBET DETAIL FOR TOP FRAME (A) AND BOTTOM FRAME (B)

DETAIL 1

BILL OF MATERIALS — The Garden Planter

Finished Dimensions in Inches

A	Frame Side	1½ x 3¼ x 16 redwood	4
B	Frame Side	1½ x 3¼ x 14 redwood	4
C	Side Piece	¾ x 3¼ x 16 redwood	16
D	Pot Support	¾ x 3¼ x 16 redwood	2
E	Cover Insert	¾ x 7⅞ x 15⅞ redwood	2

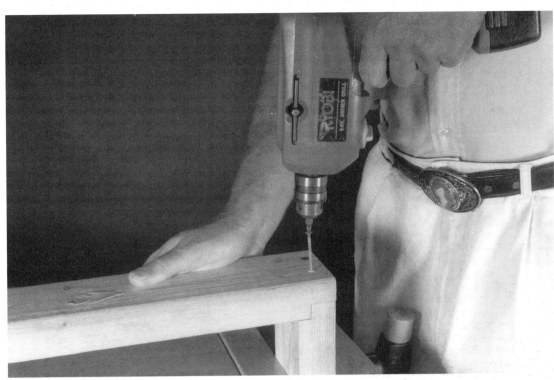

Figure 2. Secure the side frames (A, B) with No. 12 by 2½ in. flathead wood screws. Drill and countersink the screws.

pieces, each at a length of the overall pot height plus 4¾ inches.

For the pot support (D), cut two pieces of 1 x 10 stock, each at a length of the mouth diameter plus 3½ inches.

For the cover inserts (E), cut two pieces from the 1 x 10, each at a length of the mouth diameter plus 3½ inches. Next, measure each piece for the center (this marks the outer edge of a semicircle). Then, calculate the radius of the semicircle you'll be cutting. To do this, *subtract 1 in. from the mouth diameter, and divide that figure by 2 (see Detail 3).* This new figure is the radius (r). Measure and mark this distance (r) from the first mark; this provides the center of the semicircle. With a compass point in this center mark, draw the semicircle. Then use a band saw or jigsaw to cut out the centers. Once you've cut out the center of each board, cut off the edges so that its width is one-half its height (see Detail 3).

Assembly

To assemble the top frame and the bottom frame, drill two holes at the corners of each (B) workpiece and screw the frame sides together. Then drill two holes in each end of the two pot support pieces (D). Nail the pot support pieces (D) into the (A) pieces of the bottom frame, leaving a 1 in. gap between each board.

Sand the rough edges of the side pieces (C) and cover inserts (E). Drill holes for nails in the side pieces (C), (two holes 3 in. from the top and two holes 1½ in. from the bottom of each piece). Nail the side pieces (C) onto the top frame and the bottom frame so that each side piece is 1 in. from the bottom of the bottom frame, and 1¼ in. above the top of the top frame. Space the side pieces evenly, leaving a slight gap at each end, as well as ¼ in. or so between each piece. For the best fit, rasp or sand the cover pieces.

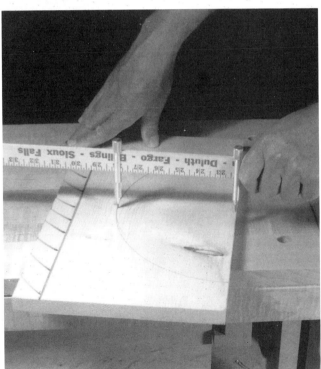

Figure 3. Lay out the radius for the cover inserts (E) using a bar compass, as shown. Then cut out the shape with a saber saw or band saw.

Finishing

Although redwood is a highly durable wood for outdoor projects, you might wish to finish your planter or planters with an exterior, transparent penetrating oil stain. ☐

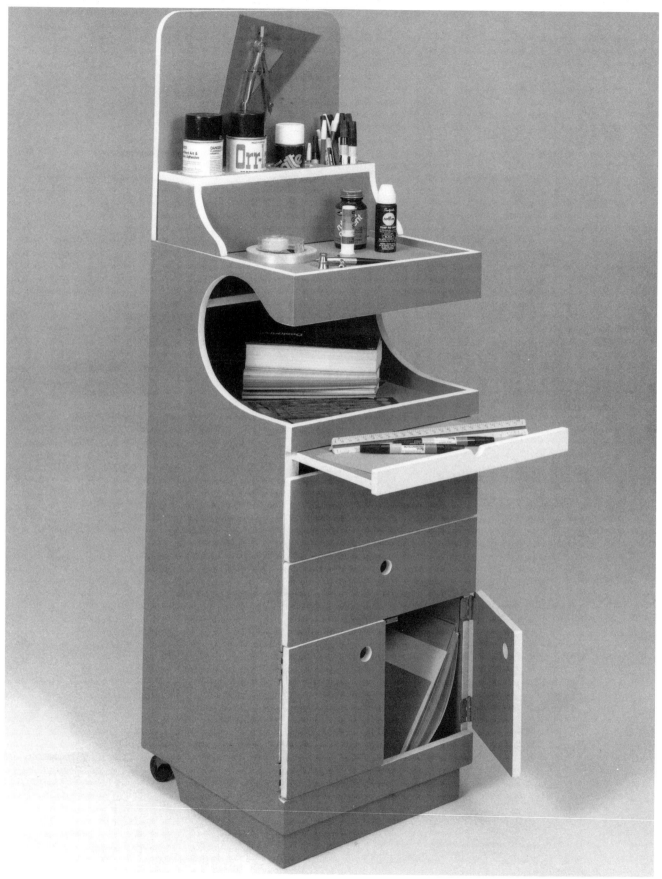

This project is courtesy of the American Plywood Association.

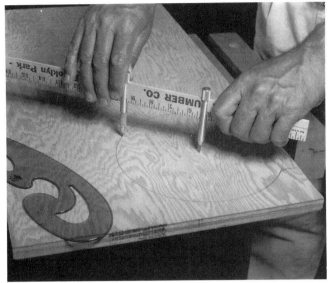

Figure 1. Carefully lay out the design in the sides (B) using a French curve and a compass.

Figure 2. Cut out the design with a saber saw equipped with a plywood cutting blade. Work slowly.

Taboret

Store your drafting or art supplies in this attractive taboret. Drawers, shelves and trays make it the ultimate organizer.

This handy taboret provides storage for all your drafting equipment, brushes, paints and other drafting or art supplies. It is ideal for both adults and children alike, and it will certainly brighten any studio, workshop or playroom.

Tips

This project uses ½ in. APA plywood sanded on both sides. Make sure that the plywood you purchase is warp-free. Otherwise, you may encounter construction problems.

Use 5d finishing nails and carpenter's glue for assembly.

BILL OF MATERIALS — Taboret

Finished Dimensions in Inches

A	Back	½ x 15 x 48 plywood	1
B	Side	½ x 14½ x 33 plywood	2
C	Shelf	½ x 14 x 14 plywood	3
D	Top Rail	½ x 3 x 15 plywood	1
E	Middle Rail	½ x 1½ x 15 plywood	1
F	Front Kick Panel	½ x 2¼ x 14 plywood	1
G	Side Kick Panel	½ x 2¼ x 12 plywood	2
H	Bottom Rail	½ x 2 x 15 plywood	1
I	Tray Front	½ x 4½ x 14 plywood	1
J	Tray Side	½ x 4½ x 7 plywood	2
K	Tray Top	½ x 4 x 15 plywood	1
L	Tray Back	½ x 4½ x 14 plywood	1
M	Sliding Shelf	½ x 13⅞ x 14 plywood	1
N	Drawer Side	½ x 3⅞ x 14 plywood	4
O	Drawer Bottom	½ x 13⅞ x 14 plywood	2
P	Drawer Back	½ x 3⅞ x 12⅞ plywood	2
Q	Drawer Front	½ x 4⅞ x 15 plywood	2
R	Shelf Pull	½ x 1⅜ x 15 plywood	1
S	Door	½ x 7½ x 8⅞ plywood	2
T	Shelf Guide	½ x 1½ x 14 plywood	2
U	Drawer Guide	½ x ½ x 14 plywood	4
V	Tray Bottom	½ x 3 x 14 plywood	1
W	Hidden Shelf	½ x 5 x 14 plywood	1
X	Door Stop	½ x 2¼ x 14 plywood	1

Construction

Begin by cutting all of the project parts to their overall size, length and width. Allow enough material for edge-jointing or sanding.

Cut out the design in the taboret sides (B) with a saber saw. Use a plywood cutting blade and hug the cutting line. Then finish sand the contour with a drum sander inserted in your drill. Now drill ¾ in. diameter holes into the doors (S) and shelf pull (R).

Next, lay out the three holes and square in the tray top (K) and drill a starting hole for each hole. Then finish waste area with a saber saw equipped with a plywood cutting blade.

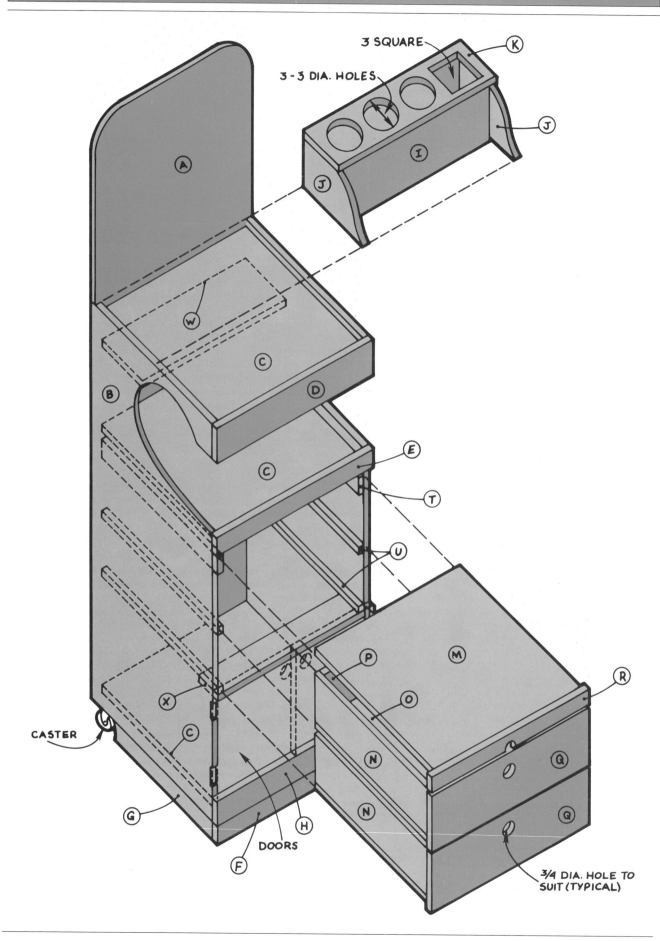

3 SQUARE

3 - 3 DIA. HOLES

CASTER

DOORS

3/4 DIA. HOLE TO SUIT (TYPICAL)

FRONT VIEW

SIDE VIEW

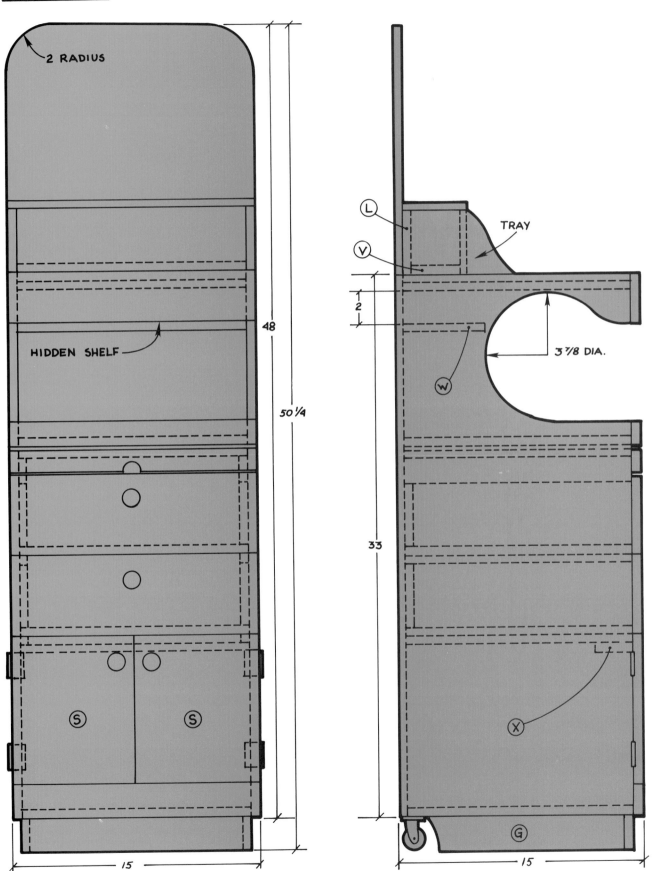

2 RADIUS

HIDDEN SHELF

48

50¼

15

S   S

TRAY

L

V

1
2

3⅞ DIA.

W

33

X

G

15

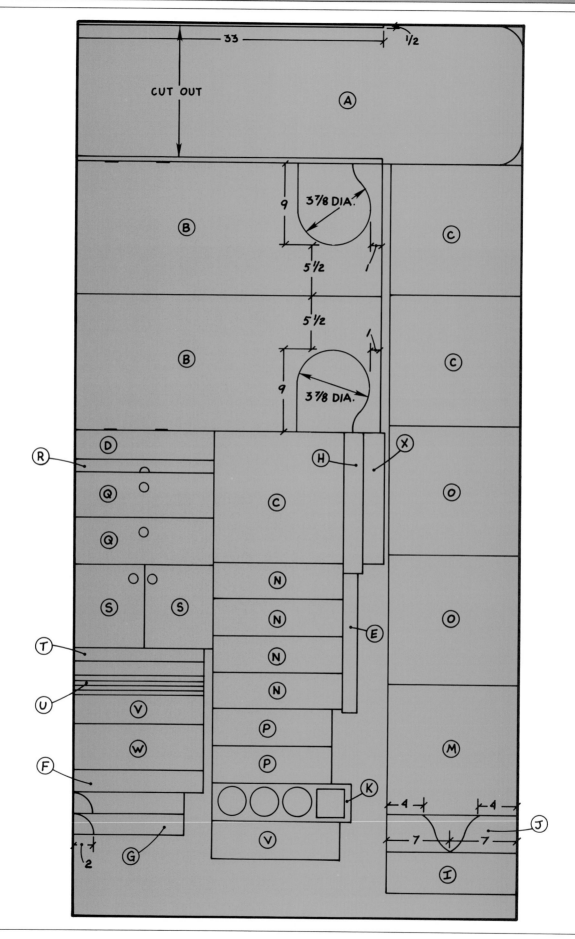

Figure 3. Lay out the shapes on the tray top (K) and drill starter holes. Cut these shapes with a saber saw.

Now cut the contours in the tray sides (J) as well as the side kick panels (G).

Mortise the areas of the side pieces (B) the thickness of the folded hinge used for mounting the doors. Don't forget to cut notches in the back panel (A) and round over the edges as shown in the illustration. Finish sand all project parts before assembling.

Assemble the sides to the back panel with nails and glue. Then attach the three shelves (C) along with the three front rails (D, E, H).

Now install the hidden shelf (W), the door stop (X), drawer guides (U) and shelf guides (T). Secure the guides with ¾ in. brads and glue.

Before installing the kick panels (F, G), make sure that the casters sit flush on the floor when the taboret is upright. You may have to trim the kick panels to suit your 2½ in. flat plate casters. When everything is perfect, install the kick plates.

Affix the doors to the cabinet assembly with two 1½ in. straight pin hinges. Make sure the doors are properly aligned and then install a magnetic catch for each door.

Assemble the shelf pull (R) to the sliding shelf (M) and slide into the unit.

Next, construct the drawers, which consist of the drawer side (N), bottom (O), back (P) and front (Q). Notice that the drawer bottom does not fit into any grooves or dadoes. As long as the drawer bottom is square, the drawer assembly will be square. Assemble the two drawers with finishing nails and glue.

Now construct the tray by assembling the top (K), front (I), side (J), bottom (V) and back (L).

Figure 4. Fill in any blemishes with a nontoxic wood filler. Make sure the filler goes on smoothly.

Finishing

Fill in all surface blemishes with a nontoxic wood filler and finish sand the entire project, making sure that all edges are slightly rounded.

An airless sprayer is ideal for spraying on a sanding coat. Lightly sand this finish when dry, and then apply a second or third final coat to suit your color scheme. ☐

This project is courtesy of Georgia-Pacific Corporation.

Figure 1. Lay out the leg (F) tapers and cut out on a band saw equipped with a ½ in. blade. Cut ¹⁄₁₆ in. short of the cutting line. Refer to next photo.

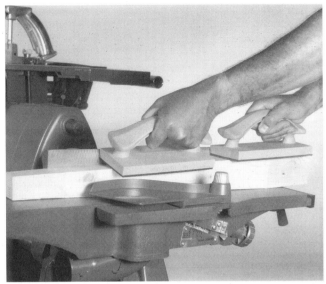

Figure 2. Joint the leg tapers on your jointer. Use a holding jig to prevent your fingers from inadvertently slipping into the cutterhead. Make light ¹⁄₃₂ in. or less passes.

Shaker Desk

Finally, the perfect desk for doing your bookkeeping, writing letters or working on your next sewing project.

This Shaker desk is as comfortable as it is attractive. A special feature is the drop-down lid that provides a large work surface. When you are finished, simply lift the lid back up and lock it upright to hide all your clutter.

Tips

We recommend constructing the project from pine or plywood. If you opt to use plywood, make sure that you cover up the edges with an appropriate edging. Use carpenter's glue and finishing nails to assemble the unit. If you opt to use fasteners, make sure that you counterbore them and cover up the holes with a wood plug.

Select only the best materials for this project, particularly for the lid. If the material selected for the lid is warped, the lid may not rest or close properly.

Desk Construction

Cut out the parts for the desk sides (A), back (B), front (C), bottom (D), rails (E, G) and legs (F). You will have to edge-glue several pieces of pine to come up with the appropriate width for the desk bottom (D). After you have

glued the workpieces, cut the bottom to its final length and width on your table saw. Cut the remaining parts out on your table saw. Note, however, that you may have to use a band saw to rip the legs.

Joint the edges of the wood on a stationary jointer, and sand all of the parts thoroughly before assembly. Round the edges of the desk bottom at this time.

Bevel the front edge of the desk front (C) to suit the taper of the sides (A). Use either a hand plane or a stationary jointer to accomplish this. Work slowly and make shallow passes.

Lay out the tapers for the legs (F) carefully and cut the tapers on your band saw. Use a ½ in. wide blade to prevent the blade from wandering. Stay on the inside of the cut and then dress the taper on your jointer.

Carefully locate the positions of the desk rails (E, G) on the legs and drill mating doweling holes. Drill two holes for each joint to accommodate a 3 in. by 1½ in. dowel. Then assemble the rails to the legs with glue, using a band clamp to clamp the assembly. Make sure that you square the assembly and set the legs on a flat surface during this step.

Secure the desk bottom to the leg assembly with glue and 4d finishing nails. Be sure to sink the nail heads.

Now assemble the sides, along with the back and front, to the desk bottom. Again, use carpenter's glue and 4d finishing nails. Make sure that this subassembly is square.

Measure the materials needed for the desk top (I), lid (H) and lid extension (X). The lid extension is needed to prevent the top lid (J, K) and the desk lid (H) from interfering with one another. Remeasure these components to suit your construction and then cut them to size. Using your table saw, cut the bevel for the lid extension (X) from wider material. Then cut it to its appropriate width. Round over all appropriate edges and sand the workpieces.

Cut stopped dadoes in the desk top (I) to accommodate two cabinet dividers (M).

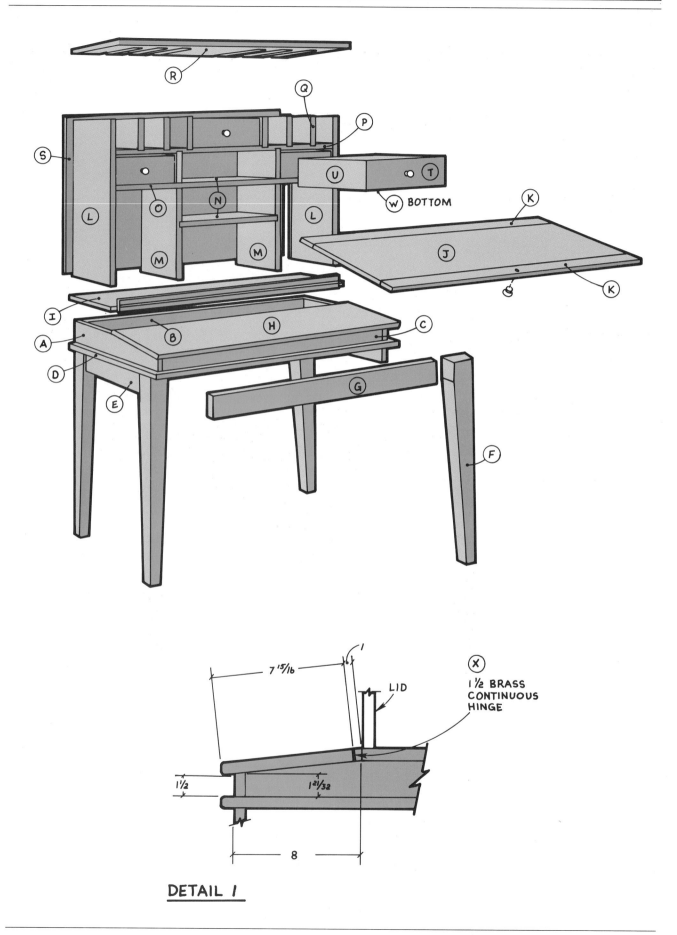

DETAIL 1

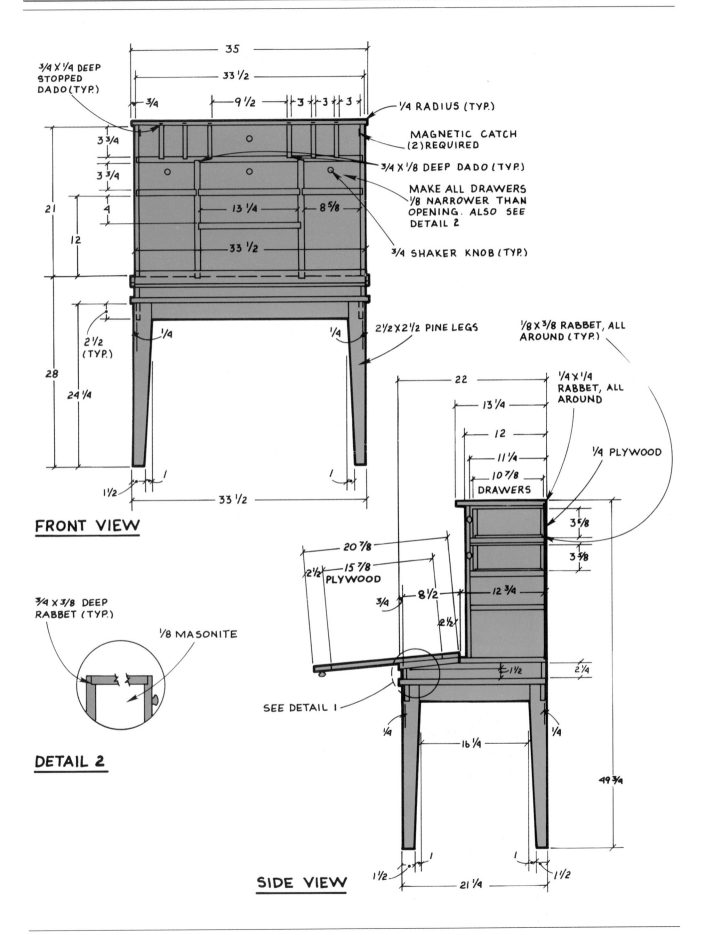

FRONT VIEW

3/4 X 1/4 DEEP STOPPED DADO (TYP.)

35

33 1/2

3/4

9 1/2

3 3 3

1/4 RADIUS (TYP.)

MAGNETIC CATCH (2) REQUIRED

3/4 X 1/8 DEEP DADO (TYP.)

MAKE ALL DRAWERS 1/8 NARROWER THAN OPENING. ALSO SEE DETAIL 2

3/4 SHAKER KNOB (TYP.)

3 3/4

3 3/4

4

21

12

13 1/4

8 5/8

33 1/2

2 1/2 X 2 1/2 PINE LEGS

1/8 X 3/8 RABBET, ALL AROUND (TYP.)

1/4 X 1/4 RABBET, ALL AROUND

1/4 PLYWOOD

2 1/2 (TYP.)

1/4

1/4

28

24 1/4

1

1

1 1/2

33 1/2

DETAIL 2

3/4 X 3/8 DEEP RABBET (TYP.)

1/8 MASONITE

SIDE VIEW

22

13 1/4

12

11 1/4

10 7/8 DRAWERS

20 7/8

15 7/8 PLYWOOD

2 1/2

3/4

8 1/2

12 3/4

3 5/8

3 5/8

2 1/2

1 1/2

2 1/4

SEE DETAIL 1

1/4

1/4

16 1/4

49 3/4

1

1

1 1/2

1 1/2

21 1/4

Figure 3. Check the jointed surfaces making up the lid (J, K) to insure they form a flat surface when doweled and edge-glued.

BILL OF MATERIALS — Shaker Desk

Finished Dimensions in Inches

A	Desk Side	¾ x 2¼ x 21¼ pine	2
B	Desk Back	¾ x 2¼ x 32 pine	1
C	Desk Front	¾ x 1²¹/₃₂ x 32 pine	1
D	Desk Bottom	¾ x 22 x 35 pine	1
E	Desk Rail	¾ x 2½ x 16¼ pine	2
F	Leg	2½ x 2½ x 24¼ pine	4
G	Desk Rail	¾ x 2½ x 28½ pine	2
H	Desk Lid	¾ x 7¹⁵/₁₆ x 35 pine	1
I	Desk Top	¾ x 14 x 35 pine	1
J	Lid	¾ x 15⅞ x 33½ plywood	1
K	Lid Edge	¾ x 2½ x 33½ pine	2
L	Cabinet Side	¾ x 12 x 21 pine	2
M	Cabinet Divider	¾ x 11 x 16⅝ pine	2
N	Cabinet Shelf	¾ x 11 x 13½ pine	2
O	Cabinet Shelf	¾ x 11 x 8⅞ pine	2
P	Cabinet Shelf	¾ x 11 x 32¼ pine	1
Q	Cabinet Divider	¾ x 4 x 11 pine	6
R	Cabinet Top	¾ x 13¼ x 35 pine	1
S	Cabinet Back	¼ x 21½ x 32½ plywood	1
T	Drawer Front	¾ x 3⅝ x opening less ⅛ pine	4
U	Drawer Side	¾ x 3⅝ x 10⅛ pine	8
V	Drawer Back	¾ x 3⅝ x opening less ⅞ pine	4
W	Drawer Bottom	⅛ x 9⅜ x opening less ⅞ Masonite	4
X	Desk Lid Extension	¾ x 1 x 35 pine	1

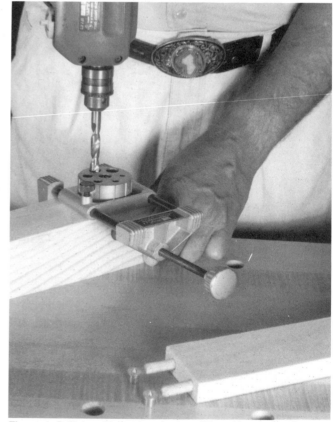

Figure 4. Drill dowel holes into the legs (F) and insert dowel centers to help mark the adjacent desk rails (E, G) for drilling.

Figure 5. Cut the dadoes in the cabinet top (R). If you do not have a radial arm saw, use a T-square guide to help you align a router equipped with a ¾ in. straight bit.

Attach the desk top and the lid extension (X) in place. Then hinge the lid with a continuous hinge as shown in the illustration. This step completes the construction of the basic desk.

Cabinet Construction

Begin constructing the cabinet by cutting the cabinet sides (L) and the top (R) to their proper lengths and widths. Next, cut stopped dadoes in the top to accommodate the dividers (Q). Do this on your table saw using a dado blade set to ¾ in. wide. and a ⅛ in. depth of cut. Also cut stopped dadoes in the sides to hold the cabinet shelves (P) and (O) in place.

Cut stopped rabbets in the backs of the cabinet top (R) and the desk top (I) in order to hold the cabinet back (S). Cut these rabbets with a rabbeting bit with pilot guide in your router. Then square the edges with a wood chisel, and assemble the parts.

Now, cut the cabinet dividers (Q), shelf (P) and dividers (M). Cut dadoes where appropriate and dry-assemble the upper cabinet.

Based on this assembly, cut the rest of the parts, which include the remaining shelves (N, O). Make sure everything fits properly.

Make dowel holes in the bottom of the cabinet sides (L), and drill mating dowel holes in the top edges of the desk top (I). Then assemble the cabinet to the desk top with glue and 4d finishing nails. It is best to have another person help you during this procedure. Use glue sparingly; otherwise it will be difficult for you to clean it up. When you do get carpenter's glue on a wood surface, use a warm, damp cloth to remove it. Allow the assembly to cure for 24 hours.

Now, cut the cabinet back (S) to size and install with carpenter's glue and 1 in. brads. Then custom cut the lid (J) and lid edge (K) to fit the opening. Allow enough material to be jointed so the lid and lid edge will fit perfectly, with no gaps. Also cut these parts oversize so the dried assembly can be cut square.

Assemble the lid edge to the lid with ⅜ in. by 1½ in. dowels spaced every 10 inches. Glue the assembly with carpenter's glue and apply light clamping pressure. Once the glue has dried, remove any excess glue with a paint scraper. Then install the lid in place with a continuous hinge, and secure two magnetic catches to the inside of the cabinet to hold the lid upright.

Carefully measure the openings for the drawers (T, U, V, W) and custom fit them. The drawers should actually be constructed so that the height and width are ⅛ in. less than the opening. Note that the drawer fronts (T) are butted next to the drawer sides (U), and that the drawer sides must be rabbeted to accommodate the drawer back (V). Groove the drawer workpieces to hold the drawer bottom (W). You will have to cut a stopped groove in the drawer front and square the groove with a wood chisel.

Assemble each drawer with glue and 4d finishing nails. Square each drawer as you go.

Finishing

Sand all of the parts thoroughly and round any square edges. Remove the hinges and magnetic catches and apply a stain suitable to your room decor. Then apply a light coat of sanding sealer and allow it to dry. After this has dried, give it a light sanding and remove the dust with a damp cloth.

Complete the unit by applying a satin finish polyurethane. Then reinstall the hardware and add knobs for the drawer. Make sure that you buy knobs that fit into the allotted space. □

This project is courtesy of Shopsmith, Inc.

Magazine Rack

Store your magazines in this handsome pine rack.

There never seems to be enough space for storing magazines. This magazine rack is inexpensive and easy to build. It can be constructed in no time at all using standard size hardwood dowels and scrap wood left over from other projects.

Tips

Use select pine and carefully check to make sure the dowels you purchase are smooth-grained and straight. Assemble the project with carpenter's glue.

Construction

Cut the base (A), feet (B) and rails (C) to their proper widths and lengths.

Mark the location of all holes to be drilled. There is a total of fourteen ½ in. diameter column holes in the base (A) and four ¾ in. diameter brace holes in the rails (C). Drill these holes at a 10 degree angle on your drill press.

Change the drill press table back to 90 degrees to drill the fourteen ½ in. diameter column holes in the top rails.

Using the patterns provided, cut the contours of the top rails and the feet (B) with a scroll saw.

With a handsaw or table saw, cut a 60 degree bevel on the edges of the base and the ends of the feet. Make sure the pieces are exactly the same width and the same angle where they join.

BILL OF MATERIALS — Magazine Rack			
		Finished Dimensions in Inches	
A	Base	¾ x 7 x 16½ pine	1
B	Feet	¾ x 2 x 8⅜ pine	2
C	Rail	¾ x 2½ x 18 pine	2
D	Brace	¾ dia. x 9¾ dowel pine	2
E	Column	½ dia. x 10½ dowel pine	14

Figure 1. Set the drill table to 10 degrees and drill the holes into the base (A). Use the drill's depth stop and a Forstner bit.

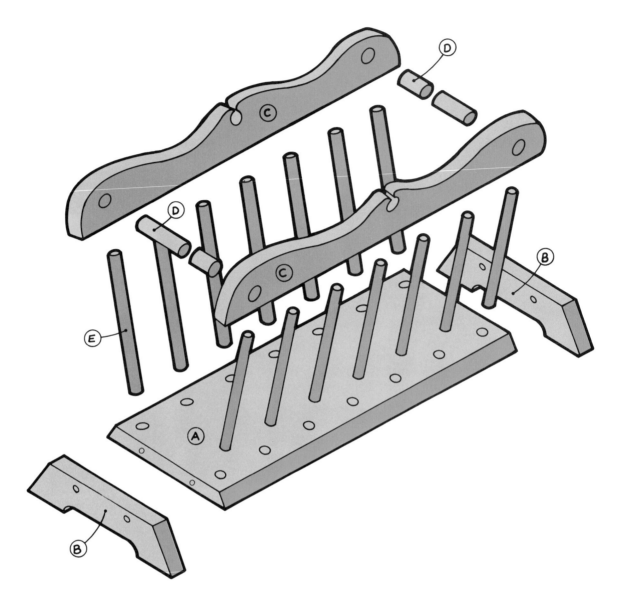

Then cut the braces (D) and columns (E) to length, making sure to knock off any burrs on the ends.

Assembly

To assemble, first attach the feet to the base using glue and No. 8 by 1½ in. flathead wood screws. Countersink the screws.

To complete the rack assembly, use glue to fasten the ends of the columns and braces. Be sure to wipe off any excess glue immediately with a damp rag.

Finishing

Use a sanding block to round over all sharp edges, including the protruding ends of the braces, and to smooth the joints between the base and legs.

Stain the rack with an Early American stain. Natural oil is recommended for the finish. ☐

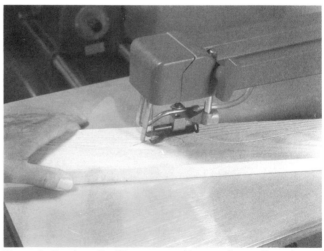

Figure 2. Cut the rail's (C) contours with a scroll saw. Keep the guard no higher than ⅛ in. above the material.

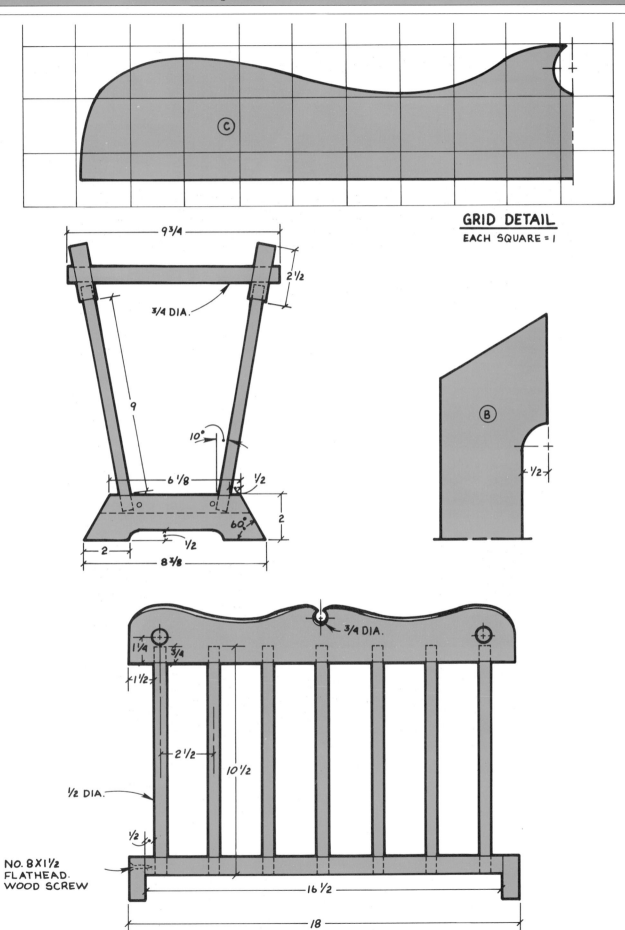

GRID DETAIL
EACH SQUARE = 1

9¾

2½

¾ DIA.

9

10°

6⅛

½

2

60°

½

2

8¾

B

½

3/4 DIA.

1¼

¾

1½

2½

10½

½ DIA.

½

NO. 8 X 1½
FLATHEAD.
WOOD SCREW

16½

18

This project is courtesy of Georgia-Pacific Corporation.

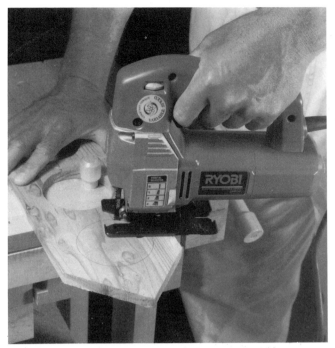

Figure 1. Lay out the front (A), then draw the circles with a compass. Drill starter holes and cut out the waste area with a saber saw.

Figure 2. Cut the sides (C) oversize and make a 45 degree miter with a saber saw. Then position the side workpieces next to the front as shown. Mark the sides to their correct length and cut.

Bird Feeder

If you enjoy the song of chirping birds, then this easy-to-build, three-story bird feeder is just for you.

This redwood bird feeder features three 4 in. diameter holes to accommodate just about any size apple, orange or suet. Made from ½ in. thick redwood, it is easy to construct with simple hand tools.

Construction

Begin construction by cutting out all of the project parts as specified in the Bill of Materials. Notice that there is no need to miter the roof (E, F), but that the sides (C) are mitered to 45 degrees.

Use a compass to draw the three 4 in. diameter holes on the front (A). Then drill three starter holes and cut out the waste area with a saber saw. Cut out the holes with a fine-tooth blade. Next, drill the ¼ in. diameter by ½ in. deep holes for the perch rods (G). Locate these holes to suit.

Then assemble the project, using No. 8 by 1¼ in. brass flathead wood screws (countersunk). Begin by attaching the bottom/divider (D) to the sides (C) and back (B) with wood screws. Then attach the front (A) and the roof (E, F). Finally, insert the perch pins (G) to complete the basic unit.

Finishing

Thoroughly sand all of the project parts, dulling all sharp edges.

An applied finish is not necessary, since redwood is naturally weather resistant. However, if desired, you can apply a clear oil stain or several coats of an exterior grade varnish. Make sure that you use a nontoxic finish.

Complete the project by installing an eye hook in the top of the roof and inserting apples, oranges or suet. Then hang the bird feeder using a length of wire. You may wish to insert two eye hooks to help keep the feeder stable. ☐

BILL OF MATERIALS — Bird Feeder

Finished Dimensions in Inches

A	Front	½ x 6½ x 18 redwood	1
B	Back	½ x 5½ x 18 redwood	1
C	Side	½ x 6 x 15¼ redwood	2
D	Bottom/Divider	½ x 5½ x 5½ redwood	3
E	Roof	½ x 6⅜ x 8½ redwood	1
F	Roof	½ x 5⅞ x 8½ redwood	1
G	Perch Rod	¼ dia. x 2½ birch	3

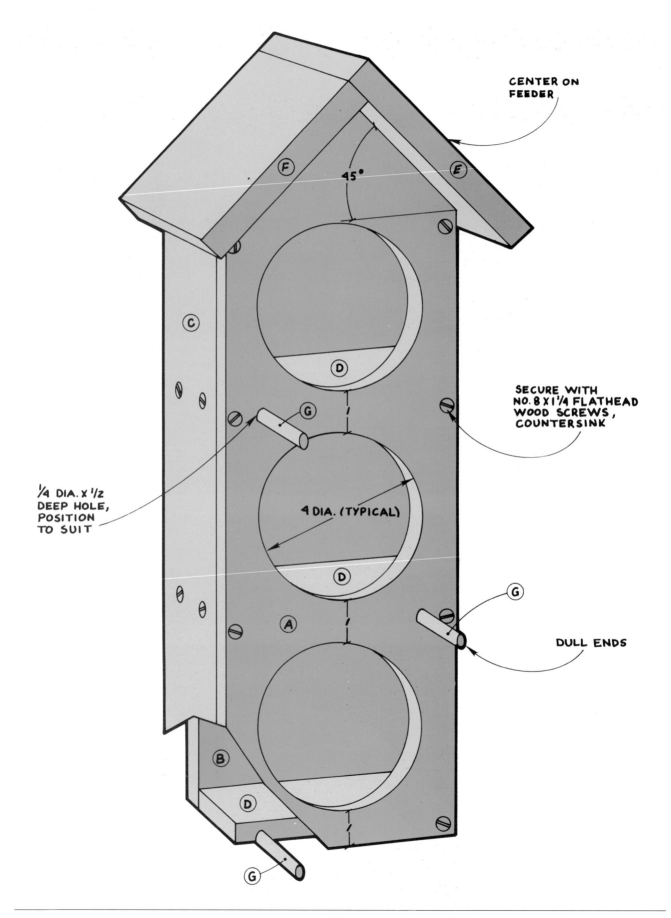

CENTER ON FEEDER

45°

SECURE WITH NO. 8 X 1¼ FLATHEAD WOOD SCREWS, COUNTERSINK

¼ DIA. X ½ DEEP HOLE, POSITION TO SUIT

4 DIA. (TYPICAL)

DULL ENDS

Figure 3. Pre-drill and countersink the fastener holes as shown to prevent splitting the redwood.

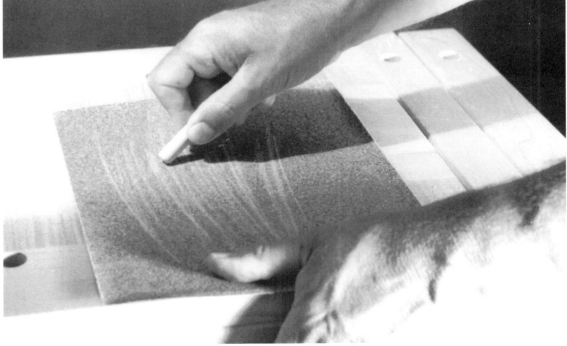

Figure 4. Round the ends of the perch rods (G) by moving the dowel tip across 100 grit sandpaper while turning the dowel

This project is courtesy of the American Plywood Association.

Curio Cabinet

This curio cabinet is charming, functional and easy to build.

This curio cabinet is quite suitable for the beginning woodworker. Basic hand tools and simple butt joints are all that is required. The project is made from one sheet of ¾ in. plywood and has five shelves for glassware, china, souvenirs or books.

Tips

Choose only APA ¾ in. plywood with both sides finished for this project. This will minimize wood filling and additional sanding. Remember that the quality of the plywood determines how good the cabinet will look.

Construction

Begin by cutting out all of the project parts to their required sizes.

Use a circular saw equipped with a plywood cutting blade to cut out the parts. Work slowly to eliminate unstraight rip.

Use a saber saw equipped with a plywood cutting blade to cut the contours in the two rails (E) and the sides (A).

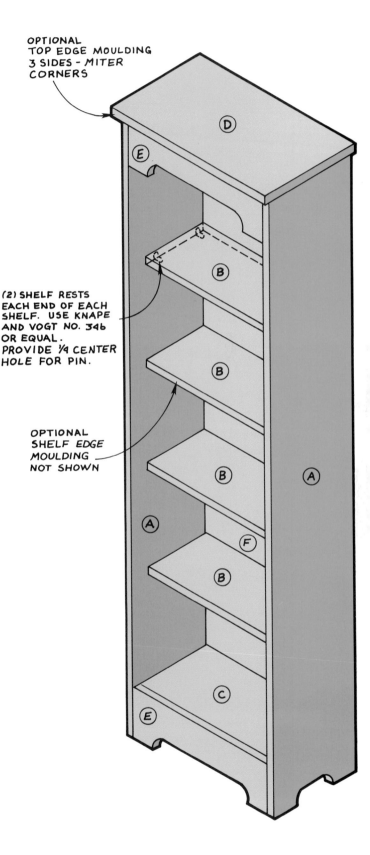

OPTIONAL TOP EDGE MOULDING 3 SIDES - MITER CORNERS

(2) SHELF RESTS EACH END OF EACH SHELF. USE KNAPE AND VOGT NO. 346 OR EQUAL. PROVIDE ¼ CENTER HOLE FOR PIN.

OPTIONAL SHELF EDGE MOULDING NOT SHOWN

Figure 1. Cut out the contours in the rails (E) and sides (A) with a saber saw. Cut with the good side down and use a plywood cutting blade.

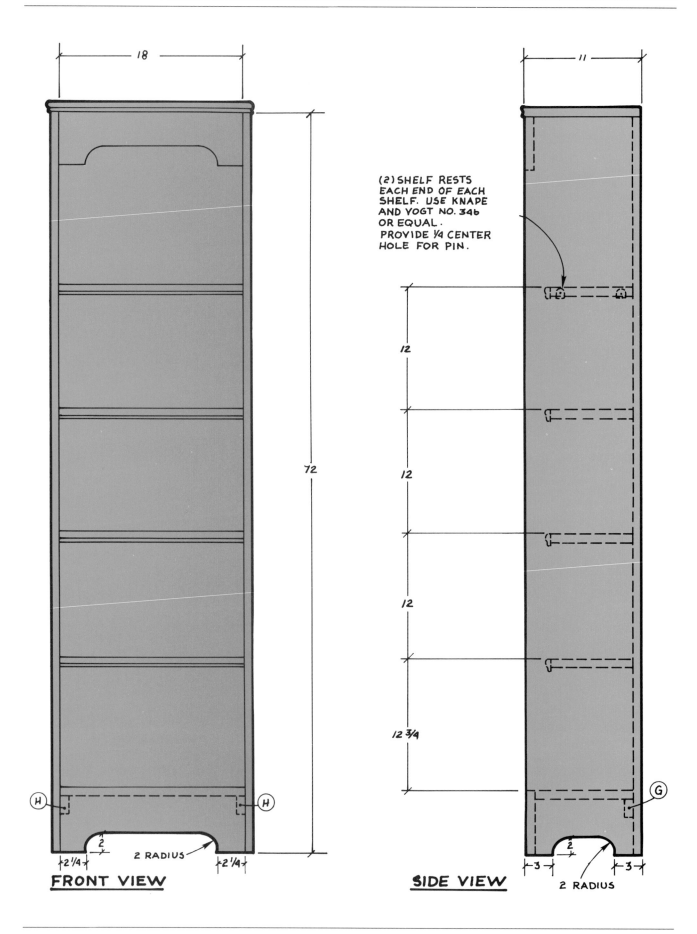

18

72

FRONT VIEW

2 RADIUS

2¼

2¼

H

H

11

(2) SHELF RESTS
EACH END OF EACH
SHELF. USE KNAPE
AND VOGT NO. 346
OR EQUAL.
PROVIDE ¼ CENTER
HOLE FOR PIN.

12

12

12

12

12 ¾

SIDE VIEW

2 RADIUS

3

3

G

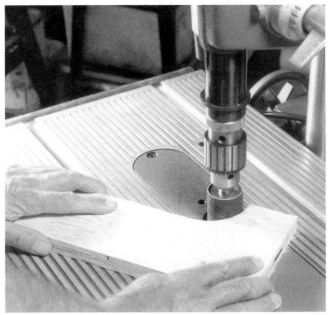

Figure 2. Sand the contours with a drum sander installed in a drill or drill press. The drum should rotate into the workpiece.

Figure 3. If you do not have a jointer or power hand plane, use a bench plane. Clamp a piece of scrap wood for an edge-guide, as shown. Take long, shallow passes.

Use a bench plane, stationary jointer or a portable hand plane to dress all of the edges so that they are straight, smooth and square.

Sand all of the project parts using a sanding block or a pad sander.

Begin construction by assembling the two sides (A) to the top (D) and bottom (C) with 4d finishing nails and carpenter's glue. Then turn the project with the backside up and insert the back (F) using 4d finishing nails and glue.

Now install the two front rails (E) along with the cleats (G, H), which fit underneath the bottom shelf.

Locate the positions of the four adjustable shelves (B) and drill appropriately sized holes for shelf rests.

Add edging to all of the showing edges of the project. Edging can be purchased at lumberyards, hardware stores and through mail order catalogs.

Finishing

Sand all project parts and apply a sanding sealer. Allow the sealer to dry thoroughly and then finish sand. Finally, add the paint of your choice to complete the project. □

BILL OF MATERIALS — Curio Cabinet

Finished Dimensions in Inches

A	Side	¾ x 11 x 72 plywood	2
B	Shelf	¾ x 8 x 17½ plywood	4
C	Bottom	¾ x 9⅜ x 18 plywood	1
D	Top	¾ x 11⅜ x 20 plywood	1
E	Rail	¾ x 5⅜ x 18 plywood	2
F	Back	¾ x 18 x 72 plywood	1
G	Back Cleat	¾ x 1½ x 17⅞ plywood	1
H	Side Cleat	¾ x 1½ x 9⅜ plywood	2

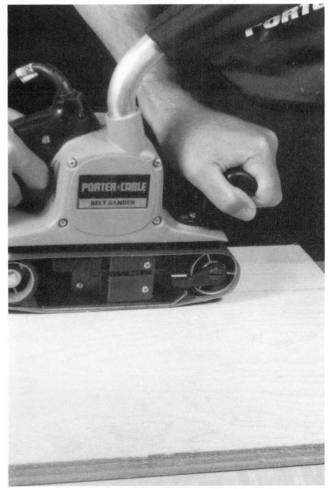

Figure 4. Sand flat surfaces with a belt sander. Always keep the sander parallel to the wood's surface and work it back and forth. Avoid keeping it stationary for too long.

This project is courtesy of Shopsmith, Inc.

Folding Party Trays

Entertain in style with these folding party trays.

You're having a cookout and your guests are arriving in fifteen minutes. You've dragged out that wobbly, old card table one more time and set it up beside your picnic table, but now you're back in the house, scrounging for an extra table. You veto an impulse to pull your heirloom coffee table out to the patio; then the doorbell rings, and several guests wind up sitting on folding chairs, balancing plates of food on their laps.

Next time, enjoy your outdoor meals in style with these handy fold-away party trays. Made of redwood, these trays are not only utilitarian, but beautifully designed and surprisingly easy to build.

Getting Started

Each fold-away party tray requires one 8 ft. redwood 1 x 10. Add brass hardware for a special touch.

To build this project, you'll need a table saw and jointer for sizing cuts. Use the drill press to make the bolt and screw holes with 3/16 in., 1/4 in., 3/8 in. and 3/4 in. brad point drill bits

and a No. 10 screw bit. You'll also need a band saw and a disk sander to round and shape the parts.

Construction

Use a table saw to cut all the pieces to size as shown in the Bill of Materials. Use a jointer to remove the sawing marks from the wood.

Lay out and drill all the bolt and screw holes. The counter-bored holes in the skirt (G) conceal the top mounting screws under the table. Access to these screws allows replacement of the top boards.

When drilling the counterbores, always drill the large diameter holes first. The recess made by the tip of the brad point bit will center the smaller bit in the large hole.

Drill 3/4 in. diameter holes in the two brace locks (F) and the waste area of the skirts (G). These holes will form the notches that accept the dowel brace (E) when the table is in either an open or closed position.

Drill 5/16 in. diameter holes into the ends of a 3/4 in. diameter dowel to form the spacers (C). Drill deep enough to form two spacers. Then cut the spacers to length on a band saw.

Also round the ends and corners on the legs (A), brace locks (F), and skirts (G). Cut away stock to form the notches in the brace locks (F) and skirts (G). Then use a disk sander to sand the sawn edges smooth.

Assembly

First assemble the two leg sets exactly square. Be sure that the counterbores are facing out on the outer leg sets and in on the inner leg sets. Fasten the dowel brace (E) in the legs (A)

Figure 1. Form the brace locks (F) from longer material to avoid getting fingers too close to cutting blades, or drill. Drill 3/4 in. diameter holes and cut out the waste area on a band saw.

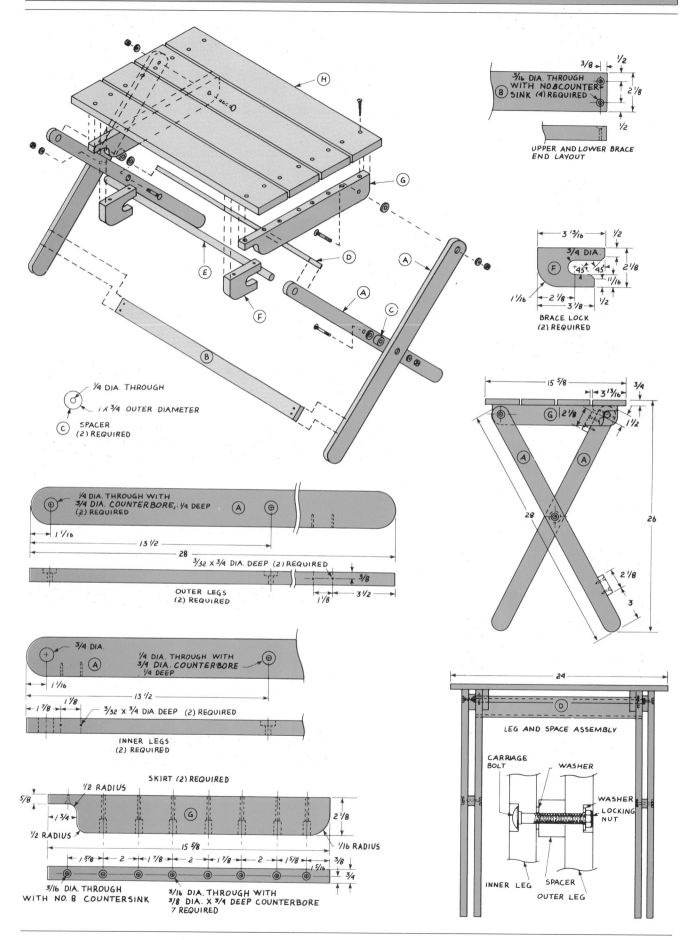

3/16 DIA. THROUGH
WITH NO.8 COUNTER-
SINK (4) REQUIRED

B

3/8   1/2
2 1/8
1/2

UPPER AND LOWER BRACE
END LAYOUT

3 13/16   1/2
3/4 DIA.
F   45°   45°   2 1/8
11/16
1 1/16   2 1/8   1/2
3 1/8

BRACE LOCK
(2) REQUIRED

H

G

D

A

A

C

E

F

B

1/4 DIA. THROUGH

1 x 3/4 OUTER DIAMETER

C   SPACER
(2) REQUIRED

1/4 DIA. THROUGH WITH
3/4 DIA. COUNTERBORE, 1/4 DEEP
(2) REQUIRED   A

1 1/16
13 1/2
28
3/32 x 3/4 DIA. DEEP (2) REQUIRED
3/8
1 1/8   3 1/2

OUTER LEGS
(2) REQUIRED

3/4 DIA.
A
1/4 DIA. THROUGH WITH
3/4 DIA. COUNTERBORE
1/4 DEEP

1 1/16
13 1/2
1 7/8
1 1/8
3/32 x 3/4 DIA.DEEP (2) REQUIRED

INNER LEGS
(2) REQUIRED

SKIRT (2) REQUIRED

1/2 RADIUS
5/8
1 3/4
1/2 RADIUS
G
2 1/8
1/16 RADIUS
15 5/8
3/8
1 5/8   2   1 7/8   1 7/8   2   1 5/8
5/8
3/4
3/16 DIA. THROUGH
WITH NO. 8 COUNTERSINK
3/16 DIA. THROUGH WITH
3/8 DIA. X 3/4 DEEP COUNTERBORE
7 REQUIRED

15 5/8   3/4
3 13/16
G   2 1/8
1 1/2
A   A
28
2 1/8
3
26

24
D
LEG AND SPACE ASSEMBLY

CARRIAGE
BOLT
WASHER
WASHER
LOCKING
NUT
INNER LEG
SPACER
OUTER LEG

Figure 2. Drill 5/16 in. diameter holes into a length of 3/4 in. diameter dowel, held in place with a wood clamp. Then cut the spacers (C) to length on a band saw.

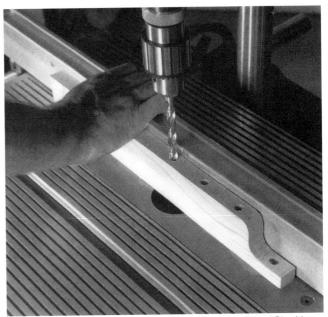

Figure 3. Pre-drill and counterbore holes into the skirts (G) with your drill press. Make sure to use a back-up board.

with 6d finishing nails and carpenter's glue. Tap them through the undersized holes in the edges of the legs (A) and the end of the dowel brace (E).

Assemble the top (H). Lay the boards on a flat surface, spacing them 1/8 in. apart with pieces of corrugated cardboard. Use the leg sets to position the skirts (G) and brace locks (F) for assembly.

Fasten the skirts (G) to the top (H) with No. 8 by 2 in. round head wood screws and flat washers. Secure each brace lock (F) to the top (H) boards with No. 8 by 2 1/2 in. round head wood screws, flat washers and two No. 8 by 1 in. flathead wood screws.

Combine the leg sets with the spacers (C), using 2 1/4 in. carriage bolts, flat washers and locking cap nuts. Fasten the leg sets to the skirts (G) with 1 1/2 in. carriage bolts, flat washers and cap nuts. Slide the carriage bolts through from the inside out.

Finishing

Sand and finish each fold-away party tray. Use an exterior-grade finish to match the patio furniture you might already have...and happy partying! □

BILL OF MATERIALS — Folding Party Trays

Finished Dimensions in Inches

A	Leg	3/4 x 2 1/8 x 28 redwood	4
B	Lower Brace	3/4 x 2 1/8 x 22 1/2 redwood	1
C	Spacer	3/4 x 1 x 1 redwood	2
D	Upper Brace	3/4 x 2 1/8 x 19 1/2 redwood	1
E	Dowel Brace	3/4 dia. x 19 1/2 redwood	1
F	Brace Lock	3/4 x 2 1/8 x 3 13/16 redwood	2
G	Skirt	3/4 x 2 1/8 x 15 5/8 redwood	2
H	Top	3/4 x 3 13/16 x 24 redwood	4

Figure 4. Smooth the ends of the legs (A) with a disk sander as shown. Use a fine grit disk.

This project is courtesy of Shopsmith, Inc.

Figure 1. A radius template is ideal for laying out the handholds in the sides (A). Draw the curves of the sides with a bar compass.

Figure 2. Drill starter holes in the area of the sides (A) where the handholds will be cut. Then cut out the openings using a saber saw equipped with a plywood cutting blade to reduce splintering the wood.

Telephone Stand

This project is easy to build and makes a great telephone stand, night stand or end table.

If you're like a lot of people, maybe the location of your telephone is such that you're forced to set the phone on your kitchen table or countertop. Or is it in your living room, sitting conspicuously on your coffee table? And what about your telephone books and note pads? They never seem to be handy when you need them. Well, here's a simple and good-looking solution to these problems — a telephone stand you can easily build yourself. One of the really nice aspects of this project is the detail designs. In several places throughout the plans we suggest certain shapes or edges. However, feel free to use your imagination to fit your particular decor.

Tips

Use carpenter's glue for this project's assembly. We used a dovetail joint to assemble the shelves to the sides, but you can substitute with dado joints.

Construction

Begin by cutting all the stock to the sizes listed in the Bill of Materials. Next, cut the four ⅜ in. stopped dovetail grooves, 11⅜ in. in length in the sides (A) as shown in Detail 1. These dovetails accommodate the shelves (B). Be sure to start the grooves at the rear of the sides for all dovetails. Cut the dovetails using a router equipped with a dovetail cutter. Guide the router along a straightedge.

Cut the four matching dovetails on the ends of shelves (B) as indicated in Detail 2. Make these tails with a dovetail cutter inserted in the router. Use an edge-guide set to the proper depth of cut.

Using a shaper or router, round over the front edge of the shelves (B), or use the design of your choice. Then notch the front edge of the shelves with a band saw.

Use a bar compass to draw a 6 in. radius in the top of each side (A). Using a band saw or jigsaw, round off the tops and cut out the openings at the bottoms of side pieces (A). Use a drum sander to finish the edges.

Drill starter holes in sides (A) at the tops where the decorative handholds are to be cut out. (See Detail 1.) Then use a jigsaw or saber saw to cut out the handholds. If you prefer, you can leave the sides solid at the top or cut out an opening to suit. You might even want to try your hand at woodburning a decoration.

Now, cut the decorative edge on the shelf facings (C) using a shaper or router. (See Detail 3.) We chose a bead and

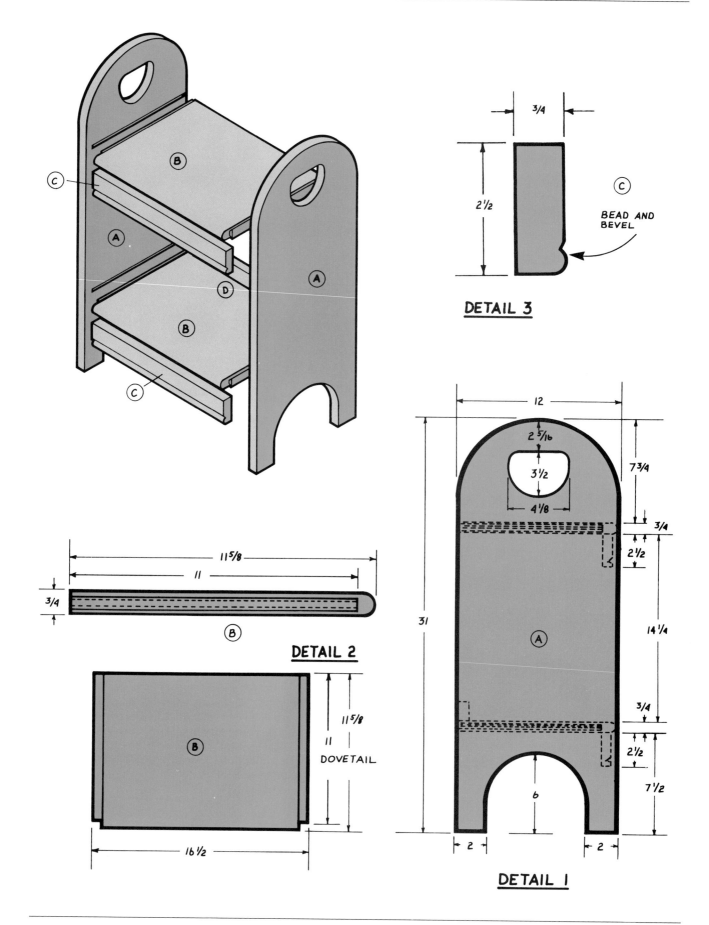

DETAIL 3

BEAD AND BEVEL

3/4

2½

Ⓒ

DETAIL 2

11⅝

11

3/4

Ⓑ

Ⓑ

11⅝

11

DOVETAIL

16½

DETAIL 1

12

2⁵/₁₆

3½

4⅛

7¾

3/4

2½

31

Ⓐ

14¼

3/4

2½

6

7½

2   2

Figure 3. Rout dovetails into the sides (A) with a dovetail cutter installed in your router. Guide the router with a straightedge.

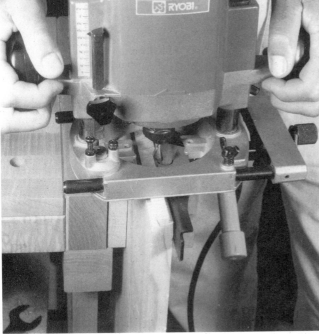

Figure 4. Make the dovetails on the shelves (B) with a dovetail cutter. Use an edge-guide to guide the router along the edge.

Figure 5. After you have finished making the dovetails for the shelves and rounded over the front edges, notch the front corners on a band saw as shown.

BILL OF MATERIALS — Telephone Stand

Finished Dimensions in Inches

A	Side	¾ x 31 x 12 pine	2
B	Shelf	¾ x 16½ x 11⅝ pine	2
C	Shelf Facing	¾ x 16 x 2½ pine	2
D	Bottom Shelf Back	¾ x 16 x 1½ pine	1

bevel edge for our stand. However, you might have other ideas for your home.

Assemble the shelves to the sides, using the dovetails, glue and clamps. Wipe away any excess glue immediately with a damp cloth.

Complete the assembly by installing the shelf facings (C) and the bottom shelf back (D) with glue and clamps. Attach the two shelf facings (C) flush with the front of the shelves.

Finishing

Finish with the stain of your choice and apply a sanding sealer. Let the sealer dry, then sand lightly before applying a final polyurethane finish. ☐

This project is courtesy of Howard Stephen and Shopsmith, Inc.

Quilt Display Rack

This quilt rack is as unique as the family heirlooms displayed on it.

Family heirlooms are precious to most people, especially those with strong family backgrounds. Such is the case with my daughter Julie. She wanted to display one of her great-great-grandmother's antique quilts. That's when I got the idea for this antique quilt display rack. I began by sketching my idea. The result was a red oak frame with simple lines and easy-to-construct plans. In my case, what makes this particular project unique is where I got the stock.

Several years ago, our family church replaced the old, hard red oak pews. I bought several of them, not really knowing what I would use them for. Here was an opportunity to give the old pews a new life. All the pieces of this project were cut from the old pews, except the stretchers. The wood you use, of course, can be of your own choosing, depending on your decor and the availability of wood. I hope you enjoy building the quilt rack. It makes a fine, long-lasting gift. Hopefully it will be passed on from one generation to the next.

Getting Started

You won't need a large amount of stock for this project. If some of the thicknesses are not readily available, such as for the bases (A) and top caps (C), you will simply have to glue up some thinner stock to size. Note: When working with glued-up stock, always allow the glue to dry for at least 24 hours before working with it.

Bases

Let's start with the bases (A). You'll need to cut two blanks to size as shown in the Bill of Materials. As mentioned earlier, if 2¼ in. stock is not available, you'll have to create it. Glue up three pieces of 1 in. stock, side to side. There is an advantage to this method as opposed to a solid piece. You'll not only get a stronger base, but also an attractive end grain pattern. Use a damp cloth to wipe away any excess glue before it dries. After the glue has dried for at least 24 hours, cut the two bases to 3 in. by 17 inches. Then if you have a thickness planer, use it to plane the bases down to an exact 2¼ in. thickness.

As shown in the diagram, the bases have a ½ in. chamfer, 3 in. from each end. And there is also a peak in the bottom,

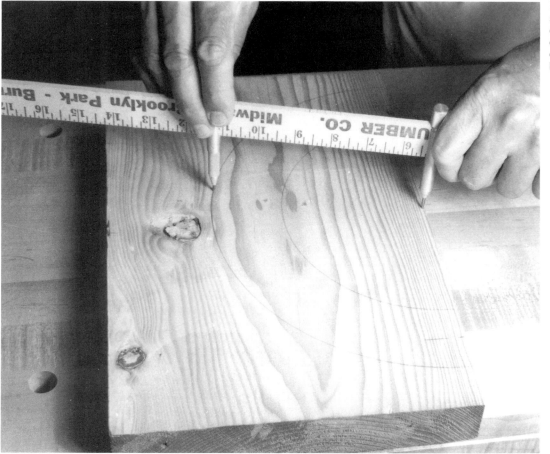

Figure 1. Draw the shape of the top caps with a bar compass and then cut to shape with a band saw.

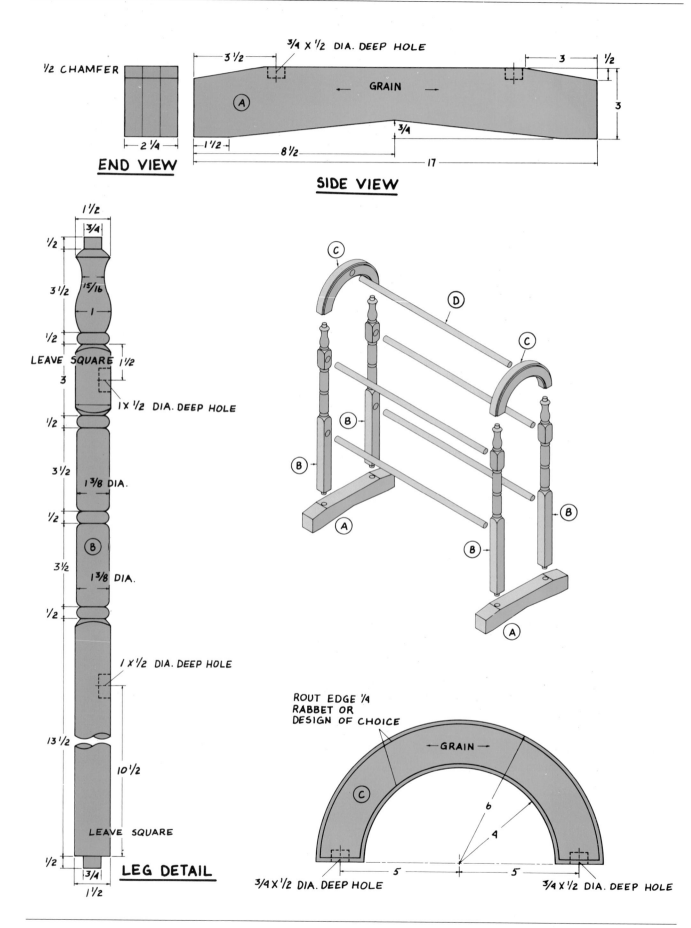

½ CHAMFER

END VIEW

2¼

3½   ¾ X ½ DIA. DEEP HOLE   3   ½

← GRAIN →

Ⓐ

3

3¾

1½

8½

17

SIDE VIEW

LEG DETAIL

1½

¾

½

3½   15/16

1

½

LEAVE SQUARE 1½

3

1 X ½ DIA. DEEP HOLE

½

3½   1⅜ DIA.

½

Ⓑ

3½   1⅜ DIA.

½

1 X ½ DIA. DEEP HOLE

13½

10½

LEAVE SQUARE

½

¾

1½

Ⓒ

Ⓓ

Ⓑ

Ⓑ

Ⓐ

Ⓑ

Ⓑ

Ⓐ

ROUT EDGE ¼
RABBET OR
DESIGN OF CHOICE

← GRAIN →

Ⓒ

6

4

¾ X ½ DIA. DEEP HOLE   5   5   ¾ X ½ DIA. DEEP HOLE

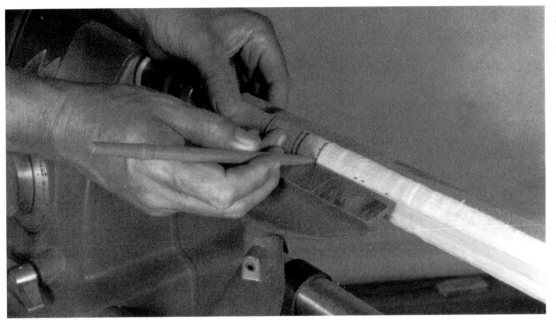

Figure 2. Mark the turning points on the legs (B) after turning the legs to a cylinder.

starting 1½ in. from each end, that rises and meets in the center ¾ in. from the bottom. Mark these lines on the base pieces and cut them using a band saw. Sand all areas smooth. Finally, drill two holes ¾ in. diameter by ½ in. deep for the leg tenons as shown in the diagram.

Top Caps

The top caps (C) need to be cut with extreme care. You'll need two pieces of stock 1½ in. by 6 in. by 12 inches. If you are not able to make them from solid stock, glue up stock using thinner pieces and follow the same procedures used for making the bases. Once your stock is ready to work with, either make a template from the diagram or use a pencil compass to mark two half circles with 4 in. and 6 in. radii.

Position and drill ¾ in. diameter by ½ in. holes for the leg tenons as shown in the diagram. A horizontal boring machine works best for this.

Using a band saw, cut out the top caps, being sure to stay just outside the pencil line. Sand the outside of the top caps with a disk sander and the inside areas with a drum sander.

As an added touch, rout a decorative edge on the top caps. The diagram shows a simple ¼ in. rabbet cut. You might prefer a ¼ in. Roman ogee or even a ¼ in. rounding over bit.

Turning the Legs

Because some of the areas of the legs (B) are to remain square, the stock needs to be cut, planed and sanded smooth to size before turning. The turning stock is to be sized to 1½ in. by 1½ in. by 30 inches per the Bill of Materials. Use the pattern (diagram) to mark your leg stock, or design your own pattern.

The legs have very simple lines; that is, the lathe chisel cuts have been kept very basic. Only a few small beads (raised areas) and a larger bead and cove (cut-in area) are required for a very stylish looking leg profile. The cuts are made using a 1 in. parting tool to control the depth, a 1 in. gouge and 1 in. skew, plus a good pair of outside calipers. If you are using a Shopsmith Lathe Duplicator, the first turned leg will serve

as your pattern, or you can make a template.

Turning Tip: Extra care must be taken when making the tenons for the ends of the legs. The tenons must be exactly ¾ in. in diameter to fit the holes in the top caps and bases. If you do remove too much stock, an easy correction is to take some straight grain wood and hand plane a ½ in. shaving about 3 in. long. Glue and wrap the curled shaving tightly around the tenon and allow it to dry for at least 24 hours. Then re-turn the tenon to the exact ¾ in. diameter.

Assembling and Finishing

The only pieces remaining to make are the stretchers (D). These are simply 1 in. diameter oak dowel rods cut to 30 in. lengths.

Now you're ready to dry-fit the project together. (See the exploded diagram.) If everything fits as it should, disassemble and then glue and clamp it back together. Be sure to wipe away any excess glue with a damp cloth immediately or your stain will not take properly.

Depending on the type of wood used, you might want to use a sanding sealer before applying your final finish. This provides good seal and makes the surfaces uniform so you will get an even coverage of stain. When the sanding sealer is properly dry, lightly hand sand with 400 grit or finer sandpaper. Remove all the dust and apply your choice of finish. I used a clear oil finish to bring out the rich color that red oak provides. □

BILL OF MATERIALS — Quilt Display Rack

Finished Dimensions in Inches

A	Base	2¼ x 3 x 17 oak	2
B	Leg	1½ x 1½ x 30 oak	4
C	Top Cap	1½ x 6 x 12 oak	2
D	Stretcher	1 dia. x 30 dowel rod oak	5

This project is courtesy of Shopsmith, Inc.

Barbecue Cart

Bring the kitchen to your backyard with this handsome, sturdy barbecue cart.

Cooking outdoors can sometimes take more effort than it really should. You always keep running indoors for some reason — preparing the meat, cutting vegetables and organizing all the other elements of your cookout. With this barbecue cart you can take all your utensils and condiments outside so you can do all the food preparation and cooking while visiting with your guests. No more wasted steps, and the cart rolls away for easy storage and cleanup. It also looks great in your kitchen during the cold weather season. Red oak was used for this cart for lasting beauty.

Tips

Cut all pieces to size according to the Bill of Materials.

Figure 1. Round the edges of the false fronts (Y) on a stationary belt sander. Work while applying light pressure.

Note: Allow all glued-up assemblies to dry for about 24 hours before using them in another step.

Construction

Begin building the cart by putting together the facing assembly (see Detail 1). Drill 3/8 in. diameter dowel holes and assemble the middle stile and the two rails (B, C, D) using glue and 3/8 in. by 1 1/16 in. dowel pins.

Next, construct the base assembly using the subassembly (B, C, D) and parts A, E, F, G. Cut a notch in left side (F) to allow for the shelf to be installed later. (See Detail 2.) Again, drill 3/8 in. diameter dowel holes and use glue and 3/8 in. diameter by 1 1/16 in. dowel pins to secure the assembly. (See Detail 2.)

Mount the cleats (L) 7 1/4 in. down from the top of the rails. (See Detail 4.)

Now cut 1/4 in. by 3/8 in. deep tongue-and-groove joints in the stiles and rails (H, I, J) for the web frame assembly. (See Detail 3.) Then glue up the web frame assembly (H, I, J). (See Detail 3.) Mount the web frame assembly on the cleats (L) using four No. 8 by 1 1/4 in. flathead wood screws.

Cut dado and rabbet joints in the drawer fronts and backs (W) and the drawer sides (V). (See Detail 5.) Next, cut notches in the drawer fronts and backs 1 in. wide by 1/4 in.

		BILL OF MATERIALS — Barbecue Cart	

		Finished Dimension in Inches	
A	Stile	3/4 x 1 1/2 x 8 oak	2
B	Middle Stile	3/4 x 1 1/2 x 4 1/4 oak	1
C	Top Rail	3/4 x 2 1/4 x 17 oak	1
D	Bottom Rail	3/4 x 1 1/2 x 17 oak	1
E	Back	3/4 x 8 x 20 oak	1
F	Side	3/4 x 8 x 14 1/2 oak	2
G	Leg	2 x 2 x 38 oak	4
H	Stile	3/4 x 2 1/2 x 17 oak	2
I	Rail	3/4 x 2 1/2 x 15 3/4 oak	2
J	Middle Stile	3/4 x 3 1/2 x 12 3/4 oak	1
K	Drawer Runner	1/4 x 1 x 16 oak	2
L	Cleat	3/4 x 3/4 x 16 7/8 oak	2
M	Side	3/4 x 1 5/8 x 22 1/4 oak	2
N	Back Brace	3/4 x 1 5/8 x 12 3/4 oak	1
O	Front Brace	3/4 x 3/4 x 12 3/4 oak	1
P	Guide	3/4 x 1 1/4 x 10 1/4 oak	2
Q	Shelf	11/16 x 10 3/8 x 11 11/16 oak	1
R	Bottom	1/8 x 14 1/2 x 11 oak	1
S	Front/Back Rail	3/4 x 1 1/2 x 20 oak	2
T	Side Rail	3/4 x 1 1/2 x 18 1/2 oak	2
U	Top (Formica)	3/4 x 17 x 18 1/2 oak	1
V	Side	5/8 x 4 1/16 x 16 oak	4
W	Front/Back	5/8 x 4 1/16 x 6 7/8 oak	4
X	Bottom	1/4 x 6 3/4 x 15 1/8 oak	2
Y	False Front	3/8 x 5 x 8 1/2 oak	2
Z	Top (Formica)	3/4 x 18 5/8 x 24 1/8 oak	1
AA	Side Rail	3/4 x 1 1/2 x 20 1/4 oak	2
BB	Front/Back Rail	3/4 x 1 1/2 x 25 3/4 oak	2
CC	Utensil Holder	3/4 x 2 x 17 5/8 oak	1
DD	Condiment Holder	3/4 x 4 x 18 oak	1

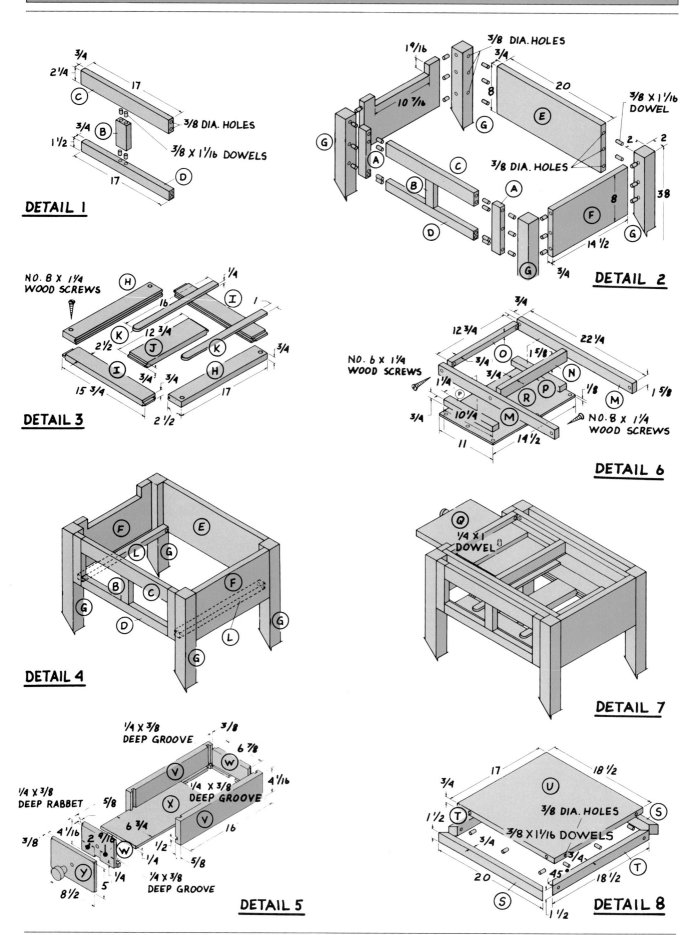

DETAIL 1

DETAIL 2

DETAIL 3

DETAIL 4

DETAIL 5

DETAIL 6

DETAIL 7

DETAIL 8

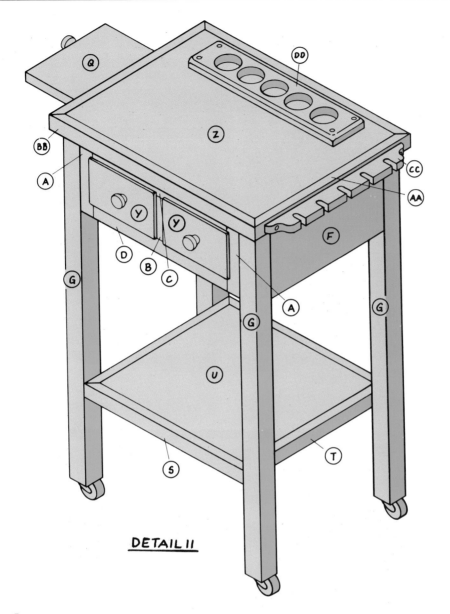

DETAIL 11

DETAIL 9

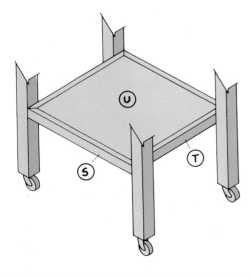

DETAIL 10

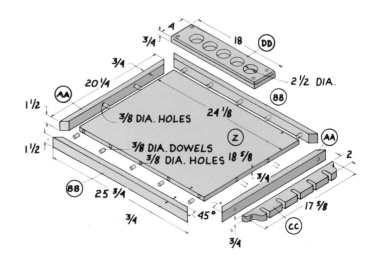

3/4
18 DD

3/4
20 1/4
AA
2 1/2 DIA.
BB

1 1/2
3/8 DIA. HOLES
24 1/8

1 1/2
3/8 DIA. DOWELS
3/8 DIA. HOLES
18 5/8
Z
AA

2
3/4

BB
25 3/4
3/4
45°
17 5/8
CC
3/4

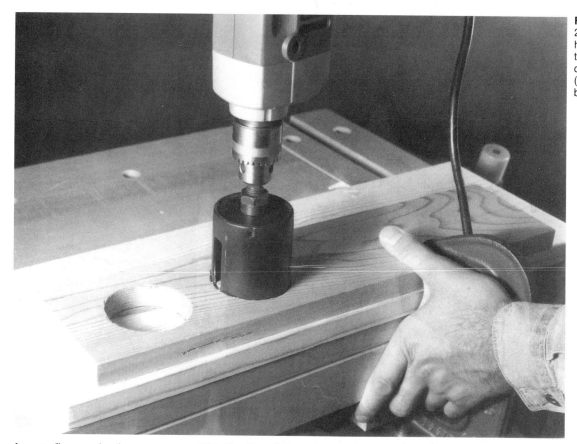

Figure 2. Use a 2½ in. diameter hole cutter to cut the holes in the condiment holder (DD). Use a backer board.

deep to fit over the drawer runners (K). (See Detail 5.)

Using glue, assemble the drawer parts (V, W, X).

Mount the drawer runners (K) on the web frame to fit the assembled drawers. (See Detail 3.)

Round over the false drawer fronts (Y) on your stationary belt sander. Then glue the false fronts to the drawer assembly (V, W, X). (See Detail 5.)

Using No. 6 by 1¼ in. flathead wood screws, construct the shelf support assembly (M, N, O, P, R). Drill pilot holes for easier assembly. (See Detail 6.)

Mount the completed shelf support assembly to the base assembly using No. 8 by 1¼ in. flathead wood screws. (See Details 6 and 7.)

Drill a ¼ in. diameter by ½ in. deep hole, ½ in. from the back edge of the shelf (Q). (See Detail 7.)

Construct the bottom shelf assembly next. Cut miters for the front and back rails (S) and the two side rails (T). (See Detail 8.)

Using glue and ⅜ in. diameter by 1¹⁄₁₆ in. dowel pins, assemble the bottom shelf (S, T, U). (See Detail 8.)

Attach the bottom shelf assembly to the legs (G) using No. 8 by 1¼ in. flathead wood screws. (See Detail 9.)

Finally, construct the top assembly. Cut miters for the side rails (AA) and the front and back rails (BB). Then cut out the utensil holder (CC) and the condiment holder (DD). (See Detail 10.)

Using glue and ⅜ in. diameter by 1¹⁄₁₆ in. dowel pins, assemble the top (Z, AA, BB). (See Detail 10.)

Mount the top assembly to the base assembly using No. 8 by 1¼ in. flathead wood screws.

Mount the utensil holder (CC) to the side of the top

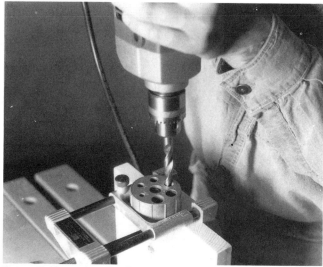

Figure 3. Use a doweling jig to position and drill all dowel holes. Use a spur point drill bit.

assembly with No. 8 by 1¼ in. flathead wood screws.

Round the edges of condiment holder (DD) and mount to the Formica top with No. 6 by 1¼ in. flathead wood screws. Cover screw heads with wooden caps. (See Detail 10.)

Sand the entire cart and finish with the stain of your choice. We used Watco natural stain.

Install the shelf (Q) and insert a ¼ in. by 1 in. dowel pin to keep the shelf from pulling completely out. (See Detail 7.)

Mount the drawer, shelf pulls and casters, and you are ready to cook out in style! □

This project is courtesy of Cherry Tree Toys, Inc.

Rolls Royce

Simple hand tools are all that is required to build this project.

Besides being fun to build, this Rolls Royce is designed to stimulate a child's development. It has animated features that children will find engrossing. You'll have as much fun making this toy as the children will have playing with it.

Tips

This Rolls Royce is constructed from cherry lumber and will take many years of abuse. Buy knot-free lumber.

Some of the parts, like the wheels, can be made or purchased. Cherry Tree Toys, Inc., offers full-size patterns, project parts, cherry workpieces and even a finished Rolls Royce. For information and a catalog, write to the address printed at the end of the Bill of Materials.

Figure 1. Lay out and then cut the fenders (J) on a band saw using a ¼ in. blade. Work slowly and stay outside of the cutting line.

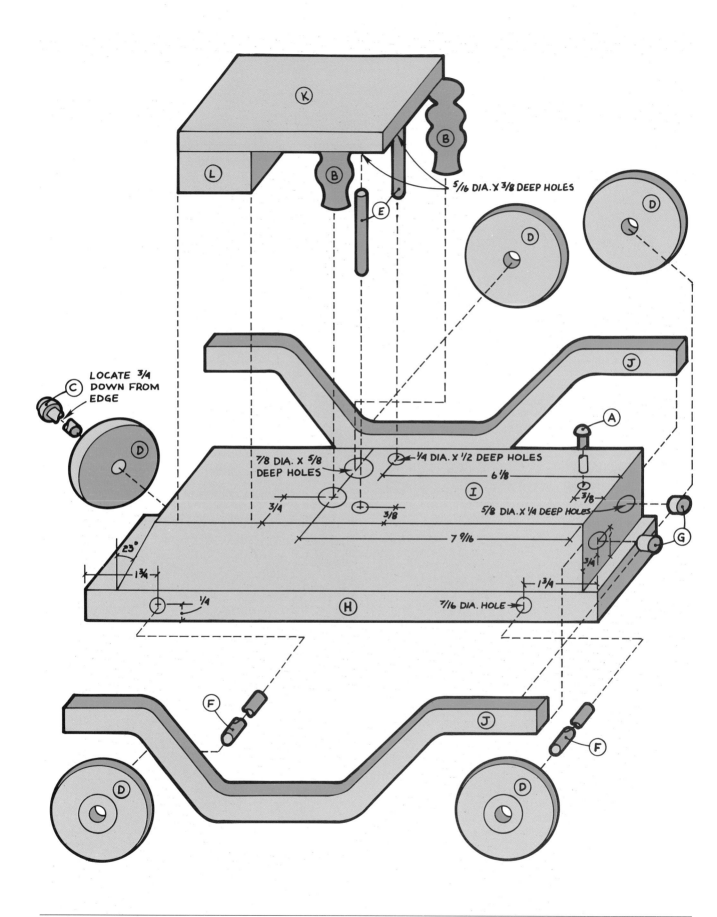

5/16 DIA. X 3/8 DEEP HOLES

LOCATE 3/4 DOWN FROM EDGE

7/8 DIA. X 5/8 DEEP HOLES

1/4 DIA. X 1/2 DEEP HOLES

6 1/8

3/8

3/4

3/8

5/8 DIA. X 1/4 DEEP HOLES

7 9/16

23°

1 3/4

3/4

1 3/4

1/4

7/16 DIA. HOLE

Figure 2. Dress the edges of the fenders (J) with an abrasive sander. Work in long, even-pressured strokes. Use a contour platen.

Construction

Transfer the grid patterns for the fenders (J) onto graph paper. Using carbon paper, trace the pieces onto nonsplintering wood of the proper thickness. Then cut out the fenders with a band saw or saber saw.

Now measure and cut the body (I), frame (H), roof (K) and roof support (L) to size on a band saw. Sand these workpieces thoroughly.

BILL OF MATERIALS — Rolls Royce

Finished Dimensions in Inches

A*	Radiator Cap	#2 ⅜ dia. x 1¼ cherry	1
B*	People	#7 ¾ dia. x 2¼ hardwood	2
C*	Spare Tire Dowel	#10 ½ dia. x 1¾ cherry	1
D*	Wheel	#16 2½ dia. x ¾ cherry	5
E	Roof Support	¼ dia. x 1⅝ dowel cherry	2
F	Axle	⅜ dia. x 4⅜ dowel hardwood	2
G	Headlight	⅝ dia. x ⅜ dowel cherry	2
H	Frame	¾ x 2¾ x 12⅞ cherry	1
I	Body	1¾ x 2¾ x 12⅛ cherry	1
J	Fender	¾ x 2¾ x 12⅛ cherry	2
K	Roof	½ x 2¾ x 5½ cherry	1
L	Roof Support	¾ x 1¾ x 2¾ cherry	1

* These parts are available from Cherry Tree Toys, Inc., Dept. PSW, 408 S. Jefferson St., Belmont, OH 43718 (614) 484-4363.

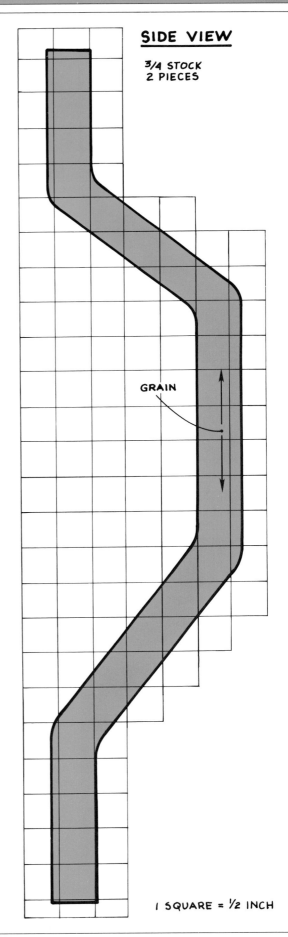

SIDE VIEW

¾ STOCK
2 PIECES

GRAIN

1 SQUARE = ½ INCH

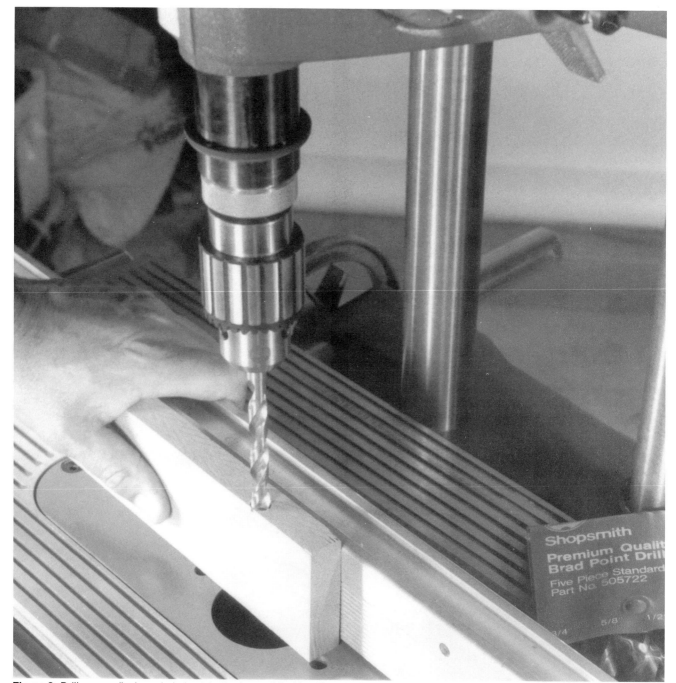

Figure 3. Drill perpendicular axle holes into the frame (H) with a Forstner bit installed into a drill press. Drill about ⅔ of the way through from one side, flip the workpiece over and drill into this side. This insures proper hole alignment.

Carefully position and drill the required holes into the frame, body and roof as shown in the illustration.

Glue the roof (K) to the roof support (L) with white glue. Then glue the body (I) in the middle of the frame (H).

Sand all the wood surfaces and round over exposed edges for safety.

Glue the fenders (J) so they protrude ¼ in. above the body. Clamp these in place until the glue dries.

Likewise, attach the headlights (G), radiator cap (A), and spare tire dowel (C) along with the spare tire (D).

Now affix the cab assembly along with the roof supports (E) and the people (B) to the body. Check to make sure everything is properly aligned.

Glue the wheels and check for alignment. The axles are glued to the wheels and are allowed to turn freely in the frame.

Finishing

Sand all the project parts, then finish with a nontoxic clear finish. ☐

This project is courtesy of Georgia-Pacific Corporation.

Early American Shelves

This is an easy, attractive solution to creating extra display space for the kitchen or dining room.

This project features shelves that are 9¼ in. deep by 48 in. long, supported by two decorative brackets. The Early American detailing makes them particularly well suited to a kitchen or dining room, but they would look great in just about any room. Each display unit is held securely to the wall with a wall mount (B) affixed to the wall with No. 8 by 2 in. flathead wood screws. You can opt to modify the design by lengthening or shortening the shelves. You can build the shelves to any length you want. If you build longer shelves, we recommend that you make additional brackets (C), spacing them every 32 inches.

Tips

Make sure you locate the position of the wall studs on which the Early American shelves will be mounted. Also run a straightedge along the area where the wall mount (B) will be positioned to insure that the wall is flat for mounting.

You should select only straight material for this project. If the shelves are slightly warped, the brackets will not set flush against the wall unless heavy objects are placed on the shelves.

If you opt to expose the fastener heads as we did, then you may wish to use drywall screws or brass screws to accent the project. If you don't want the fastener heads to show, counterbore the fastener holes, mount the shelves and fill the hole recesses with wood caps or plugs that have been stained to match the project.

Construction

Begin by cutting the shelves to length from 1 x 10 pine.

Figure 1. Draw the corner radii for the bracket (C) with a large can if you have difficulty transferring grid designs or do not have French curves.

Crosscut them to length on your radial arm saw. Then cut the blanks for the brackets (C), and rip the material for the wall mounts (B) to width and length.

Use a circle template, compass or base of a can to draw the radii for the shelves and wall mounts. Then carefully lay out the bracket design on graph paper and correlate the grid pattern used in our illustration with your graph paper. You must accurately measure the width and height of the wall mount on this bracket.

Cut out the bracket shape with a saber saw or band saw, being careful to stay on the edge of the pencil line. Then transfer this design to the other bracket workpieces and cut out each one in a similar manner.

Now, cut the radii for the shelves and wall mounts with your saber saw or band saw. Sand all of the workpieces carefully. Once the workpieces meet your satisfaction, begin assembly.

Assemble the wall mount to the shelf with carpenter's glue and No. 8 by 2 in. flathead wood screws, countersunk.

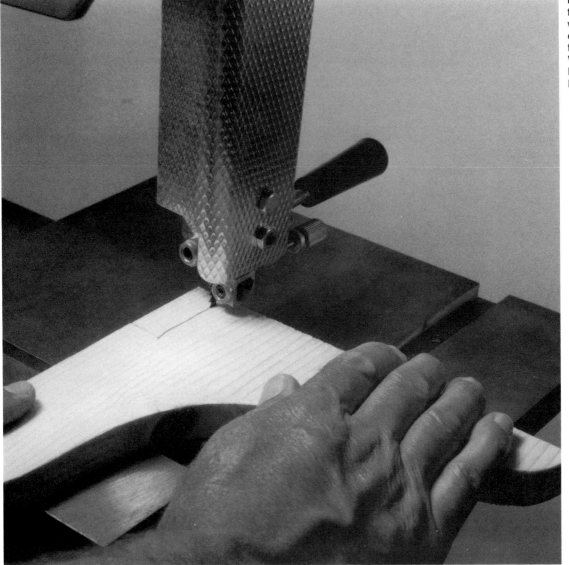

Figure 2. Cut out the bracket (C) with a saber saw equipped with a fine-tooth blade. Work slowly and hug the cutting line.

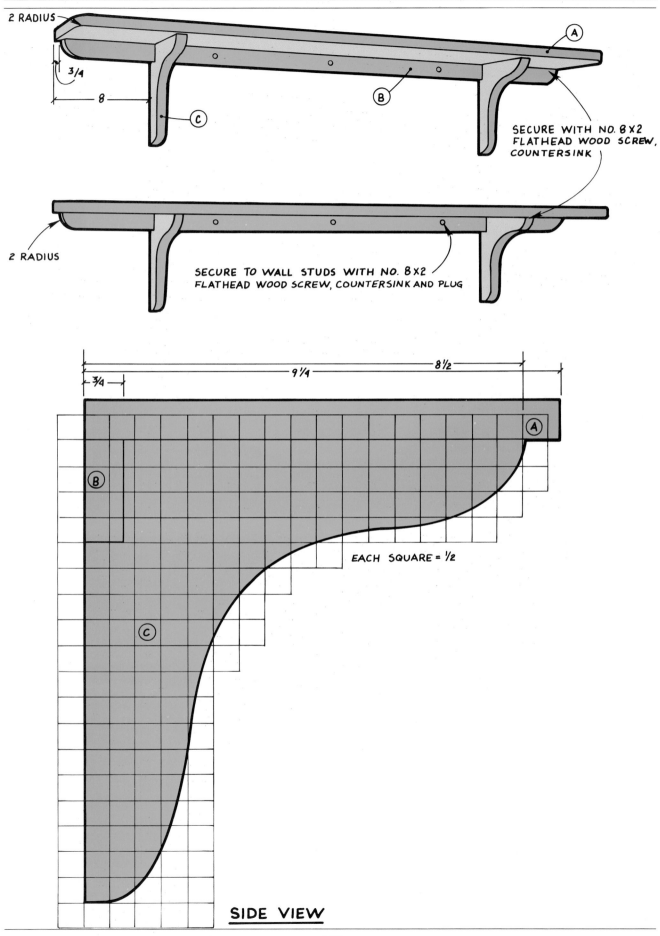

2 RADIUS

3/4

8

A

B

C

SECURE WITH NO. 8 X 2
FLATHEAD WOOD SCREW,
COUNTERSINK

2 RADIUS

SECURE TO WALL STUDS WITH NO. 8 X 2
FLATHEAD WOOD SCREW, COUNTERSINK AND PLUG

9 1/4

8 1/2

3/4

A

B

EACH SQUARE = 1/2

C

SIDE VIEW

Figure 3. Finish sand the edge of the bracket (C) with a half-round file or dowel wrapped with sandpaper (as shown).

Drive the wood screws in the top of the shelf. Make sure you pre-drill these holes. Be careful not to over-glue. If you do, wipe the excess with a warm, damp cloth. Then secure the brackets to the shelf assembly in a similar manner. Use a combination square or a carpenter's square to insure that the brackets are perpendicular to the surface of the shelves.

Now drill mounting holes into the wall brackets to correlate with your wall stud locations.

Finishing

Apply a light Early American stain to the shelf surface. After this has dried, apply a satin polyurethane finish to all of the project's surfaces. Let dry, then sand lightly before applying a final coat.

Mount the shelves to the wall studs with No. 8 by 2 in. flathead wood screws. Use a level to insure the units are parallel to the floor, or a tape measure to measure up from the floor. □

Figure 4. Here the holes for the screws are being pre-drilled and countersunk at the same time. One such handy tool is made by Stanley and called the Screw-Mate. It comes in a variety of sizes, suited to the fastener size used.

BILL OF MATERIALS — Early American Shelves

Finished Dimensions in Inches

A	Shelf	¾ x 9¼ x 48 pine	2
B	Wall Mount	¾ x 2 x 46½ pine	2
C	Bracket	¾ x 8½ x 9 pine	4

This project is courtesy of the American Plywood Association.

Adjustable Desk Unit

Build a desk unit that grows with your child, from toddler to teenager.

This desk, bookshelf and chair grows with your child. Initially, the desk and chair are put together to fit his or her small size. Later, both the seat and work surface can be moved 7½ in. higher to accommodate the growing adolescent. The shelves are large enough to accept everything from toy trucks to tape players.

Tips

Use two sheets of APA ¾ in. plywood that has been sanded on both sides. Follow the illustrations to lay out all of the required workpieces on two plywood sheets. If you follow these patterns, you need to consider the space taken up by your saw kerfs.

Assembly requires the use of flathead wood screws, which allow the project to be disassembled and reorganized to accommodate the adolescent or young child. Pre-drill all screw holes and counterbore.

Construction

Carefully lay out all of the project parts on two sheets of plywood as indicated in the illustrations. You will need to use a saber saw equipped with a plywood cutting blade as well as a handheld power circular saw also equipped with a plywood cutting blade. Carefully plan your cuts until all of the project parts have been cut to size.

Joint the long plywood edges with a handheld jointer. If you do not have a power jointer, then use a bench plane.

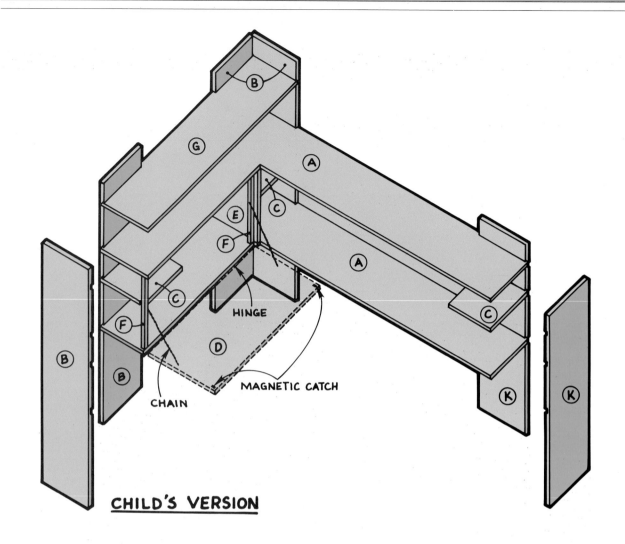

CHILD'S VERSION

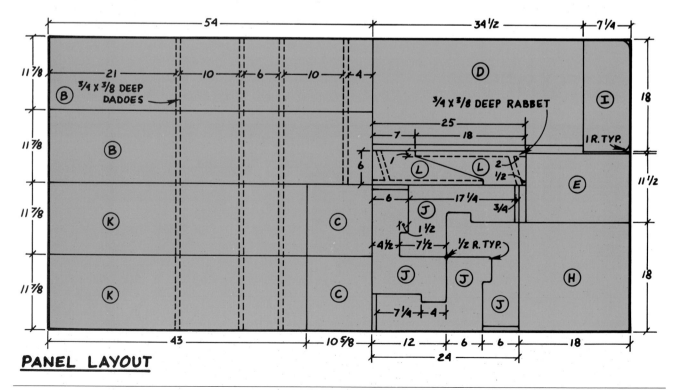

PANEL LAYOUT

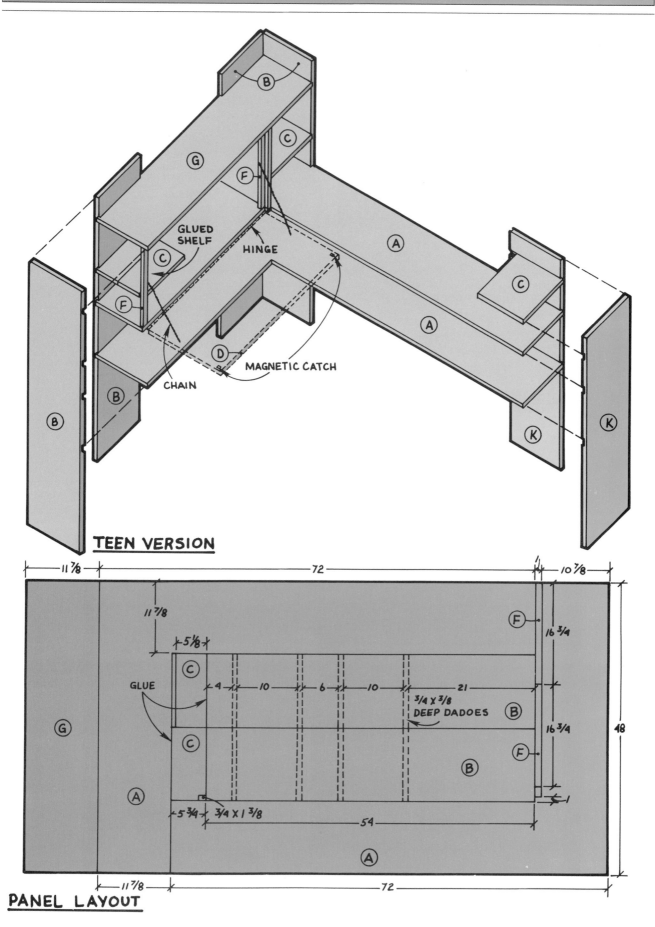

TEEN VERSION

GLUED SHELF

HINGE

MAGNETIC CATCH

CHAIN

PANEL LAYOUT

11 7/8

72

10 7/8

11 7/8

5 1/8

16 3/4

GLUE

4   10   6   10   21

3/4 X 3/8 DEEP DADOES

16 3/4

48

5 3/4   3/4 X 1 3/8

54

72

Figure 1. Use a portable hand plane to joint the plywood edges. Use the tool's edge-guide to keep the jointer perpendicular to the wood's edge.

Figure 2. Use a router equipped with a straight bit to cut dadoes into the sides (B, K). Make progressively deeper passes with the router until it reaches final cutting depth.

CHILD'S VERSION

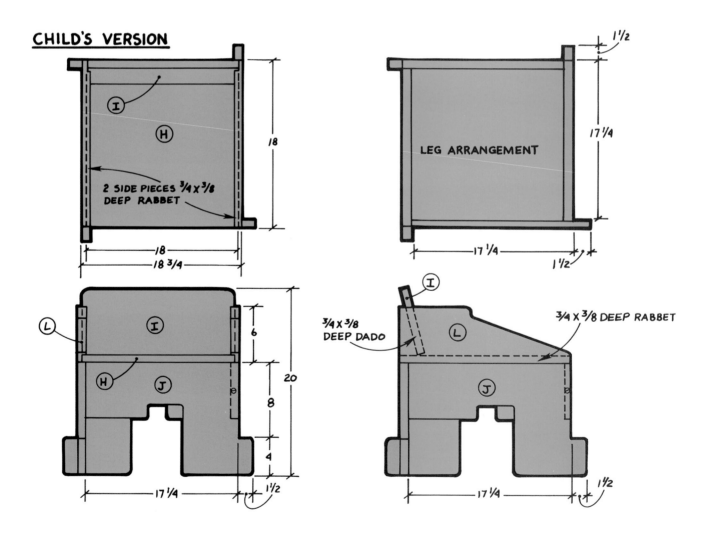

2 SIDE PIECES ¾ x ⅜ DEEP RABBET

18

18

18 ¾

LEG ARRANGEMENT

1½

17¼

17¼

1½

6

20

8

4

17¼

1½

¾ x ⅜ DEEP DADO

¾ x ⅜ DEEP RABBET

17¼

1½

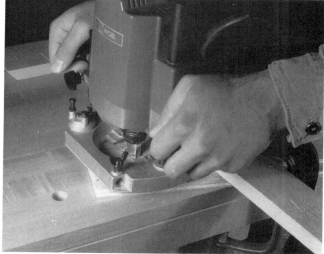

Figure 3. Rabbet the seat side (L) with a rabbeting bit installed in your router. Then cut the dado with a straight bit. Guide your router with a clamped straightedge, as shown.

Determine whether you are going to build the children's version or the teen version of the desk and chair.

Carefully dado the side workpieces (B, K) as indicated in the illustration. Now carefully dado and rabbet the seat sides (L).

Shelf and Desk Assembly

Assemble the sides (B, K) along with the L-shaped shelves (A) and top shelf (G). Secure the assembly with No. 8 by 1½ in. flathead wood screws. Countersink all screw heads, but do not glue this assembly.

At this point, the unit should be standing on a flat surface. Now install the desk side (E) along with two corner shelves (C). Again, secure these with No. 8 by 1½ in. flathead wood screws.

Secure two cleats (F) with No. 8 by 1¼ in. flathead wood screws. Make sure that you countersink all screw heads.

Check to make sure that the lid (D) fits properly. Then install a continuous hinge and add a chain at each end of the lid for hanging. Mount the chains with appropriate round head

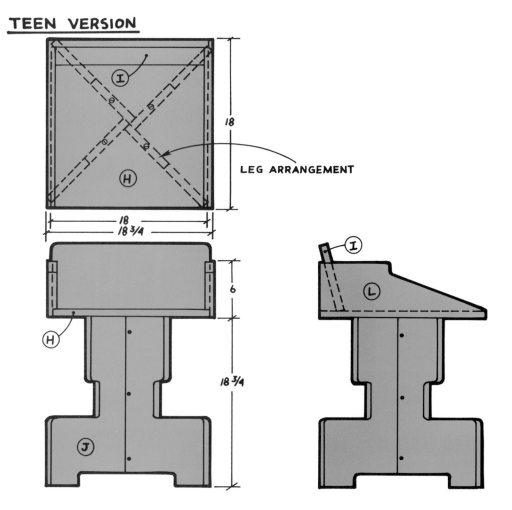

TEEN VERSION

LEG ARRANGEMENT

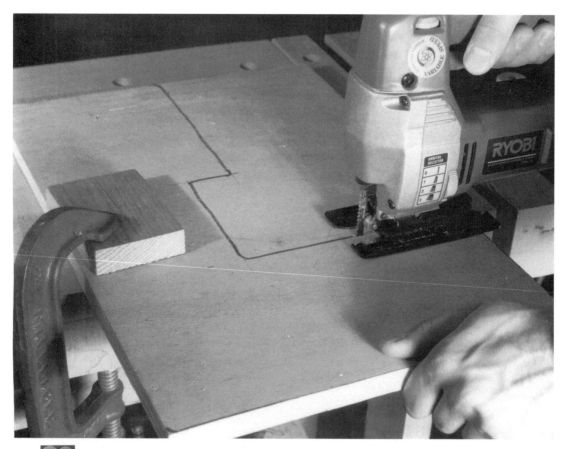

Figure 4. Lay out the chair's leg (J) patterns and cut out with a saber saw. Use a sharp plywood cutting blade.

	BILL OF MATERIALS — Adjustable Desk Unit		
	Finished Dimensions in Inches		
A	Shelf	¾ x 48 x 72 plywood	2
B	Side	¾ x 11⅞ x 54 plywood	4
C	Corner Shelf	¾ x 10⅝ x 11⅞ plywood	3
D	Lid	¾ x 17¼ x 34½ plywood	1
E	Desk Side	¾ x 11½ x 16¾ plywood	1
F	Cleat	¾ x 1 x 16¾ plywood	2
G	Top Shelf	¾ x 11⅞ x 48 plywood	1
H	Seat	¾ x 18 x 18 plywood	1
I	Seat Back	¾ x 7¼ x 18 plywood	1
J	Leg	¾ x 12 x 17¼ plywood	4
K	Side	¾ x 11⅞ x 43 plywood	2
L	Seat Side	¾ x 6 x 18 plywood	2

screws. Then install two magnetic catches underneath the top shelf to secure the lid.

Seat Assembly

Begin by installing the legs (J) and the seat with No. 8 by 1½ in. flathead wood screws. Notice that the legs are secured to one another in one of two arrangements, depending on whether you are building the children's version or the teen version of the chair. Then install the back (I) along with the two sides (L) with No. 8 by 1½ in. flathead wood screws. Do not glue this assembly.

Finishing

Remove the lid along with its hardware and sand all of the project parts, including the seat, thoroughly. Slightly round all edges and corners to avoid injury, and fill in all blemishes with a nontoxic wood filler. Once the project parts are finish sanded, remove all of the dust from the workpieces with a damp cloth.

Apply a sanding sealer to the project and then give it its final coat or coats. You may opt to use two or more colors as we did. Save these plans so you can convert the child's version to the teen version. ☐

This project is courtesy of Dennis Watson and The Family Handyman magazine.

Butler's Table

Build this beautiful butler's table made from solid cherry with brass table hinges.

Afternoon tea? You may not have the butler, but you can still enjoy the beauty and elegance of a butler's table. Like the original butler's table, the tray is removable and easily carried, along with its contents of after-dinner drinks or half-time snacks. Two small dowels help align the tray and prevent it from being accidentally knocked off the base.

Tips

Carefully select the cherry lumber you will use for this project. It is important that the top, in particular, be comprised of unwarped wood. Use quarter-sawn cherry for the top to minimize movement due to humidity changes. Wood will shrink or swell across the grain with changes in room humidity but is stable along the grain. Quarter-sawn stock, because of the orientation of the growth rings, is more stable than plain-sawn stock.

If you are unable to obtain quarter-sawn cherry, use cherry-veneered plywood for the top (G) and solid cherry for the leaves. However, make sure that the grain and color of the plywood closely match the leaves.

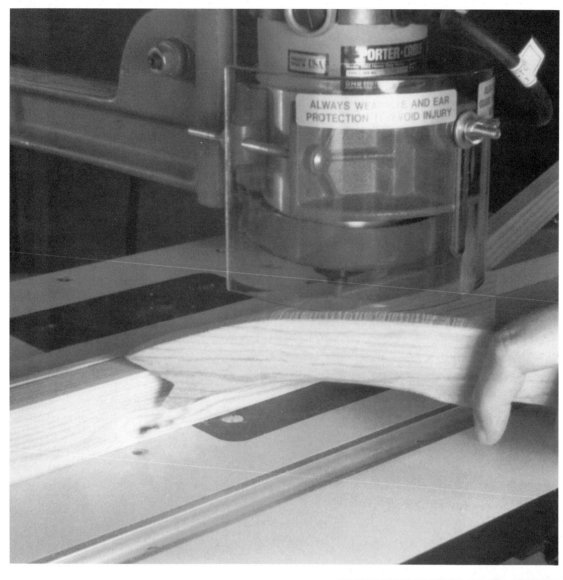

Figure 1. When routing the veining for the legs, push each piece from left to right. Rout the outside vein first, flip the material around, and then rout the other outside vein.

Construction

Rip the legs (A) slightly oversize on a table saw, and then use either a jointer or a hand plane to finish the legs to their final widths of 1⅝ in. square.

Cut the upper rails (B, C) from ¾ in. cherry. Rip these 2⁹⁄₁₆ in. wide, then joint or hand plane to 2½ in. wide. Crosscut rail (B) to 26¾ in. long and rail (C) to 16¾ in. long. In a similar manner, cut the lower rails (D) and stretcher (E) to size.

Join the upper rails (C) and lower rails (D) to the legs with dowels, but don't glue at this time. Use a doweling jig or dowel centers and drill press to assure the holes are drilled straight and accurately. Use a Forstner bit or spur point bit.

Next, add the upper rails (B) and stretcher (E) to the assembled sides and fasten with dowels. Make sure that all the joints pull up tight and the base is square.

Now take the table base apart. With your router, run a ¼ in. veining on the legs and a ⅛ in. veining groove along the lower edge of the upper rails (B, C). Use a router table to rout the veins.

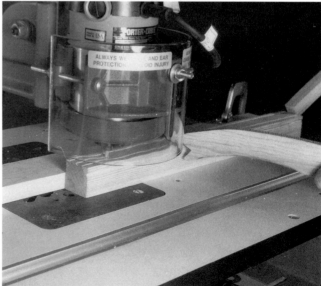

Figure 2. Adjust the fence to rout the inner leg vein. Rout the vein and finish the remaining surfaces.

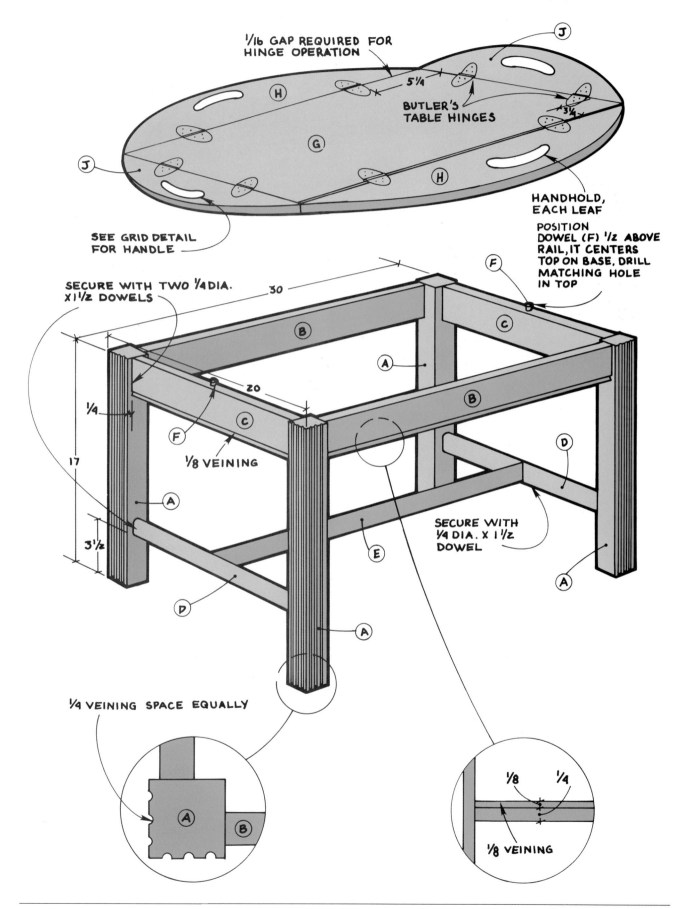

1/16 GAP REQUIRED FOR HINGE OPERATION

J

5 1/4

BUTLER'S TABLE HINGES

H

3 1/4

G

J

H

HANDHOLD, EACH LEAF

SEE GRID DETAIL FOR HANDLE

POSITION DOWEL (F) 1/2 ABOVE RAIL, IT CENTERS TOP ON BASE, DRILL MATCHING HOLE IN TOP

SECURE WITH TWO 1/4 DIA. X 1 1/2 DOWELS

30

F

B

C

A

1/4

20

B

17

C

F

1/8 VEINING

A

D

A

E

3 1/2

SECURE WITH 1/4 DIA. X 1 1/2 DOWEL

D

A

A

1/4 VEINING SPACE EQUALLY

A

B

1/8   1/4

1/8 VEINING

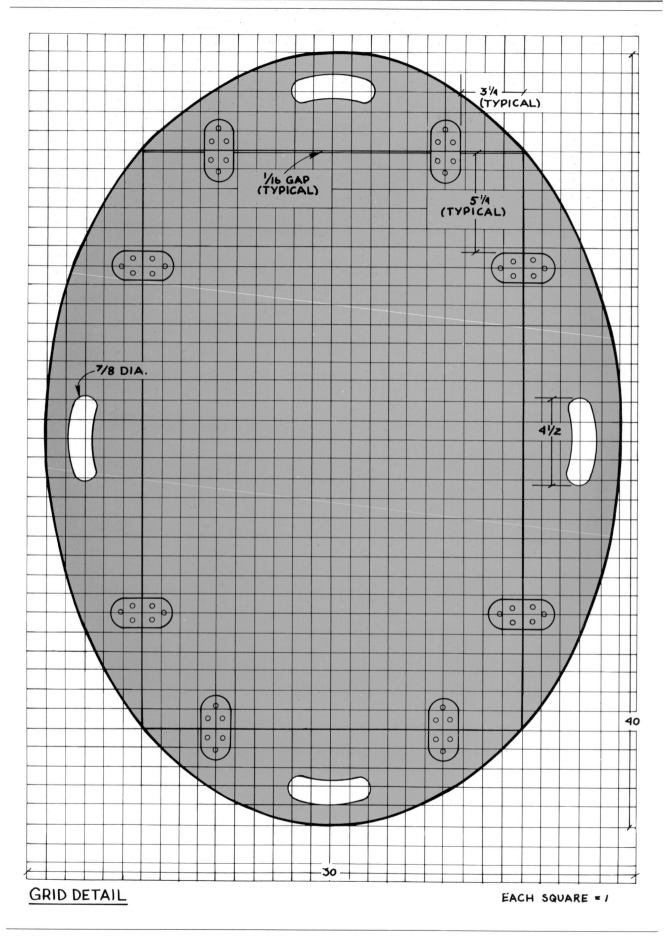

3¼
(TYPICAL)

¹⁄₁₆ GAP
(TYPICAL)

5¼
(TYPICAL)

7/8 DIA.

4½

GRID DETAIL

EACH SQUARE = 1

40

30

Figure 3. Cut the leaves carefully on your band saw. Use a ½ in. band saw blade to prevent wandering.

Next, round over the top of the lower rails (D) and stretcher (E). Use a ¼ in. rounding over bit with pilot guide. If you have never routed right up to an edge, practice on scrap material before you attempt the real thing. As an alternative, rout the rails (D) and stretcher (E) from longer materials, then cut them to size.

Give the parts a thorough sanding with 150 grit sandpaper followed by 220 grit, then glue and clamp the base together. Two cloth band clamps are ideal for gluing this assembly. Check to be sure that the base is square.

Make the top (G) 1 in. wider and longer than the finished size. If you are using solid cherry, you'll probably have to edge-glue two or three boards to make the top. Select your wood carefully. Try to match the color and grain so the top looks like one solid piece.

Rip the boards a little wide, then run the boards through the jointer or hand plane to remove the saw marks and true the edges. Dry-fit the top together, using pipe or bar clamps to apply pressure. The joints should all pull up tightly with moderate pressure; don't force the boards. Then glue the top together.

After the top has dried, scrape the dried glue off with a paint scraper or old wood chisel. Plane the top flat, using a hand plane. Or, if you prefer, a large cabinet shop will run the glued-up top through their planer or sander for a small fee. Rip the top to width and crosscut to 30 in. long.

Match up the leaves (H, J) to the top for color and grain, then enlarge the squared drawing and transfer the design to the leaves. Cut to shape and round over the corners using a router with ¼ in. rounding over bit and pilot guide.

Next, install the table hinges. Use a router with bushing guide and hardboard template to cut a mortise slightly smaller than the hinge. Then make the final fitting with a gouge and chisel. Make the template large enough so you can clamp it to the top.

BILL OF MATERIALS — Butler's Table

Finished Dimensions in Inches

A	Leg	1⅝ x 1⅝ x 17 cherry	4
B	Upper Rail	¾ x 2½ x 26¾ cherry	2
C	Upper Rail	¾ x 2½ x 16¾ cherry	2
D	Lower Rail	⅝ x 1¼ x 16¾ cherry	2
E	Stretcher	⅝ x 1¼ x 27¾ cherry	1
F	Locating Pin	⅜ dia. x 1½ dowel hardwood	2
G	Top	¾ x 20 x 30 cherry	1
H	Leaf	¾ x 5 x 30 cherry	2
J	Leaf	¾ x 5 x 20 cherry	2

Clamp the leaf to the top with a pipe clamp and a 1/16 in. spacer between the top and leaf edges. Now, clamp the template to the top and leaf, then rout the mortise.

We used cast brass hinges that were not precisely identical; therefore, custom fit each one with a sharp wood chisel and gouge. Some wood will also have to be removed to allow for the spring and hinge barrel. Screw the hinges in place with steel screws that are the same size as the brass screws provided with the hinges. (Brass screws have a tendency to break off and the heads become marred when installing them in new wood.) Now, remove the steel screws and install the brass screws. Sand the piece carefully, top and bottom.

Locate the center of the upper rail (C) and drill a 3/8 in. diameter hole 1 in. deep for locating dowels (F). Use a dowel center to transfer the hole location to the top. Carefully drill a 1/2 in. deep hole into the top.

Glue the dowel into the rail and taper the top of the dowel with a wood file. Now remove the hinges.

Finishing

Most of the original butler's tables were stained dark. Cherry will darken with age, though, so you'll want to take this into consideration. Since this is a table that probably will be used for drinks and receive hard use, finish it with two coats of a semi-gloss polyurethane sealer, sanding lightly between coats. Be sure to finish both sides of the top and the leaves; otherwise one side will pick up or lose moisture faster than the other, causing the wood to bow. □

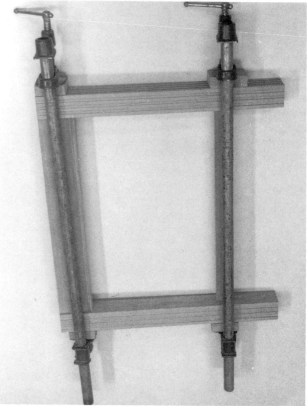

Figure 5. Use bar clamps to glue up two legs (A) to one upper rail (B).

This project is courtesy of Georgia-Pacific Corporation.

Sewing Table

This hideaway sewing table is ready when you are, yet can be rolled out of sight when not in use.

This unique sewing table features two drawers on each side that are perfect for storing seam rippers, pins, threads and scissors. We have added casters to the legs so that you can easily move your sewing table to any spot in the room. The sewing table is also specially designed to fit within a standard closet. However, its narrower width makes the table somewhat unstable. You will need to hold onto the sewing table while you are moving it. Definitely keep young children away while the sewing table is not in use.

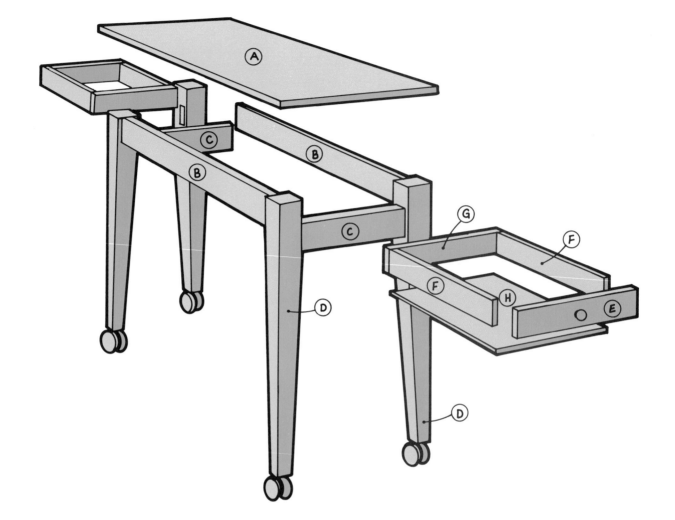

Figure 1. Edge-glue pine lumber to form the top (A). Use bar clamps, but do not overtighten. Keep the assembly as flat as possible. Remove dried glue with a paint scraper.

Figure 2. If you do not have a band saw to cut the tapers in the legs (D), use an extra long blade in your saber saw. These blades can be purchased in most home centers, lumberyards and hardware stores.

SIDE VIEW

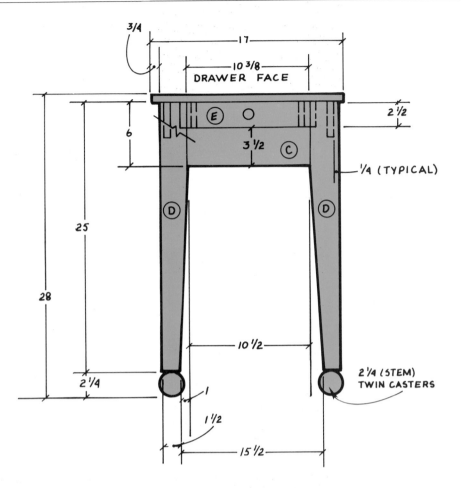

3/4

17

10 3/8
DRAWER FACE

2 1/2

E

6

3 1/2   C

1/4 (TYPICAL)

D   D

25

28

10 1/2

2 1/4 (STEM)
TWIN CASTERS

2 1/4

1

1 1/2

15 1/2

FRONT VIEW

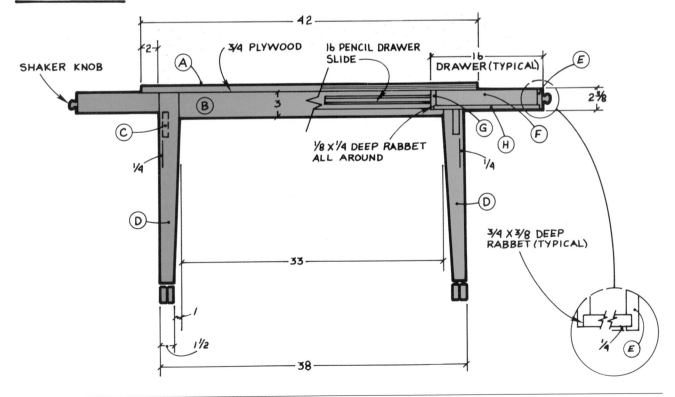

42

2

3/4 PLYWOOD

16 PENCIL DRAWER
SLIDE

16
DRAWER (TYPICAL)

E

SHAKER KNOB

A

B

1
3

2 3/8

C

G   F

1/4

H

1/8 X 1/4 DEEP RABBET
ALL AROUND

1/4

D

D

33

3/4 X 3/8 DEEP
RABBET (TYPICAL)

1

1 1/2

38

1/4   E

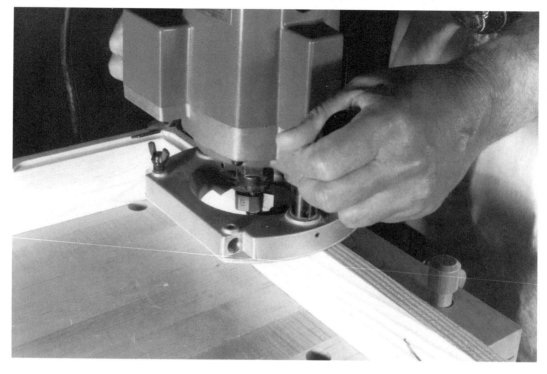

Figure 3. Rabbet the bottom of the drawers using a bit installed in your router. You also need a pilot to guide the bit along the wood's edge. Move the router clockwise.

Tips

Buy straight, dry pine lumber for this project. It is easy to build and requires simple hand tools to construct.

Construction

Edge-glue ¾ in. pine to form the table top (A). Joint the edges on a stationary jointer or a portable hand plane. Edge-glue the surfaces using carpenter's glue and bar clamps. Snug up the joints but do not overtighten. After the glue has dried, remove the excess with a paint scraper.

Likewise, edge-glue the workpieces forming the legs (D). Now cut the remaining parts to their proper width and length and dress all edges. Then sand all of the project parts for assembly.

Lay out the leg tapers (D) and cut these out with a band saw or hand saw. Then joint the tapers on your stationary jointer.

The rails (B, C) and legs are doweled together. Drill two

dowel holes for each joint to accommodate the ⅜ in. diameter by 1½ in. dowels.

Dry-assemble the rails to the legs. Once everything fits perfectly, glue the assembly. Use a band clamp or bar clamps to snug up all the joints, and make sure the unit is absolutely square.

Now secure the top to the rails and legs with carpenter's glue and 4d finishing nails. Sink all nail heads.

The next phase includes drawer construction and assembly. Cut a rabbet into the drawer back (G) and a dado into the drawer face (E) with your saw. Then attach the drawer sides (F) to the drawer face and drawer back with carpenter's glue and 4d finishing nails. Do not drive finishing nails near the area where the drawer bottom (H) will be inserted. Square both drawer assemblies and allow to dry.

Now cut a rabbet into the bottom of each center drawer with a rabbeting bit installed in a router. You will need a pilot guide in order to accomplish this. Then square the edges of the rabbeted bottom and insert a ⅛ in. Masonite bottom (H) with carpenter's glue and ¾ in. brads.

Drill holes into the leg bottoms to accommodate 2¼ in. (stem) twin casters and into the drawer faces for an appropriate knob. Then install the drawers into the sewing table with 16 in. pencil drawer slides.

When everything fits perfectly, remove the hardware and finish sand the entire project.

Finishing

Apply an appropriate stain to the project or a sanding sealer. Finish sand this coat after it dries and then apply either a polyurethane or latex paint as a final coat.

Reinstall the drawer hardware, and insert the stem casters in place to complete the project. □

BILL OF MATERIALS — Sewing Table

Finished Dimensions in Inches

A	Top	¾ x 17 x 42 pine	1
B	Rail	¾ x 3 x 33 pine	2
C	Rail	¾ x 3½ x 10½ pine	2
D	Leg	2½ x 2½ x 25 pine	4
E	Drawer Face	¾ x 2⅜ x 10⅜ pine	2
F	Drawer Side	¾ x 2⅜ x 15¼ pine	4
G	Drawer Back	¾ x 2⅜ x 9⅞ pine	2
H	Drawer Bottom	⅛ x 8⅞ x 15 Masonite	2

This project is courtesy of the American Plywood Association.

Picnic Table

This attractive, sturdy table is a great project for the beginning woodworker.

I f the high price of a store-bought picnic table has kept you indoors, here's an affordable solution to your problem. This project is as good looking as it is easy to build. With built-in seats on both sides, there is plenty of room for four adults. The slotted workpieces and angle-bracing construction make the table sturdy yet easy to take apart and store.

Tips

Make the project using one sheet of APA ¾ in. exterior grade plywood. To lay out the workpieces on the plywood for

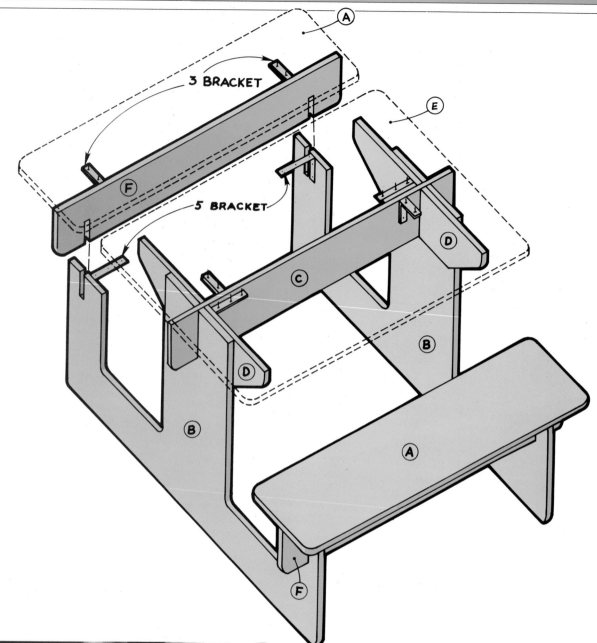

3 BRACKET

5 BRACKET

cutting, follow the technical illustration provided. The kerf reduces the overall dimensions of some of the workpieces, but only slightly.

Construction

Examine the cutting diagram carefully, taking note of the

Figure 1. Cut the supports (D) to their overall size and then lay out the cutting pattern. Next, cut out the pattern with a saber saw equipped with a plywood cutting blade.

BILL OF MATERIALS — Picnic Table

Finished Dimensions in Inches

A	Seat	¾ x 12 x 42 plywood	2
B	Side	¾ x 27 x 48 plywood	2
C	Cross Brace	¾ x 6 x 42 plywood	1
D	Support	¾ x 6 x 24 plywood	2
E	Top	¾ x 30 x 42 plywood	1
F	Seat Cross Brace	¾ x 6 x 42 plywood	2

PANEL LAYOUT

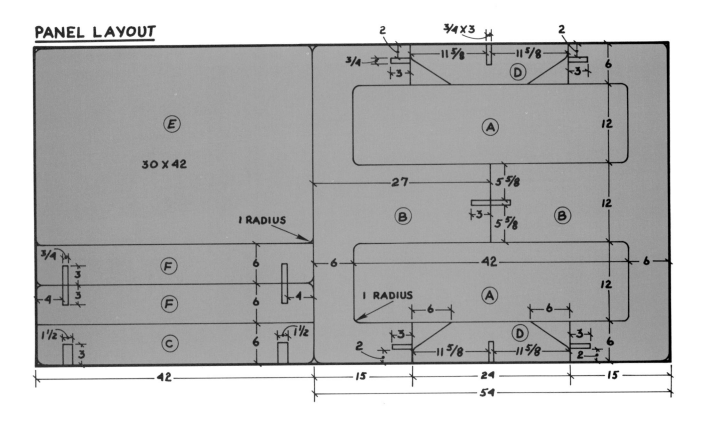

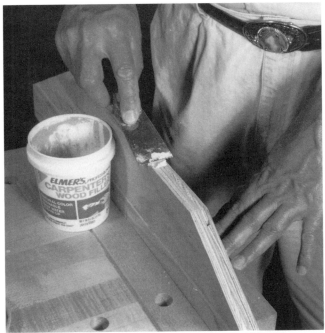

Figure 2. Fill in all blemishes with a nontoxic wood filler. Then sand flush with a belt sander.

many interlocking project parts. Begin by carefully laying out the project parts and then cutting them out to their proper width and length. Lay out the pattern on the blemished side. Cut out the seats (A), sides (B) and supports (D) with a saber saw equipped with a plywood cutting blade. Work slowly and stay on the cutting line.

Rip the cross brace (C) and seat cross braces (F) on your handheld circular saw. Rout the corners of the respective parts and cut the required slots with a saber saw or band saw.

Dry-assemble the picnic table by connecting the cross brace (C) and seat cross braces (F) to the picnic table sides. Check for fit and make sure that the top areas of interconnected parts are flush. Then position the supports (D) to insure that the fit is snug and flush with the top of the sides.

Now disassemble the picnic table and finish sand all parts. Fill in all blemishes with an exterior grade nontoxic wood filler. Use a belt sander to sand the wider surfaces and make sure you dull all edges with a sanding block.

Finishing

Remove all dust from the workpieces and apply a sanding sealer. Once dry, lightly sand this coat and paint the project its final color.

Secure the supports (D) to the sides with No. 8 by 1¼ in. brass flathead wood screws (countersunk). Make sure that the matching sides are symmetrical. Now insert the cross braces (C, F) and position the table top (E) and seats (A). Secure them with 3 in. and 5 in. angle brackets as shown in the illustration.

To store the picnic table, remove the top and seats from the angle brackets and slip out the cross braces. □

FRONT VIEW

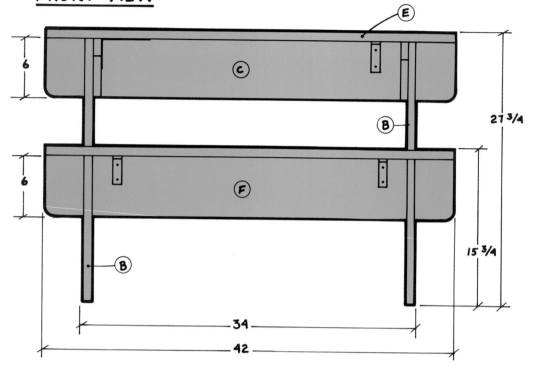

SIDE VIEW

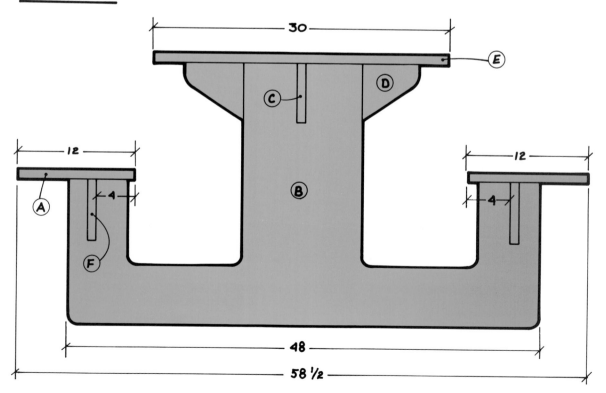

This project is courtesy of Cherry Tree Toys, Inc.

Door Harp

Give your guests a warm welcome with this decorative door harp.

Welcome guests with this charming door harp. When the door opens or closes, four wooden balls strike the musical wire of the door harp at random to create an unusual, pleasant melody. This door harp is quick and easy to construct, and fun to paint. Only simple hand tools are required to build the project. The plan contains full-size traceable patterns for the door harp, along with color painting patterns.

Tips

This door harp is constructed from ¾ in. pine and ⅛ in. plywood. Some of the parts, like the tuning pins (E), can be made or purchased. Cherry Tree Toys, Inc. offers full-size patterns, project parts, complete workpieces and even a finished door harp. For information and a catalog, write to the address listed at the end of the Bill of Materials.

Construction

Trace out the sound box (A) and the front sounding board (B) on wood of the proper thickness using graphite transfer paper. All of the pieces should be traced out in the same position on identically shaped rectangular pieces of wood so they can be properly positioned on top of one another when they are glued together. Do not trace out the painting pattern at this time.

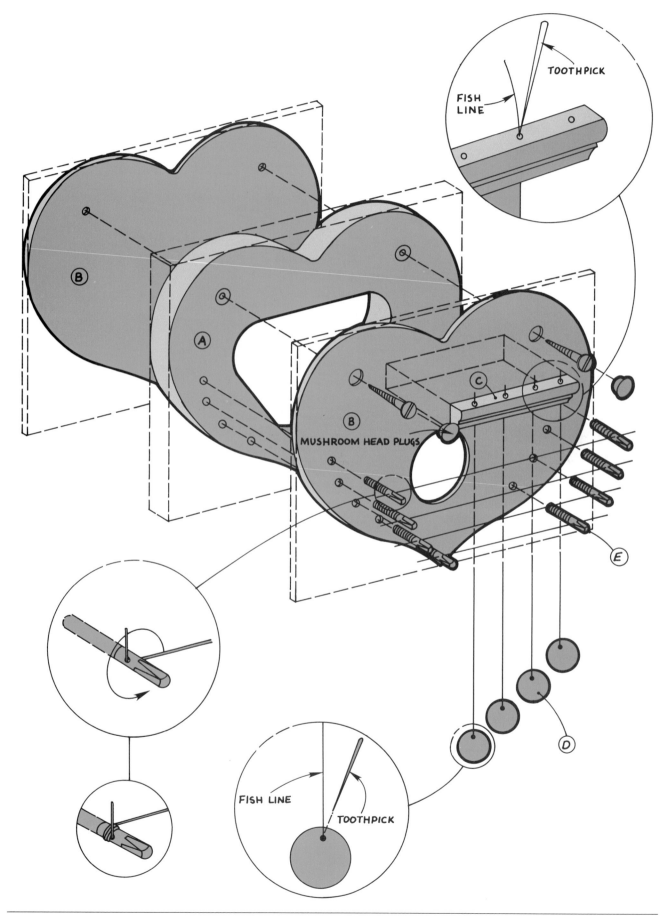

TOOTHPICK

FISH LINE

B

A

B

MUSHROOM HEAD PLUGS

C

E

FISH LINE

TOOTHPICK

D

FRONT VIEW
1/8 PLYWOOD

FULL-SIZE PATTERN

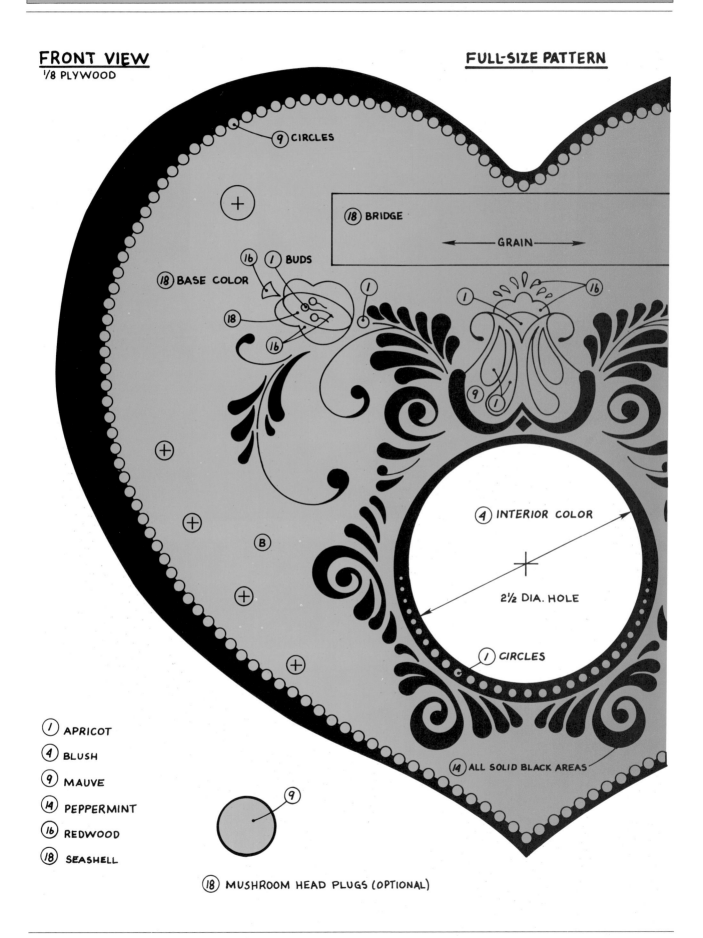

⑨ CIRCLES

⑱ BRIDGE

GRAIN

⑯ ① BUDS

⑱ BASE COLOR

⑱

⑯

①

①

⑯

⑨

①

④ INTERIOR COLOR

2½ DIA. HOLE

① CIRCLES

B

C

⑭ ALL SOLID BLACK AREAS

① APRICOT
④ BLUSH
⑨ MAUVE
⑭ PEPPERMINT
⑯ REDWOOD
⑱ SEASHELL

⑨

⑱ MUSHROOM HEAD PLUGS (OPTIONAL)

FRONT VIEW
¾ STOCK

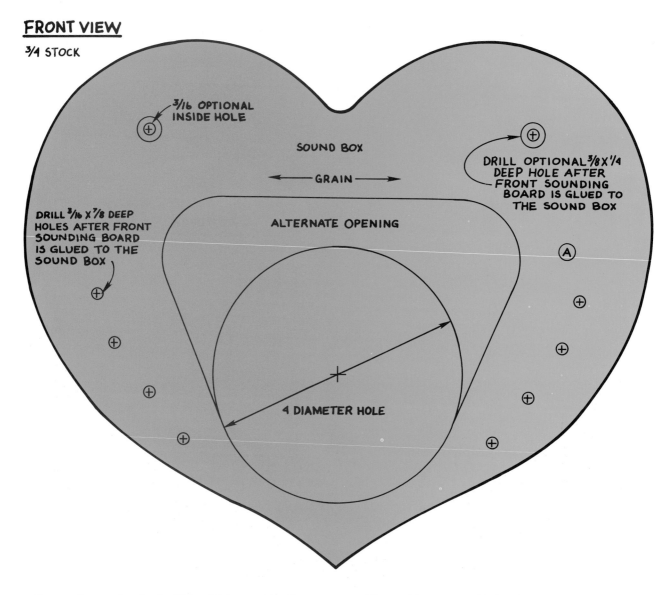

3/16 OPTIONAL INSIDE HOLE

SOUND BOX

◄— GRAIN —►

DRILL OPTIONAL ⅜ X ¼ DEEP HOLE AFTER FRONT SOUNDING BOARD IS GLUED TO THE SOUND BOX

DRILL 3/16 X ⅞ DEEP HOLES AFTER FRONT SOUNDING BOARD IS GLUED TO THE SOUND BOX

ALTERNATE OPENING

(A)

4 DIAMETER HOLE

Cut out the opening in the ¾ in. thick core (A). Cut out the 4 in. diameter hole. Use a circle cutter or drill a pilot hole and then use a coping saw, jigsaw or saber saw to remove the remainder of the wood from the hole.

In the front panel (B) drill a 2½ in. diameter hole through the ⅛ in. thick plywood. This hole can be drilled with a Forstner bit, circle cutter or by drilling a pilot hole and then removing the remainder of the wood with a coping saw or a jigsaw.

Glue the ⅛ in. thick front and back boards (B) to the ¾ in. thick core (A) with white glue. Make certain the three pieces of wood are properly positioned on top of one another before they are glued together.

Once the glue has dried, cut out the basic heart-shaped pattern with a coping saw, band saw, saber saw or jigsaw. Then sand all of the project parts.

Drill the eight 3/16 in. diameter by ⅞ in. deep holes for the tuning pins (E) with a drill press.

If you wish to mount the door harp to a door with screws, drill optional countersunk holes as shown in the plan. An alternative mounting technique is to rout a keyhole opening in the back. Glue the bridge (C) to the front of the door harp.

Painting the Project

Apply primer to the door harp and clapper balls. Next, paint the harp with its base color. Refer to the paint chart to see what colors the numbers represent. When the base paint has dried, use graphite transfer paper to transfer the painting pattern onto the door harp. Be sure to center the pattern on the 2½ in. diameter hole.

Finish painting the door harp and clapper balls. The sides of the door harp should be painted the same color as the adjacent color of the face. If you will be mounting the door harp with countersunk screws, prime and paint the mushroom head plugs while you are painting the door harp. The mushroom head plugs are used to cover the screw holes.

Figure 1. Make the hole in the core (A) by drilling a starter hole and cutting out the waste area with a scroll saw.

Hammer in the tuning pins until they reach the full drilled depth. Use a tuning pin wrench, a small adjustable wrench, or pliers to turn the four tuning pins on the right side two or three revolutions counterclockwise.

Tuning the Harp

Cut four 11 in. long pieces of music wire with wire cutters. Insert one end of the music wire through the hole in one of the tuning pins on the left side with about 1/4 in. extending out of the pin. Then bend this 1/4 in. of wire at a 90 degree angle. Using a clockwise motion, wrap the wire around the tuning pin two times, then insert the end of the wire through the hole in the corresponding tuning pin on the right. Leave enough slack in the wire so the tuning pin on the right side can be turned two revolutions clockwise before all the slack is out of the wire.

Bend the wire protruding out of the tuning pin at a 90 degree angle. Then slowly turn the tuning pin on the right side clockwise until all of the slack is out of the wire. **Be careful**: The wire will break if it is turned too tightly. Wear eye goggles while doing this as a precaution. Continue slowly, turning the

tuning pin and picking the wire as you would a guitar. If the music wire makes only a dull thud, it is not tight enough. Turn the pin until the music wire makes a pleasing tone. The pitch rises very quickly at this point.

Attach the three remaining music wires to the tuning pins in the same manner. After the door harp has been tuned, cut off any excess wire with a wire cutter.

BILL OF MATERIALS — Door Harp			

Finished Dimensions in Inches

A	Core	3/4 x 8 1/4 x 9 3/4 pine	1
B	Front/Back	1/8 x 8 1/4 x 9 3/4 plywood	2
C*	Bridge	5/8 x 3/4 x 4 pine	1
D*	Clapper Ball	#6020 3/4 dia. pine	4
E*	Turning Pin	#6010 3/16 dia. x 1 5/8 steel	8

* These parts are available from Cherry Tree Toys, Inc., Dept. PSW, 408 S. Jefferson St., Belmont, OH 43718 (614) 484-4363.

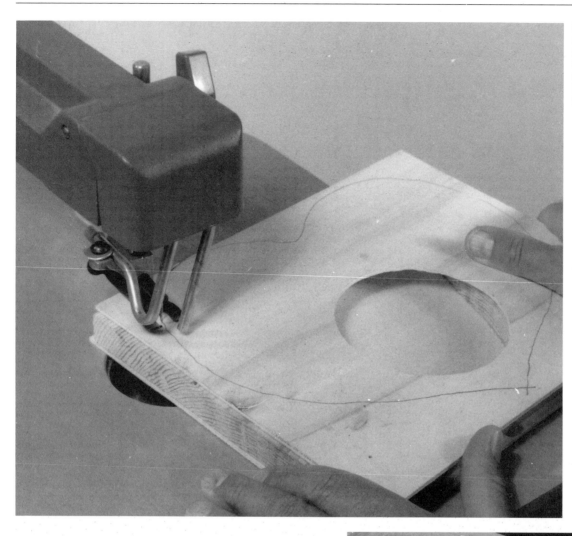

Figure 2. Glue the core (A) to the front/back (B) with white glue. When dry, cut out the heart shape on your scroll saw.

Finishing Touches

Cut four 7 in. long pieces of fishline for the clapper balls. Push one end of the fishline into the hole in one of the clapper balls. With the fishline in place, push the end of a pointed toothpick, which has been dipped in glue, into the hole, along with one end of the fishline. Then break off the toothpick. This should firmly attach the fishline to the clapper ball. Push the other end of the string through one of the holes in the bridge so it protrudes out the top of the bridge. Then adjust the length of the string so the clapper ball is centered on one of the music wires.

We suggest placing the balls on the music wire as they are shown in the photo on page 147. Push the other end of the same toothpick (which also has been dipped in glue) into the hole in the top of the bridge, with the fishline protruding, and break off the toothpick. Use the same procedure for securing the other three clapper balls to the bridge. Cut off the excess fishline.

If you are mounting the door harp to a door with screws, use the appropriate screws and glue the mushroom head plugs to the front of the door harp to cover up the countersunk screw holes. The door harp also can be attached with a single screw if you rout a keyhole opening in the back of the door harp. Your door harp is now ready for use. ☐

Figure 3. Thread the wire through the tuning pins (E) as shown and turn slowly. Make sure you wear eye goggles for protection in the event the wire breaks.

This project is courtesy of Georgia-Pacific Corporation.

Sewing Cabinet

Get organized with this cheerful fold-up sewing cabinet.

This sewing cabinet project puts an end to confusion. Only a few seconds are needed to fold down the table and set up your sewing machine. Thread, patterns and material can be stored on this project's handy shelves and its three spacious drawers. The table is supported by two legs that fit into round holes. The legs are tenoned where they fit into the table holes.

Tips

The lines of this project are clean and do not require more than straightedge cuts. Buy good quality plywood, sanded on both sides. Check the edges when cutting out the workpieces to insure that the edges are well glued and solid.

You might want to paint the sewing cabinet in contrasting colors for a bright, cheerful effect. Add decorative porcelain or wood knobs to the drawers and fold-down table to suit.

Use carpenter's glue and finishing nails for assembly. Remember to sink all nail heads.

Construction

Rip all the pieces to width first, then cut to length. Rip with the plywood's good side up.

Cut the two sides and one center panel to length on your radial arm saw, or use a circular saw guided by a straightedge.

Likewise, cut the top and bottom workpieces to length. Now cut dados and rabbets into the bottom, top, sides and center panel as indicated in the illustration. If you do not have a table saw, then use a router equipped with a ¾ in. straight

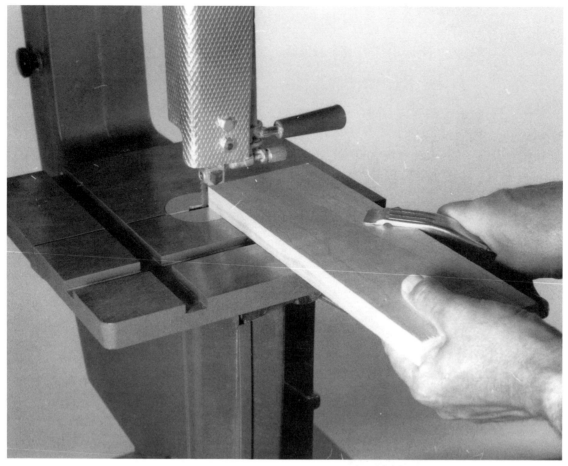

Figure 1. Cut each leg's (I) round tenon by first setting the depth of cut on your band saw as shown. Clamp the wood stop onto the band saw table.

bit. Use a straightedge to guide the router, and make progressively deeper passes to achieve final depth.

Assemble the sides and center panel to the top and bottom workpieces with carpenter's glue and 6d finishing nails. Assemble the unit on a flat surface and make sure that the assembly is square. Cut and install the various lengths of shelves, glue them in place and secure them with 6d finishing nails.

Cut the base rails and the pine corner blocks to their proper sizes. Assemble them to one another with glue and 4d

BILL OF MATERIALS — Sewing Cabinet

Finished Dimensions in Inches

A	Side	$3/4$ x 15 x $50\frac{1}{2}$ plywood	3
B	Shelf	$3/4$ x $12\frac{1}{4}$ x 15 plywood	4
C	Shelf	$3/4$ x 15 x $24\frac{1}{2}$ plywood	2
D	Top/Bottom	$3/4$ x 15 x $38\frac{1}{2}$ plywood	2
E	Base Rail	$3/4$ x $2\frac{1}{2}$ x $34\frac{1}{2}$ plywood	2
F	Base Rail	$3/4$ x $2\frac{1}{2}$ x $10\frac{1}{4}$ plywood	2
G	Corner Block	$3/4$ x $2\frac{1}{2}$ x $2\frac{1}{2}$ plywood	4
H	Table	$3/4$ x 24 x $24\frac{7}{8}$ plywood	2
I	Leg	$1\frac{1}{2}$ dia. x $28\frac{3}{4}$ pine	2
J	Drawer Face	$3/4$ x $7\frac{3}{8}$ x $11\frac{7}{8}$ plywood	2
K	Drawer Back	$3/4$ x 6 x $10\frac{3}{8}$ plywood	2
L	Drawer Side	$3/4$ x 6 x $13\frac{3}{4}$ plywood	4
M	Drawer Bottom	$1/4$ x $10\frac{1}{2}$ x $13\frac{1}{2}$ plywood	2

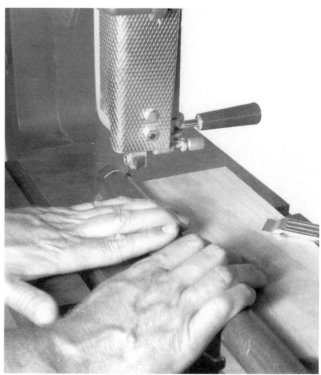

Figure 2. Now, move the leg into the blade and rotate the leg clockwise so the wood is moved into the cutting blade and not with the cutting blade. Hold the dowel firmly and keep fingers well away from the blade.

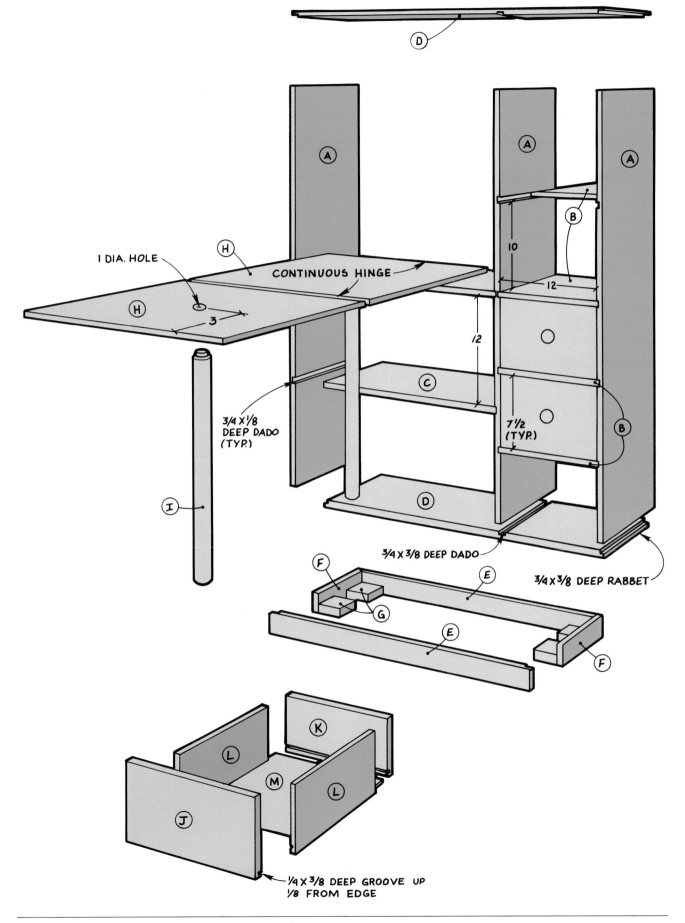

1 DIA. HOLE

CONTINUOUS HINGE

3

3/4 X 1/8
DEEP DADO
(TYP.)

10

12

12

7 1/2
(TYP.)

3/4 X 3/8 DEEP DADO

3/4 X 3/8 DEEP RABBET

1/4 X 3/8 DEEP GROOVE UP
1/8 FROM EDGE

Figure 3. Lightly clamp the leg in a bench vise, being careful not to damage the wood. Then use a sharp 1 in. wood chisel to make the round tenon. Finish sand with a sanding block or file. The tenon should fit snugly into the table's hole.

Figure 4. Dado the sides and the center panel (A) with a circular saw. Cut the material to the proper depth.

finishing nails. Pre-drill nail holes into the corner blocks to prevent the pine blocks from splitting.

Assemble the base to the upper assembly with glue and nails driven in through the top of the bottom shelf. Make sure that the base is symmetrically positioned.

Set the unit upright and measure the cavity for the fold-out panels. Make these panels identical. Then drill 1 in. diameter holes for the leg pegs. Use a back-up board on the bottom to prevent wood tear-out when drilling.

Custom measure the leg pegs and form a pin that fits up into the table and supports the table. Form this pin with a lathe or with wood chisels.

Install the continuous hinges onto the fold-out panels and position the leg pegs in place. Then examine the unit to make sure everything fits properly.

Next, custom cut and fit the drawers. Measure the cavity for the three drawers and cut the workpieces to size. Note that the drawer back fits between the two side pieces and that the drawer front is flush with the outside of the two side pieces.

Cut enough workpieces for three drawers, and groove the bottom of each drawer as shown in the illustration. Now custom cut the plywood bottoms and dry-assemble the drawers to insure that everything fits properly.

Assemble each drawer with carpenter's glue and 4d finishing nails. Square each of the drawers and allow them to dry on a flat surface.

Finishing

Sand the entire project using a pad sander and sanding block. Carefully round over all of the exposed edges and use wood filler where appropriate.

Apply a sanding sealer to the entire project. An airless sprayer or spray gun is ideal for this type of application. When

this coat is dry, lightly sand it and wipe off the dust with a damp cloth.

Spray on several coats of your desired paint, sanding between coats.

After the finish has dried, apply two double-roller catches with springs to the fold-up assembly. *Do not use magnetic catches.* Then complete the project by installing door knobs and a pull-down knob for the fold-out table. □

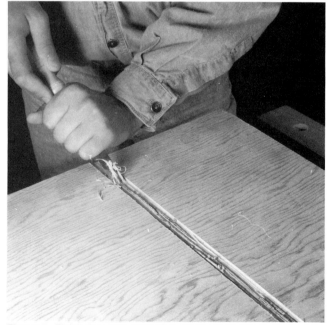

Figure 5. Finish the dado cut with a sharp wood chisel. Never put your hand in front of the area you are cutting.

This project is courtesy of George Campbell.

Colonial Cradle

Build a special gift that can be passed down from generation to generation.

I t's the dream of every parent or grandparent to build a cradle for the newest member of the family. This Colonial cradle is sure to become a family heirloom. Constructed from pine, it accepts standard cradle bedding, rocks gently on safe, wide rockers and is easy to transport. (As with all cradles, the baby should not be kept in it once he begins to crawl or lift himself up. At this stage the cradle becomes hazardous because the child may fall out of it.)

Tips

Make sure you buy the bed mattress and bumper pad before *you build this project.* Check for these items at children's furniture stores or mail order catalogs.

Construction

Begin by cutting out all the components to their overall widths and lengths. Cut the cradle ends (B1, B2, B3, C1, C2) first because the rest of the construction depends on their dimensions.

Starting with the bottom piece (B1), set your saw or miter gauge to $7\frac{1}{2}$ degrees, then cut the angles. Place the other two end pieces (B2, B3) together as they will be in the completed cradle, mark the ends to indicate mating edges, and cut the $7\frac{1}{2}$ degree angles.

Use a doweling guide to drill mating dowel holes in the edges, then join the boards with glue and dowels. Clamp until dry. Do not overtighten the clamps, and keep the workpieces flat to prevent warping.

Assemble the cradle's remaining end (C1, C2), sides (A1, A2, A3) and bottom (F) in the same way.

Once the assemblies have dried, rip beveled edges into the cradle's end, sides and bottom, as shown in the diagram. Remember that the cradle's sides are mirror images of each other. The beveled edges face in opposite directions. Next,

Figure 1. Drill holes into adjoining boards with a doweling jig. Use a brad point bit with a depth stop.

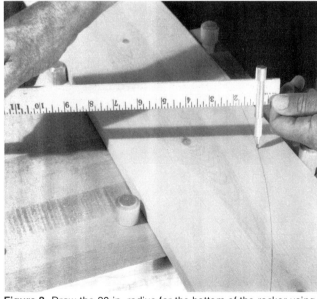

Figure 2. Draw the 30 in. radius for the bottom of the rocker using a bar compass attached to a yardstick. This compass attachment is available through numerous mail order sources.

Figure 3. Cut out the rocker's silhouette on a band saw using a ¼ in. fine-tooth blade. Work slowly and keep fingers well away from the unforgiving blade.

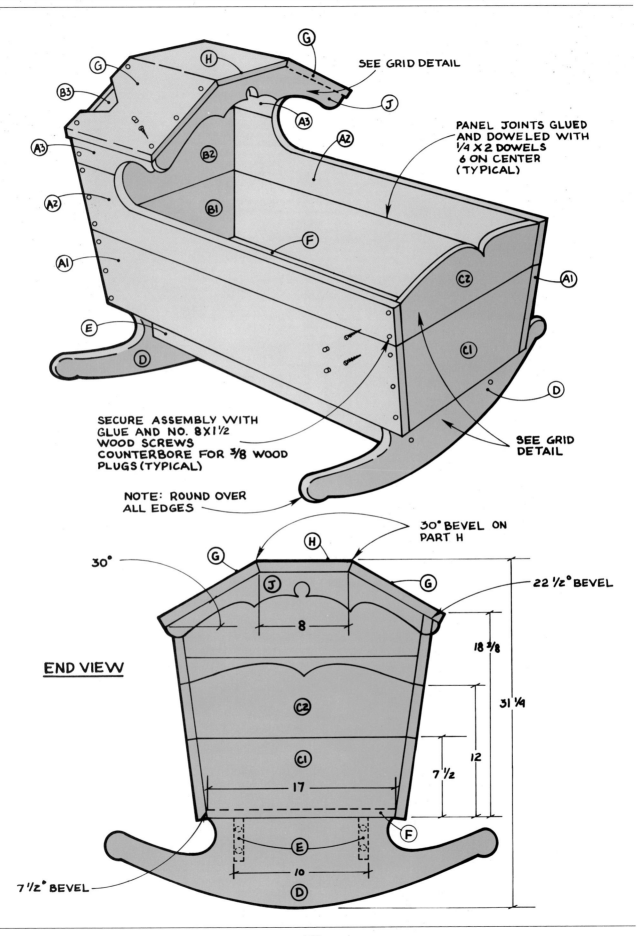

SEE GRID DETAIL

PANEL JOINTS GLUED
AND DOWELED WITH
1/4 X 2 DOWELS
6 ON CENTER
(TYPICAL)

SECURE ASSEMBLY WITH
GLUE AND NO. 8X1 1/2
WOOD SCREWS
COUNTERBORE FOR 3/8 WOOD
PLUGS (TYPICAL)

SEE GRID
DETAIL

NOTE: ROUND OVER
ALL EDGES

30° BEVEL ON
PART H

22 1/2° BEVEL

30°

END VIEW

8

18 3/8

31 1/4

12

7 1/2

17

10

7 1/2° BEVEL

GRID DETAIL

EACH SQUARE = 2

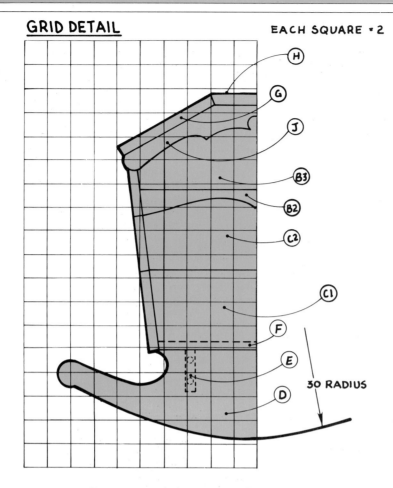

30 RADIUS

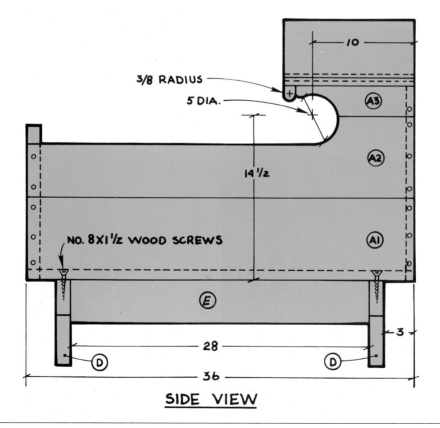

3/8 RADIUS

5 DIA.

10

14 1/2

NO. 8 X 1 1/2 WOOD SCREWS

28

36

3

SIDE VIEW

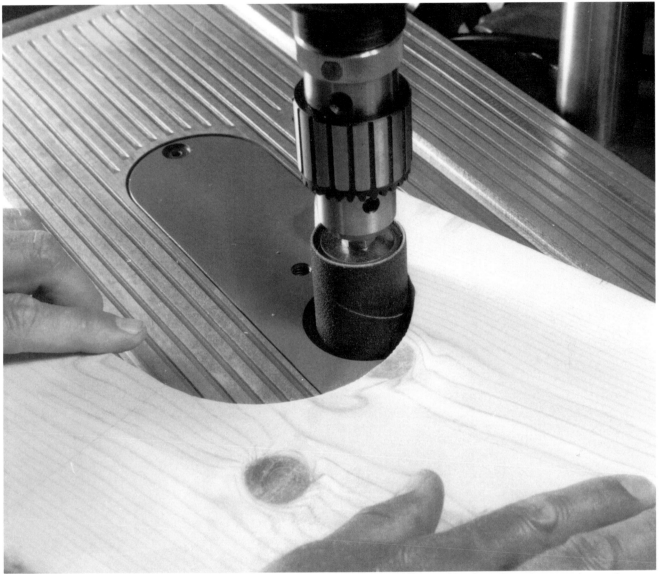

Figure 4. Sand the circular areas of the sides with a drum sander installed in your drill press. Use fine grit sandpaper and move the wood into the rotating drum.

BILL OF MATERIALS — Colonial Cradle

Finished Dimensions in Inches

A1	Side	¾ x 7½ x 36 pine	2
A2	Side	¾ x 7½ x 36 pine	2
A3	Side	¾ x 4 x 11¼ pine	2
B1	End	¾ x 7½ x 19 pine	1
B2	End	¾ x 7½ x 21 pine	1
B3	End	¾ x 7½ x 24 pine	1
C1	End	¾ x 7½ x 19 pine	1
C2	End	¾ x 7½ x 21 pine	1
D	Rocker	¾ x 8 x 36 pine	2
E	Rail	¾ x 4 x 28 pine	2
F	Bottom	¾ x 8⅝ x 34½ pine	2
G	Roof	¾ x 9¼ x 12 pine	2
H	Roof	¾ x 8 x 12 pine	1
J	Fascia	¾ x 6½ x 24 pine	1

cut the angles for the roof on the rear end panel (C1, C2) of the cradle with a saber saw. Make certain the outer edges match the sides.

Once these basic assemblies are complete, enlarge the patterns shown in the diagrams. Lay out a grid of 2 in. squares on a sheet of paper, and draw the patterns to correspond with our diagrams. Then, using carbon paper, transfer the designs to the respective cradle parts.

Cut out the rockers (D) and the sides. Clamp each group together, cutting the multiple pieces at one time. This helps keep them identical.

Use a saber saw or band saw to form the fascia (J). Do not cut this piece until the assembled end (B1, B2, B3) is cut to shape. Then match it with the end's multi-angled top.

Next, lay out and drill the holes for the screws in each part. Because wood plugs will be used to cover all of these screw heads, each hole needs to be counterbored with a ⅜ in. bit to a depth of ⅜ inch. Test-fit the plugs by drilling a hole in scrap material first.

Before assembly, use a ¼ in. rounding over bit, with pilot, in your router to round over the exposed edges on components J, D and E. Securely clamp the materials before routing.

Begin assembly by attaching the ends to the cradle's bottom, then add the sides. Use carpenter's glue along with the No. 8 by 1½ in. screws for added strength.

Cut and test-fit the roof (G, H). Then attach the roof, first to the fascia board (J), then to the back. The edges of the center board (H) will protrude slightly. This will be leveled during sanding.

Assemble the rocker base components (D, E) to one another, then carefully center the cradle on its base and fasten it securely with wood screws, countersunk to be flush with the cradle's bottom. Do not glue the cradle to the base, since you may want to disassemble the unit for simpler transportation or storage.

Glue the ⅜ in. wood plugs in place. These are available at most home supply outlets, and are slightly tapered for easy insertion.

Next, use your router to round over the cradle's remaining exposed edges. Again use a ¼ in. rounding over bit, with pilot.

Finishing

Sand the entire cradle, finishing with 150 grit paper. Apply stain (we used Carver Tripp's Provincial Maple), then finish with three coats of satin finish polyurethane varnish. Sand lightly between coats with 600 grit wet or dry emery paper for the smoothest possible finish.

Add a cradle mattress and bumper pad (available at children's furniture stores) and your heirloom-to-be is ready for the first of its long line of happy babies. ☐

This project is courtesy of California Redwood Association; design by Deck Masters; lead photo by John Rogers.

Redwood Bench/Planter

Smell the flowers as you read a book on this combination bench and planter.

This project features an L-shaped bench that is 48 in. long on each side and built around a square planter. Made of redwood, you can bet the bench/planter will be around for many years to come.

Tips

Use noncorrosive fasteners like galvanized nails. Pre-drill fastener holes located close to the wood's edges to prevent splitting the wood. Make sure you sink the nail heads located on and around the seat to avoid injury.

Assemble the bench/planter on a flat surface, like a garage floor, to help maintain squareness. Build the bench and planter separately. Then assemble them on site and install the slats at that time. Otherwise the unit will be too heavy to carry.

Construction

Cut and miter the four rails (A). Make sure these parts fit perfectly or you will have unsightly gaps. Now, secure the rails with 12d galvanized finishing nails.

Custom measure, cut and install the main brace (B), planter brace (C) and bench brace (D). Drive 12d nails in from the rail side, into the workpieces. Toenail the joints where the braces join the support, using 8d nails.

Double miter the ends of the diagonal bench support (E) and nail in place. Note that this is positioned flush with the bottom to allow room for the bench slats (G, H).

Now custom cut and install the bench supports (F). The two bench supports that adjoin the diagonal bench supports must be mitered to 45 degrees.

Cut the planter sides (I) and the corner braces (J) to length. Dowel the running edge of each of the planter's sides. Then miter both ends of this assembly to 45 degrees. Attach the sides to the corner braces with 12d nails. Make sure the

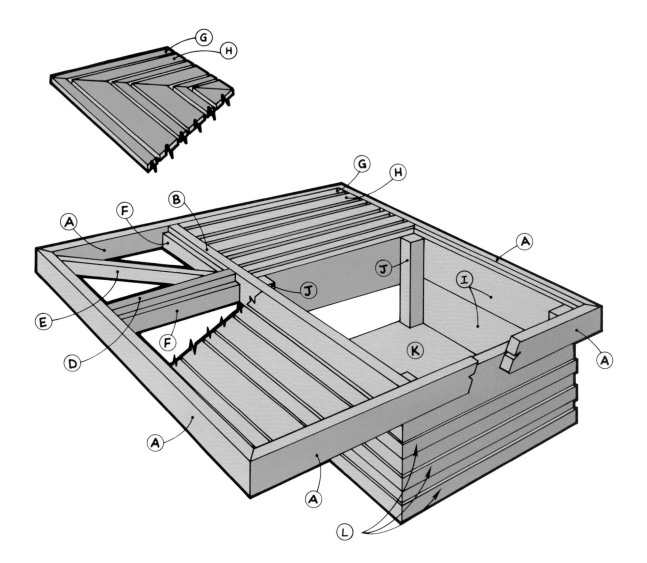

BILL OF MATERIALS — Redwood Bench/Planter

Finished Dimensions in Inches

A	Rail	1½ x 3½ x 48 redwood	4
B	Main Brace	1½ x 3½ x 45 redwood	1
C	Planter Brace	1½ x 3½ x 26¾ redwood	1
D	Bench Brace	1½ x 3½ x 16¾ redwood	1
E	Diagonal Bench Support	1½ x 2 x 23¾ redwood	1
F	Bench Support	1½ x 2 x 16¾ redwood	7
G*	Bench Slat	1½ x 1½ x 48 redwood	6
H*	Bench Slat	1½ x 3½ x 48 redwood	6
I	Planter Side	1½ x 9¼ x 26¾ redwood	8
J	Corner Brace	3½ x 3½ x 17 redwood	4
K**	Planter Base	1½ x 9¼ x 23¾ redwood	5
L	Trim	¼ x 1½ x 27¼ redwood	12

*The length for each bench slat will vary. To save lumber, cut from longer lengths and use remaining scrap for bench supports, etc.

** Dowel and cut to width.

assembly is square and that the top of the corner brace is flush with the top of the assembled planter side.

Likewise, dowel the workpieces forming the planter base (K) and cut the assembly to fit the bottom of the planter. Drill four ¾ in. diameter holes in the base to allow for water drainage. Secure the base to the planter by driving 12d nails into the planter sides.

Position the bench assembly over the planter, making sure the bench is level. Then secure the assembly by driving 12d nails from inside the planter, into the bench. Now, drill ⅜ in. diameter holes, every 6 in., for the ⅜ in. stovebolts. Install the bolts with one flat washer and nut.

You must secure the planter base to the deck to prevent the project from tipping when someone sits on the bench. Toenail the planter base to the deck with 12d nails, nailing from outside of the planter.

Next, cut and secure the bench slats (G, H) with 8d nails. Carefully miter the ends where they join the diagonal bench support. Space the slats ¼ in. from one another. Refer to the illustration. It is a good idea to sand the slats before you install them.

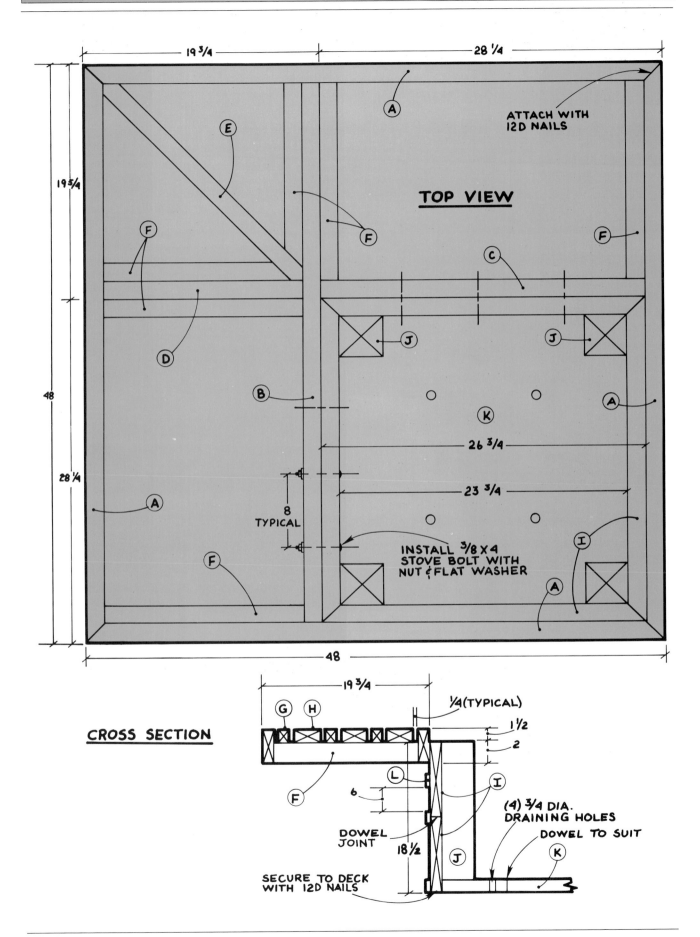

TOP VIEW

ATTACH WITH
12D NAILS

19 3/4

28 1/4

19 3/4

48

28 1/4

A

E

F

F

F

D

C

J

J

B

K

A

8
TYPICAL

26 3/4

23 3/4

INSTALL 3/8 X 4
STOVE BOLT WITH
NUT & FLAT WASHER

A

I

A

F

CROSS SECTION

19 3/4

1/4 (TYPICAL)

G   H

1 1/2

2

L

I

6

F

DOWEL
JOINT

18 1/2

J

(4) 3/4 DIA.
DRAINING HOLES

DOWEL TO SUIT

K

SECURE TO DECK
WITH 12D NAILS

Figure 1. Cut the rail miters (A) on your table saw. Make sure you clamp the workpiece down firmly to prevent kickback. Make a test cut and check for a perfect 45 degree miter. Here, the blade guard is removed for clarity.

Figure 2. Mark the location where the cut is to begin by placing a piece of tape on the table saw. Make sure the tape is well away from the blade so you can position the next piece for cutting.

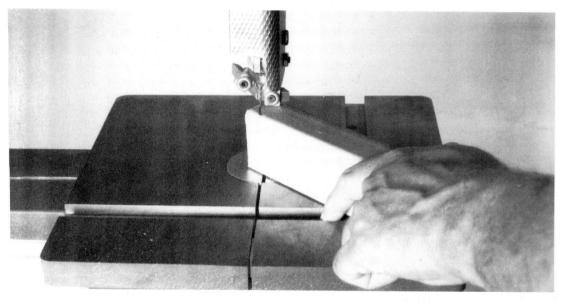

Figure 3. A band saw is ideal for cutting the double miters on each end of the diagonal bench support (E). Use a ½ in. blade to prevent the blade from drifting, and work slowly.

Custom miter the trim (L) and attach with 4d finishing nails to complete the assembly.

Finally, line the inside of the planter with a polyethylene liner, and punch out the drainage holes.

Finishing

Use a belt sander to smooth the project's showing surfaces, then round over any sharp edges with sandpaper. To soften the project's design, rout the showing edges with a ¼ in. rounding over bit, with pilot guide.

Apply a clear, nontoxic finish, suitable for outdoor use. Use a spray gun to finish hard-to-reach areas. If you use a spray gun, wear protective glasses, mask, etc. and apply at least three coats.

Finally, pour about 2 in. of gravel into the planter to provide drainage, and then add soil. Now all you have to do is sit down, pour yourself a beverage and admire your good work. □

Figure 4. It is best to dowel the edges where the planter sides abut. Then miter both ends using a circular saw, guided by a straightedge guide, as shown.

TECHNIQUES

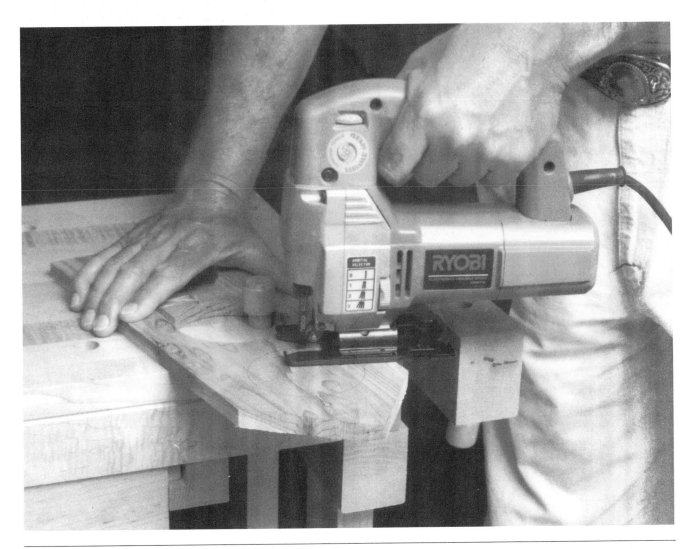

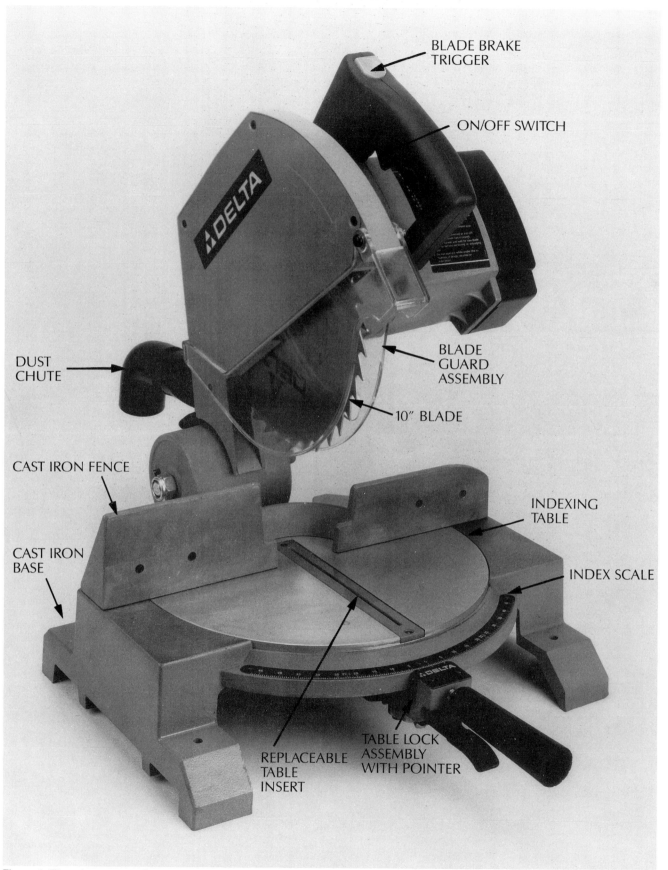

Figure 1. The primary parts of a typical motorized miter box.

Using a Power Miter Box

Learn how to set up, operate and adjust your power miter box to get the most out of this versatile tool.

For the home, workshop or construction site the motorized miter box is the ideal power tool for crosscutting everything from picture frames to 2 x 4s. A rotating index table positions anywhere between and including 45 degrees left and right of center and allows quick setup and accurate mitered cuts. With a simple jig, compound angles can be easily accomplished with this power tool.

Cutting capacities will vary with each unit. The more popular units, which feature 10 in. blades, can cut completely through a 4 x 4 at 90 degrees.

A crosscut combination blade works nicely for cutting construction materials. If you plan on cutting moulding or picture frames, get a hollow-ground novelty combination blade for an extra fine finish.

Most motorized miter boxes are designed with a heavy-duty motor that pivots downward, plunge-cutting into a pre-slotted index table as shown in Fig. 1. The index table usually features a lockable pointer assembly that has positive stops at 0, 45 and 22½ degrees. Some units let you set up to the nearest ¼ degree. In the down position the motor can be locked as shown in Fig. 2. The material is placed on the base where the index system is inserted and held next to the fence for cutting. All units are equipped with a blade guard system to help protect fingers and hands from harm. These tools spew a lot of dust, so a dust chute is usually attached for a vacuum connection.

A blade brake is a feature that does not come with all motorized miter boxes. Buy a unit with this feature to quickly bring the blade to a halt in case of accident or for quick setup. (The blade should come to a complete stop before setup.)

Best of all, the motorized miter box is portable and accurate. You can carry it to the job, and it will cut accurately time after time.

Installation

Closely follow the manufacturer's instruction manual for assembling and operating the tool. Keep the instructions, along with the tool's detailed diagram close at hand to serve as reference. When replacing parts, just refer to the part number on the diagram.

Most installations require that you install the blade along with the blade guard. Before using the tool, make sure everything is in place and that, where appropriate, all the screws and nuts are tight.

Some manufacturers offer stands that can be used to mount the motorized miter box. You can, however, construct

This story is courtesy of Delta International Machinery Corp., excerpted from the book Getting the Most Out of Your Radial Saw.

Recommended Extension Cord Sizes — Use with Portable Electric Tools

Name Plate Ampere Rating

Cord Length	0 to 5	6	7	8	9	10	11	12	13	14	15	16	17	18	19	20
25 ft.	18	18	18	18	18	18	16	16	16	14	14	14	14	14	12	12
50 ft.	18	18	18	18	18	18	16	16	16	14	14	14	14	14	12	12
75 ft.	18	18	18	18	18	18	16	16	16	14	14	14	14	14	12	12
100 ft.	18	18	18	16	16	16	16	16	14	14	14	14	14	14	12	12
125 ft.	18	18	16	16	16	14	14	14	14	14	14	12	12	12	12	12
150 ft.	18	16	16	16	14	14	14	14	14	12	12	12	12	12	12	12

Table 1. Wire sizes shown are AWG (American Wire Gauge), based on a line voltage of 120 and maximum voltage drop (loss) of 10 volts or when cord carries rated current.

Troubleshooting Guide

In spite of how well a power miter box is maintained, problems do come along. The following troubleshooting guide will help you solve the most common problems:

Trouble: Tool will not start.

Probable Cause	Remedy
1. Saw not plugged in.	1. Plug in saw.
2. Fuse blown or circuit breaker tripped.	2. Replace fuse or reset circuit breaker.
3. Cord damaged.	3. Have cord replaced.

Trouble: Tool makes unsatisfactory cuts.

Probable Cause	Remedy
1. Dull blade.	1. Replace blade.
2. Blade mounted backward.	2. Turn blade around.
3. Gum or pitch on blade.	3. Remove blade and clean with turpentine and coarse steel wool.
4. Incorrect blade for work being done.	4. Change the blade.

Trouble: Blade does not come up to speed.

Probable Cause	Remedy
1. Extension cord too light or too long.	1. Replace with adequate size cord.
2. Low voltage supply.	2. Contact your electric company.

Trouble: Machine vibrates excessively.

Probable Cause	Remedy
1. Saw not mounted securely to stand or workbench.	1. Tighten all mounting hardware.
2. Stand or bench on uneven floor.	2. Reposition on flat, level surface. Fasten to floor if necessary.
3. Damaged saw blade.	3. Replace blade.

Trouble: Does not make accurate 45 and 90 degree cuts.

Probable Cause	Remedy
1. Positive stop not adjusted correctly.	1. Check and adjust positive stop.
2. Blade is "heeling."	2. Check and adjust cutting head.
3. Table not square with fence.	3. Check and adjust table.

Trouble: Material pinches blade.

Probable Cause	Remedy
1. Cutting bowed material in wrong position.	1. Position bowed material as shown in Fig. 30.
2. Sag in table.	2. Level table.

Trouble: Saw blade cuts too deeply into worktable.

Probable Cause	Remedy
1. Adjustable stop not set correctly.	1. Check and adjust stop screw.

Trouble: Saw blade does not return to up position.

Probable Cause	Remedy
1. Spring tension out of adjustment.	1. Adjust return spring tension.

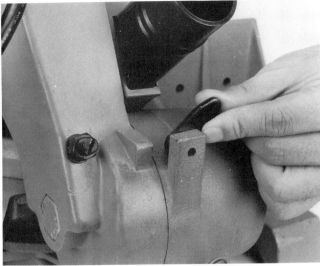

Figure 2. Locking the blade in a down position.

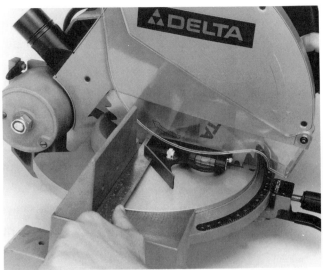

Figure 3. Checking to make sure the blade is 90 degrees to the fence.

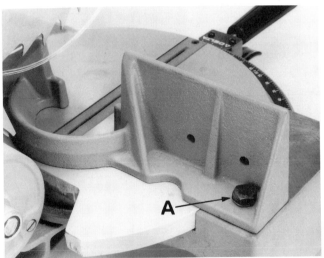

Figure 4. Adjusting the fence to the blade by loosening two screws, one of which is shown at (A).

your own stand or extension table for shop or field use. Construction information is provided with some instruction manuals.

Because the motorized miter box is portable and ideal for on-site cutting, you will need an appropriate size extension cord in order to prevent an excessive drop in voltage, resulting in loss of power and possible motor damage. Table 1 lists the proper wire gauge (rated in amperes) needed to safely operate the tool. If your tool requires a ground plug, make sure you buy an extension cord with a ground.

Safety First

Read all the manufacturer's safety instructions and exercise common sense when operating this tool. Here are some basic safety tips:

1. Always wear adequate eye protection when operating this tool. You may need ear protection as well.

2. Always unplug the tool before performing any tool adjustments, including blade changing.

3. Allow the blade to come to a complete stop before removing the workpiece or before setting up the next workpiece.

4. Keep the workpiece firmly against the fence. If it is away from the fence, the workpiece will be pulled in, perhaps along with your fingers. This situation can also bind the blade and shatter the workpiece.

5. Keep fingers well away from the blade, and plan your cuts so you cut from longer lengths of material instead of shorter lengths.

6. Never use a blade rated slower than the tool's RPM (revolutions per minute) rating.

7. Neither you or the tool should be situated on wet ground or other moist areas.

8. Do not wear loose clothing, rings, ties, watches, other jewelry or anything else that can get caught in the unforgiving blade.

9. Be sure the blade is sharp, free cutting and free from vibration.

10. When not in use, unplug the tool and keep it locked in the down position.

Adjustments

At the time of your purchase, as well as periodically, check the tool's adjustments in order to insure the tool's accuracy. Though the motorized miter box is pretty rugged, rough handling can throw off some adjustments.

The following are general instructions for making adjustments and are not intended to cover all units available. For specific adjustment information, refer to the tool's instruction manual. *When checking or making adjustments, remove the electrical cord from the power source.*

Adjust the fence 90 degrees to the blade. The blade needs to be precisely at 90 degrees to the fence. To check the tool's squareness, disconnect the electrical cord, lock the blade down, and place a square so one surface is against the blade and the other is against the fence. Refer to Fig. 3. If the fence is out of square, you will have to readjust the fence by loosening two screws or bolts located on the fence's back.

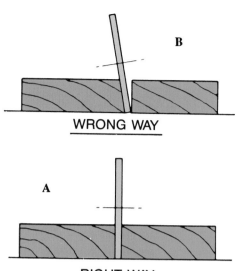

WRONG WAY

RIGHT WAY

FRONT VIEW

Figure 5. (A) The proper position of the blade as it makes a straight crosscut. (B) An unsquare condition called heeling.

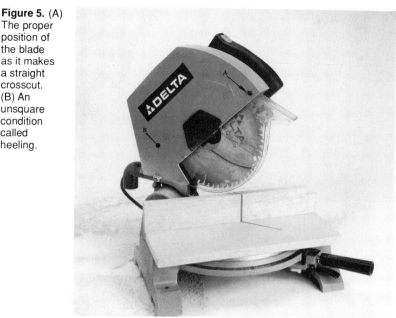

Figure 6. Removing the blade guard's side cover (B) by removing the screw (A)

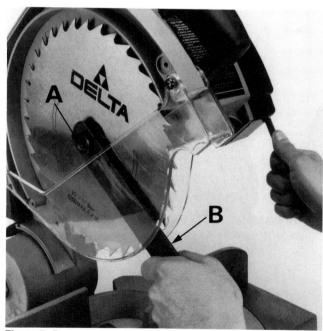

Figure 7. Removing the saw blade by turning arbor nut (A) with wrench (B) clockwise

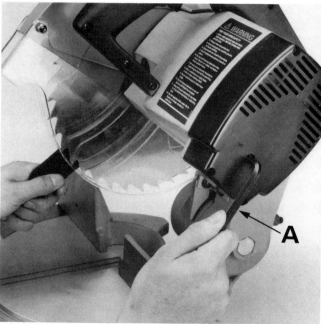

Figure 8. Holding arbor shaft stationary with a special hexagon wrench (A) to remove saw blade

Refer to Fig. 4. Move the fence into its proper place and tighten the screws or bolts.

Remove "heeling." The blade should be perpendicular to the saw table, as shown in Fig. 5A. If it is not perpendicular, the blade will not cut squarely and thus will produce what is called "heeling," as shown in Fig. 5B.

The quickest way to check for heeling is to cut a test piece of material about 3 in. or more high at 90 degrees and check the edge with a square. If the edge is slightly beveled, you will have to adjust the unit.

To make the adjustment, unplug the electrical cord and remove the screw that secures the blade guard (refer to Fig. 6). Remove the blade by holding the arbor nut with a wrench and turning it clockwise. Refer to Fig. 7. You will need to insert a hexagon wrench as shown in Fig. 8 to keep the arbor from turning. The arbor locking location will vary with the unit.

Next, loosen three bolts that connect the motor to the arm (refer to Fig. 9). Snug the bolts so the motor can be turned with mild force. Reinstall the blade, snug down the locking

Figure 9. Adjusting motor (B) so it is perpendicular to table by loosening three bolts (A)

two screws (B) located under the table. Then tap the arm (C) to the right or left as needed to bring the blade square with the fence. Conclude by tightening the screws when the unit is properly aligned. Once adjusted, the remaining positive stops will automatically be corrected.

You may have to readjust the index pointer so it points to 0 degrees. Do this by loosening the two screws that secure the pointer. Then shift the pointer left or right so it is properly aligned and retighten the screws.

Adjust blade travel and spring tension. Downward travel of the blade is adjusted to prevent the blade from contacting metal surfaces. In the event that an adjustment needs to be made, loosen locknut (A) as shown in Fig. 12 and turn the adjustment screw clockwise or counterclockwise until the blade stops at the proper location. When the blade stops at the desired position, short of obstructions, tighten the locking screw. Then double check to make sure the blade does not contact any obstructions. Only then should you reconnect the electrical cord and operate the tool.

nut (counterclockwise) and place a square so one surface rests on the unit's table and the other up against the blade as shown in Fig. 10. Turn the motor until the blade is perpendicular to the table. Then remove the blade and tighten the bolts. Finally, install the blade and check for heeling again with a square. Reassemble the blade and guard only when the blade is correctly aligned.

Keep in mind that the blade's teeth should face toward the fence where the teeth are nearest the table.

Adjust table squareness. Most motorized miter boxes with cast iron tables and fences are precision ground so the fence is precisely set at 90 degrees to the table. Some units, however, come with a wooden composite table that requires adjustment. To check for square, place a square so one surface is up against the fence and the other is resting on the table. Then tighten or loosen screws which are set into the table and adjust until the table is square with the fence.

Level the table. If your tool has a table constructed of a wooden composite material, then the table will probably sag over repeated use. To level the table, place a straightedge on the table. Underneath the table there is an adjusting screw that lifts or lowers the working surface. Turn this screw in or out until the table is flush with the straightedge. If the table is severely worn, replace it with one made by the manufacturer.

Adjust table's positive stops. The index table should automatically lock at one of the 0, 45 and 22½ degree positive stops. If, when at a positive stop, the angle is not correct, you need to make an adjustment.

To check, move the table lock assembly with the pointer to 0 degrees until the index table stops. Then tighten the handle. Use a square to insure the blade is square with the fence. If it is not square, you may be able to adjust the fence until it is 90 degrees to the blade. Refer to the previous section on adjusting the fence.

If the index table is too far out of adjustment, you will have to adjust the positive stop mechanism. Begin by setting the table at the 0 degree positive stop. Refer to Fig. 11 for the following instructions. Loosen the lock arm handle (A) and

Figure 10. Checking to make sure blade is perpendicular to table

You may need to adjust the spring that automatically returns the motor with blade to the upright position. If the unit does not return upright or returns slowly, adjustment is necessary. Again refer to Fig. 12. Loosen the locking nut (B) and turn the adjusting screw clockwise to increase tension. When it is at a suitable tension, retighten the locking nut and check the tension.

Check the drive belt. Most motorized miter boxes do not have arbors that are directly driven by the motor. Instead, toothed or cogged belts drive the arbor. Once a year, check the drive belt to make sure it is not worn. Refer to Fig. 13. Follow the tool's instruction manual for replacing the drive belt.

Maintenance and Troubleshooting Tips

Most units have sealed bearings that require no lubrication, so the unit is basically maintenance free. However, over time you will have to check blades and brushes.

Figure 11. Adjusting the table's positive stop mechanism.

Figure 12. Adjustments for blade travel and spring tension.

Figure 13. Removing drive belt for replacement.

Dulled blade. If the blade takes additional pressure to perform a cut, do not force the cut. More than likely the blade requires sharpening. Burn marks on the wood are another indication that the blade needs replacement. As with all adjustments and maintenance checks, unplug the electrical cord from the power source. Remove the blade and replace.

Accumulated gum and pitch creates friction that will quickly dull a blade. Before each day of use, check the blade and, if necessary, clean with turpentine and coarse steel wool. Make sure you are in a well ventilated area before using these solvents and wear gloves.

Check the brushes. After every 50 hours of use or the period of time specified by the tool's manufacturer, check the two replaceable brushes (see Fig. 14). Then check after every 10 hours of use until the brushes require replacement.

Located on the motor housing, turn the slotted, plastic retainer caps counterclockwise. Out will pop the spring-loaded brush. When the black carbon brush is worn to 3/16 in.

in length or if either spring or shunt wire is burned or damaged in any way, replace both brushes. If the brushes are satisfactory, reinstall them.

Replace table inserts. Some motorized miter boxes come with a replaceable table insert that is preslotted at the factory to accommodate the tool's blade. It fits into the table and is slotted to accept the blade when it is in the down, cutting position, as shown in Fig. 15. It helps to support the material underneath and thereby reduces splintering.

Every time you add a different blade it is a good idea to cut a new slot in a new table insert. Table inserts can be purchased to suit the tool or constructed from 1/4 in. plywood. If you make the new table insert, use the old one as a template. Keep the old inserts and use them with the appropriate blades.

Troubleshooting. If you experience problems in operating your machine, refer to the Troubleshooting Guide on page 170 to help you target the remedy.

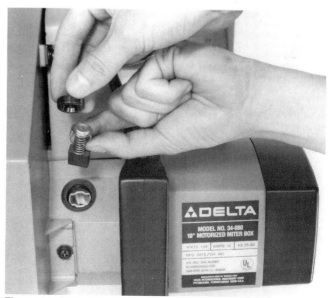

Figure 14. Inspecting the motor brushes.

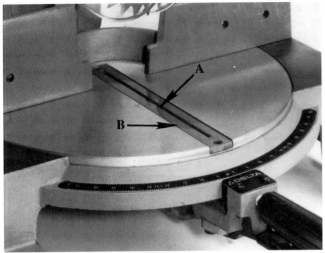

Figure 15. Blade slot (A); table insert (B).

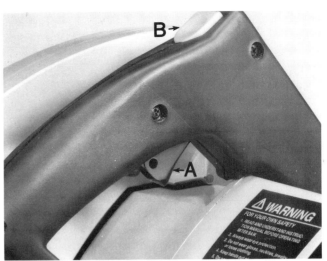

Figure 16. The switch trigger (A) and the brake button (B).

Figure 17. Aligning the blade with the cutting line.

Figure 18. Mitering a 2 x 4 laying flat.

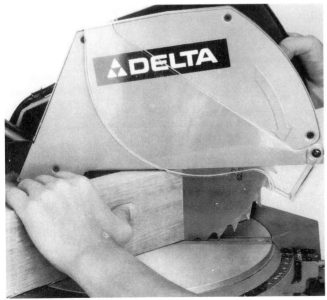

Figure 19. Mitering a 2 x 4 placed upright.

Figure 20. Crosscutting a 4 x 4 in one pass.

Figure 21. Mitering crown moulding with existing fences.

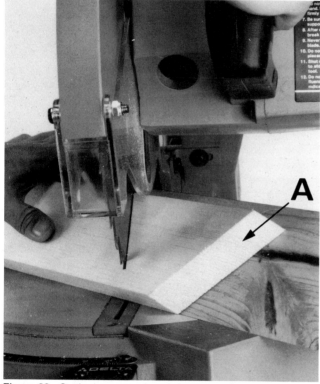

A

Figure 23. Cutting compound angle in rectangular material (A) against filler block.

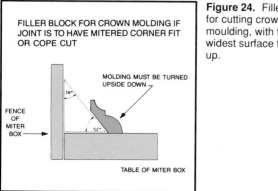

FILLER BLOCK FOR CROWN MOLDING IF JOINT IS TO HAVE MITERED CORNER FIT OR COPE CUT

MOLDING MUST BE TURNED UPSIDE DOWN

FENCE OF MITER BOX

38°

52°

TABLE OF MITER BOX

Figure 24. Filler block for cutting crown moulding, with the widest surface facing up.

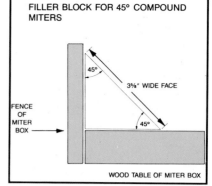

FILLER BLOCK FOR 45° COMPOUND MITERS

45°

3⅝" WIDE FACE

45°

FENCE OF MITER BOX

WOOD TABLE OF MITER BOX

Figure 22. Filler block for 45 degree compound miters.

Tool Operation

The cutting operation is simple: pull the trigger using one hand while using your other hand to secure the workpiece tightly against the table and fence. With the blade running at full speed, push the handle downward into the material until the pivoted unit stops. Do not force the cut. Then return the motor to the upright position while continuing to secure the workpiece. With your thumb, press the blade brake (refer to Fig. 16). Remove the workpiece only after the blade has stopped. Then set up the next cut.

Basic crosscutting. When possible, lay all wood material so the widest surfaced face is flat on the table. This technique allows you to place more holding pressure on the workpiece. Keep the other, dressed edge against the fence. This procedure works well for cutting 2 x 4s and mouldings that require a straight 90 degree cut. However, when cutting miters (cutting at any angle other than 90 degrees), you will have to place the workpiece to suit the surface you need cut.

If you do not have a wooden table or fence, you will have to make sure the workpiece is located precisely for cutting. To accomplish this, draw a line with a square and lower the blade until it contacts the edge of the cutting line. Make a cut on scrap material to insure the blade will cut to the line. If making a miter cut, cut a scrap piece of lumber first, and then trace the angle on the workpiece to be cut. Similarly, lower the blade until it contacts the edge of the cutting line as shown in Fig. 17.

The motorized miter box should be able to cut a 2 x 4 at a 45 degree miter, as shown in Fig. 18 and Fig. 19. Many motorized miter boxes with 10 in. blades can even sever a 4 x 4 in one pass, as shown in Fig. 20.

Compound miters. With the right jigs you can cut compound miters for windows, moulding, picture framing, roof framing and much more. For example, you can make a compound cut through crown moulding by placing the surfaces of the moulding that contact the wall and ceiling against the table and fence as shown in Fig. 21. Set the index table at the desired angle. Hold the moulding firmly and make the cut.

Use of filler blocks for compound cuts. Making compound cuts into square or rectangular material is possible with the aid of filler blocks. For example, if you want to make a picture frame with a 45 degree miter, joined at a 45 degree angle, cut a triangular filler block to angles and size as shown in Fig. 22. Place the workpiece so its widest surface rests against the filler block while its base rests on the table (refer to Fig. 23). Now, make the cut.

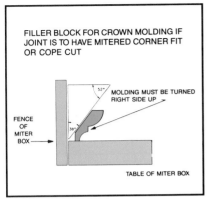

FILLER BLOCK FOR CROWN MOLDING IF
JOINT IS TO HAVE MITERED CORNER FIT
OR COPE CUT

52°

MOLDING MUST BE TURNED
RIGHT SIDE UP

FENCE
OF
MITER
BOX

38°

TABLE OF MITER BOX

Figure 25. Filler block for cutting crown moulding, with the widest surface facing downward, toward the table.

Figure 26. Cutting crown moulding in the upside-down position.

Figure 27. Cutting moulding in the upright position.

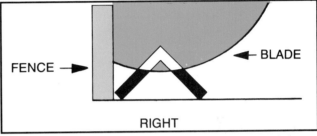

FENCE →   ← BLADE

RIGHT

Figure 28. Be sure to cut soft aluminum extrusions through the smallest section.

the smallest section of stock, as shown in Fig. 28. The wrong setup for cutting aluminum is shown in Fig. 29. Also, make sure you lubricate the saw blade with stick wax, made specifically for this purpose, before each cut. Stick wax can be purchased at most industrial mill supply houses. It helps minimize the accumulation of metal chips from adhering to the blade. Before applying lubricant to the blade, always unplug the electrical cord.

Cutting bowed material. As a general rule, do not cut severely bowed material. However, if a workpiece has a slight bow, it should be placed on the tool's table as shown in Fig. 30A. The blade pulls the material it is cutting toward the fence and thus will pull in the bowed material if it is placed as shown in Fig. 30B.

Optional Items

Dust bag. Many motorized miter boxes come with a dust chute that attaches to a vacuum. Dust bags are also sold separately by most manufacturers. Some sort of dust

Then make the filler block and secure the surface to the motorized miter box fence with round head wood screws. Make sure you drive in a total of four wood screws, two on each side of the fence.

The majority of crown mouldings are angled at 52 and 38 degrees from the wall, instead of 45 degrees. To obtain these angles, cut filler blocks as shown in Figs. 24 and 25. When using the filler block in the typical position, with the widest face showing upward, the crown moulding must be positioned on the table in the upside-down position (see Figs. 24 and 26). This means that the surface that will contact the ceiling rests against the table.

Similarly, when the filler block is reversed so the widest surface faces downward, as shown in Figs. 25 and 27, the crown moulding is placed on the table in the same position as it would be when nailed between the ceiling and wall.

Cutting plastic and aluminum. It is easy to cut plastic pipe and channel with a power miter box. A plywood blade or other fine-tooth blade is recommended to help control the cut. Blades with fewer teeth will cut faster and can shatter the material or bind if fed too quickly.

Similarly, use a fine-tooth blade or specialty blade to cut soft aluminum. Make sure you set up the stock to cut through

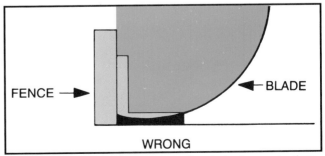

FENCE →   ← BLADE

WRONG

Figure 29. This shows the wrong way to cut aluminum extrusions.

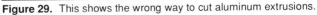

collection system is recommended for indoor use because these tools expel a lot of sawdust.

Auxiliary table. When cutting workpieces where the waste is 1 in. or less in width, there is a danger that the saw blade will grab the cutoff and propel it at great speed. This

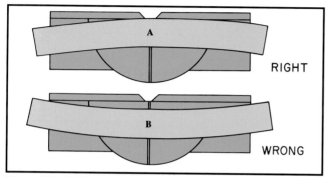

Figure 30. (A) Bowed workpieces should be placed with the convex side against the fence; (B) the workpiece will pinch the blade if the concave side is against the fence.

situation can create a hazardous situation for both you and the machine. If you frequently have small waste pieces, it is a good idea to build an auxiliary table. Secure a wood base to a wood fence so the fasteners fall safely outside of the tool's cutting zone. Attach the auxiliary table to the tool's fence with four round head wood screws.

If the auxiliary table is to be used for cutting 45 degree right and left miters, build an additional auxiliary table so you can use one for cutting a 45 degree right miter and the other table for cutting a 45 degree left miter.

An auxiliary table is also recommended for aligning moulding for cutting. Make the cut into the auxiliary table and align the workpiece with the cut slot instead of trying to align it with the blade.

Extended table. Build an extended worktable or stand to support long, unwieldy workpieces. Refer to Figs. 31 and 32. Some manufacturers include tips on constructing a suitable support table for their units.

Never cut a long workpiece without supporting the outboard end. This can cause dangerous binding. If you have to place excessive pressure on the workpiece to keep it against the table, you need a support table or stand. □

Figure 31. Build an extended table for cutting long, hard-to-manage workpieces.

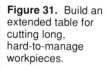

Figure 32. Work support extensions can be readily constructed from standard 2 x 6s and 2 x 4s.

This story is courtesy of Earl Richards and Shopsmith, Inc.

Sharpening Techniques

Here's how you can sharpen chisels and hand planes just like the pros.

Sharpening hand tools mystifies and intimidates many people. Some tools are better sharpened by professionals; however, some tools, such as plane blades and chisels, must be sharpened so frequently during their use that it is impractical to leave the sharpening to someone other than yourself.

Now you can sharpen your own chisels and blades with confidence. All it takes are two grit stones, good technique and a little practice. Confidence begins with simple knowledge and grows with practice — which brings success. (While oil stones may be used with equal success, we have used water stones here to illustrate the proper sharpening techniques.)

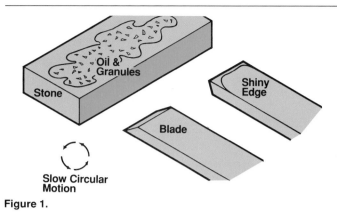

Figure 1.

Getting Started

A new blade or chisel must be prepared for sharpening. There are three steps to good preparation: (1) the back of the blade must be flattened; (2) the edge must be ground to specific angles; and (3) the cutting or ground edge must be honed and de-burred.

You will need a coarse stone, such as an 800 or 1000 grit to remove metal quickly and renew the proper angle on the cutting edge. A very hard stone, such as a 4000, 6000 or 8000 grit, is needed to polish and de-burr the cutting edge. (An 800 grit and a 4000 grit will give excellent results.) A polished edge is smoother, sharper and lasts longer.

Step one. The backs of most blades and chisels are not flat when purchased; therefore, the ground edge may not be of value. Check the back of the blade near the cutting edge, using a perfect straightedge (an engineer's square is good). If

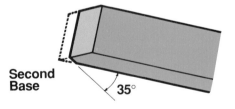

Figure 3.

any light is visible, the back is not flat. Frankly, you can assume that the back is *not* flat. To flatten a back which is only slightly off, place the back of the blade (or chisel) on a coarse stone chosen for sharpening. Make circular passes over the stone. A shiny area will develop along the cutting edge and the sides of the blade.

If the shiny area does not appear quickly, a lapping plate may be needed. A lapping plate is a piece of hard steel ¼ in. by 2 in. by 8 in. (plus or minus). Sprinkle granules of silicone carbide on the flat plate, adding a little light oil for lubrication, then place the back of the blade on the plate. Move the blade

with slow, even circular motions to get a good level back. (See Fig. 1.)

Step two. With a level back on the blade, grind the cutting face of the blade (or have the blade ground). The angle of grinding should be 25 degrees, and the cutting edge must be kept at a 90 degree angle to the sides of the blade (or chisel). (See Fig. 2.)

Step three. When the back is flat and the angles are properly ground, you now are ready to sharpen the blade. A sharp blade can only be achieved through honing on good, true stones. The honing angle is approximately 35 degrees.

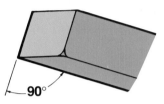

Figure 2.

This angle will produce a second face on the cutting edge. It will begin very narrow and grow with subsequent honing. (See Fig. 3.)

Tips on Honing

The stones used for honing must be perfectly flat. Check the surface frequently. To level a water stone, you need a piece of ¼ in. plate glass about 14 in. by 18 in., some 400 grit wet/dry silicone paper, a little water — and patience. Wet the glass, lay the 400 grit paper on the wet surface, add water to the face of the paper and hone the stone's face on this surface. Circular or figure eight motions are best, and you'll need to practice until your motions are consistent and even.

Always use a stand or table when honing. The height of the table is critical. When you're standing before the table, holding the blade firmly in both hands with the edge touching the stone at a 35 degree angle, then the table height is correct for you.

Fine-Tuning Your Honing Technique

The technique for honing the ground edge is simple. While honing a newly ground cutting surface on a stone, there is a tendency to dig into the stone. To minimize this problem, hold the blade in both hands, keep both wrists straight, and move your arms back-and-forth from the shoulder. Start with the blade on the end of the stone farthest away from you and draw the blade toward yourself. Repeat this action twice to start the second face before continuing a back-and-forth motion. Once started, push and pull the blade on the stone five or six times.

Lift the blade and feel the back edge of the blade. If a slight burr appears, then turn to the polish stone. Perform the same push-and-pull action for several strokes. Finally, turn the blade over, lay it flat on the fine stone and with a circular motion, remove the burr. When the second face reaches approximately 3/32 in., then the blade should be reground. □

This story is courtesy of Gene Hamilton in cooperation with The Family Handyman magazine.

Power Tool Tune-Up

Professional maintenance tips from the people at Skil help you extend the life of your power tools while getting maximum performance.

E ven though power tools are generally a bargain, cumulatively they represent a sizable investment for most do-it-yourselfers. It only makes sense, then, to learn how to maintain your tools so they last longer.

Like any mechanical device, power tools perform best when given "TLC." We had the opportunity to sit down with Roy Hanberg, the former technical coordinator of the service division at the Skil Corporation, and discuss some simple tips about extending the life of your power tools.

Roy began his career at Skil by working in the company's service centers and has had years of experience with every type of power tool maintenance problem imaginable. He agreed that preventive maintenance is the only significant step the homeowner can take to extend tool life.

"First, you can extend the life of any power tool by using sharp accessories," explains Roy. "The most dramatic example of dull accessories we see in the service centers is the case of the circular saw. The customer buys a circular saw and goes to work. The blade starts to get dull and he doesn't realize it so he keeps using it until the blade is as dull as a hoe. If he keeps horsing the tool through the cut on a long rip, he can actually overheat and damage it. At best the abuse will shorten the tool's life."

If overheating shortens the life of a tool, how hot can a drill or sander get before damage is done? "All power tools will heat up," Roy says. "When the tool is uncomfortable to hold, stop. Run it without load for a few seconds. It will cool down faster running free than if you set it down. *But stay alert. Spinning drills, wire wheels, sanding belts and blades can cause serious injury*," cautions Roy.

Actually, overheating should not be a problem, explained Roy, since all power tools are designed to be self-cooling under their rated load. "Let the tool do the work!" counsels Roy. "Don't force it and don't ask it to do a job it is not designed to handle." Skil's largest selling hand drills have a 3/8 in. chuck capacity and can easily handle 3/8 in. holes in steel and up to 1/2 in. in hardwood.

However, if you use a long, light-duty extension cord, you can burn out the motor. Don't rely on the thickness of the cord. When choosing an extension cord, think of it as part of the tool. For a 3/8 in. drill, a standard 18 gauge heavy-duty cord is good for at least 50 feet. If you use a cord over 50 ft. long, especially with a circular saw, consult your owner's manual for the proper wire gauge.

Dust buildup can cause a tool to overheat, so it is important to keep your tools clean. But just how should we clean our tools? "Vacuuming a tool is a common tactic," says Roy, "but it is easier to blow the tool clean. Use the exhaust end of a shop vac and turn the air on the tool while it is running. Direct the air through the intake ports and use the air flow of the tool to help. Dust builds up and collects moisture, resins and oil until it starts making a glue. It can actually form a solid mass. That makes a tool run hot by changing the air flow and the design of the insulation."

How often should you clean your tools? "Skil has always had a problem with *specific recommendations*," Roy ex-

Maintenance Schedule and Operating Tips

Note: All tools should be unplugged prior to maintenance.

Drills
1. Use sharp drills and accessories.
2. Don't overload the tool.
3. Use a recommended extension cord.
4. Keep both tool and cord clean (avoid strong solvents).
5. Store out of direct sunlight.
6. After 10 hours of operation, oil the bearings at end of armature.
7. After 10 hours of operation blow out tool.
8. After 20 to 25 hours of operation check brush wear.
9. After 20 to 25 hours of operation repack gear case with approved lubricant.

Sanders
1. Change sandpaper often.
2. Do not force tool.
3. Use recommended extension cord.
4. Keep tool and cord clean (avoid strong solvents).
5. Store out of direct sunlight.
6. After 10 hours of operation oil bearing at top of armature opposite fan.
7. After 10 hours of operation blow out tool.
8. After 20 to 25 hours of operation check brush wear.

Belt Sanders
1. *Change sanding belt often.*
2. Do not force tool.
3. Use recommended extension cord.
4. Keep tool and cord clean (avoid strong solvents).
5. Store out of direct sunlight.
6. After 10 hours of operation oil bearing lightly in front pulley (some belt sanders have sealed bearings on front pulley).

7. After 10 hours of operation blow out tool.
8. After 10 hours of operation inspect drive belt if so equipped.
9. After 20 to 25 hours of operation check brush wear.

Saber Saws
1. *Change blade when dull.*
2. Do not force tool.
3. Use recommended extension cord.
4. Keep tool and cord clean (avoid strong solvents).
5. Store out of direct sunlight.
6. After 10 hours of operation oil bearing at end of armature opposite fan.
7. After 10 hours of operation blow out tool.
8. After 10 hours of operation clean and oil plunger arm (arm that holds blade).
9. After 20 to 25 hours of operation check brush wear.
10. After 20 to 25 hours of operation repack gear case with approved lubricant.

Circular Saws
1. Change blade often.
2. Do not force tool.
3. Use recommended extension cord.
4. Keep tool and cord clean (avoid strong solvents).
5. Store out of direct sunlight.
6. After 10 hours of operation oil bearing at end of armature opposite fan.
7. After 10 hours of operation blow out tool and clean air outlet by blade.
8. After 10 hours of operation remove blade, clean out and inspect blade guard. (Guard should snap and remain closed when saw is held inverted.)
9. After 20 to 25 hours of operation check brush wear.
10. After 20 to 25 hours of operation repack gear case with approved lubricant.

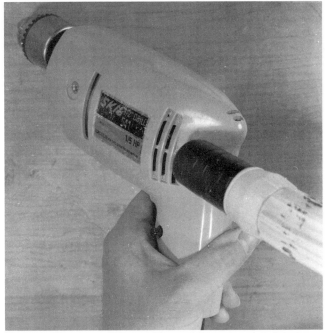

Figure 1. After every 10 hours, blow out the accumulated dust and dirt by directing a stream of air into the air intake port as the tool is run.

Figure 2. Most consumer-grade tools have sleeve bearings at the end of the armature. Oil lightly every 10 hours with No. 20 oil.

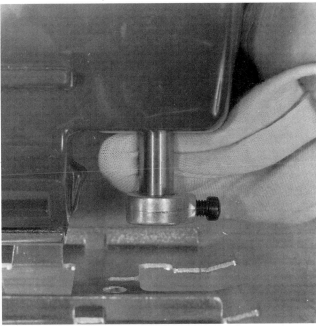

Figure 3. Keep the plunger arm of a saber saw clean and well lubricated. Wipe with an oily rag occasionally.

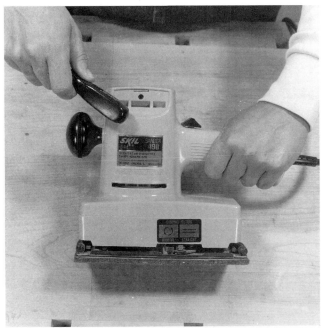

Figure 4. If a sander stops or runs rough, the brushes may be hung up. Before replacing, tap the housing (at the opposite end from the fan) to free the bushing.

plains. "Some owners use their tools a few times a year, while others use them regularly. Those who use their tools frequently should clean them once a month or more. I would feel better with a recommendation of, say, every 10 hours of use."

Roy also recommends that the cord and body of the tool be kept clean. Check your owner's manual for instructions on cleaning your tool. Many cleaners, especially those that con-

tain carbon tetrachloride, chlorinated cleaning solvents and ammonia, should not be used to clean tools because they will damage the plastic housing. Also, plastic and rubber wear longer if they are stored out of direct sunlight.

What about the brushes and bearings inside the tools? Don't they need periodic attention? "They sure do," Roy says. "Many of our popular-priced tools have sleeve bearings.

Figure 5. Most drill brushes are easily replaced; they are located at the end of the armature, opposite the fan. The gear case at the front of the drill also should be lubricated with grease every 20 to 25 hours of operation.

There is nothing wrong with a sleeve bearing when it is lubricated. You will find them at the end of the armature shaft opposite the cooling fan. I would recommend oiling after every 10 hours of use," Roy says.

"On most of our popular-priced sanders, for example, there is an oil reservoir, a felt pad that holds oil and secretes it to the bearing as it gets warm," explains Roy. "The pad holds only about 10 drops, so be careful about over oiling. *The excess may run inside the tool and could cause problems.*"

What about the brushes? Aren't these high-wear points in all electric tools? "The brushes are usually the first thing to wear out," said Roy. If the tool stops, and you suspect the brushes are at fault, try a trick Roy suggested before taking the tool in for service or replacing the brushes yourself. "As the brushes wear, they have to move in. Sometimes a brush will hang up in its channel. Many times tapping the top of the housing will free the stuck brush," advises Roy. If that doesn't work, the brushes probably will have to be replaced.

Most of the owner's manuals, including those of Skil, *don't recommend replacing brushes and lubricating the tool.* Your new tools are even held together by a screw with a special star-like key head. Are power tools being designed to keep the owner out of the tool? "Not exactly," says Roy, "but

Figure 6. Service the gear case of a saber saw at least after every 20 to 25 hours of use, and replace the brushes if necessary. The front cover of the gear case must be removed to lubricate.

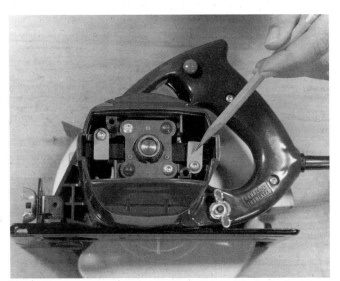

Figure 7. The brushes are located in the end of the motor housing opposite the blade on most top-handle circular saws. The brushes are accessible by removing the end cover.

things have changed industry-wide over the last 10 years. We are designing tools that must meet strict safety regulations. Today all our consumer tools are double insulated and we use different types of brush systems. The brushes certainly can be serviced and the gear case lubricated by the owner, but we don't recommend it in the owner's manual for his own safety. *Even so, we still sell more than half of our parts to the consumer*, and our service centers are there to assist him," Roy said.

Roy explained that a customer who wants to perform his own maintenance can obtain a parts list from Skil and most of the other manufacturers or get help over the counter at their service centers. "This is true throughout the industry. We encourage preventive maintenance," explained Roy.

If you want to maintain your tools yourself, you may have to buy some specialty wrenches. Those funny-looking cap screws holding the tools together are called TORX fasteners. To remove them, you need a TORX wrench. "TORX wrenches are available at our service centers," Roy said. "In fact, they are becoming so widely used, many hardware stores are now beginning to stock TORX wrenches."

The self-contained rechargeable tool is becoming popular. Roy says that Skil's rechargeable drill is one of their most used tools. His experience at the service centers has also shown that there are things the homeowner can do to get the most out of his rechargeable tool. "The best advice I can give is to use the tool," said Roy. "Since most of these tools are completely sealed," he cautioned, "there is little to be done

Figure 8. The gear case of the circular saw should be greased after every 20 to 25 hours of use. Remove the blade and the screws holding the shaft bearing in place. Repack with manufacturer recommended grease.

Figure 9. Most belt sanders have a sleeve bearing on the front idler pulley. Oil it lightly after every 10 hours of operation.

and we don't recommend they service the battery."

Roy recommends that the tool be kept fully charged. Remember that the battery will lose some of its charge when it is sitting on the shelf, so *recharge it after a long period of non-use.*

If the tool doesn't seem to hold a charge like it did when new, it might be suffering from "nicad memory." This forms in the battery if the tool is discharged to about the same point every time it is used. Roy suggests discharging the batteries completely and then fully recharging them. Complete this cycle several times. This will help erase the memory and restore full capacity to a battery that may seem faulty.

By keeping the battery fully charged, and storing the tool out of temperature extremes, battery life can be maximized.

By following Roy's recommendations faithfully, the ser-

RECOMMENDED EXTENSION CORDS

Name Plate Amps.	25 ft.-50 ft.	51 ft.-100 ft.	101 ft.-200 ft.
0-2	18	18	18
2-3	18	18	**16**
3-4	18	18	**16**
4-5	18	18	**14**
5-6	18	**16**	**14**
6-8	18	**16**	**12**
8-10	18	**14**	**12**
10-12	**16**	**14**	**10**
12-14	**16**	**12**	**10**

The smaller the gauge number, the heavier the wire. The bold-type gauge numbers are extra heavy-duty cords.

vice life of most tools will be significantly increased. "A guy who builds a rec room one year and then works on a fence the next can expect a life of at least 10 years from our consumer-grade saw, if he follows our tips. Our upgraded saw could last the homeowner his lifetime. The keys in the life of any tool are the hardness of its shafts and gears, the quality of the armature, and the bearings. But most important, it must be serviced," stated Roy.

Regular maintenance is important for the type of tools most homeowners own. Popular-priced tools usually have sleeve bearings. These will last almost indefinitely, but they must be lubricated on a regular schedule. By following these expert tips, you can increase the life of all your power tools. Give your power tools the care they deserve, and you won't ever have to experience that expensive screech a bearing makes as it cries for oil. □

Figure 10. Change the blade often on a circular saw. When the blade is off, clean the blade guard and see that it snaps shut and remains there when the saw is inverted. Oil lightly if it binds.